Country Cop

Country Cop

True Tales from a Texas Deputy Sheriff

Barry Goodson

Number 11 in the North Texas Crime and Criminal Justice Series

UNT Press

Denton, Texas

10 9 8 7 6 5 4 3 2 1

Permissions:
University of North Texas Press
1155 Union Circle #311336
Denton, TX 76203-5017

The paper used in this book meets the minimum requirements of the American National Standard for Permanence of Paper for Printed Library Materials, z39.48.1984. Binding materials have been chosen for durability.

Library of Congress Cataloging-in-Publication Data

Names: Goodson, Barry L., 1949- author.
Title: Country cop : true tales from a Texas deputy sheriff / Barry Goodson.
Other titles: North Texas crime and criminal justice series ; no. 11.
Description: Denton : University of North Texas Press, [2020] | Series: Number 11 in the North Texas Crime and Criminal Justice Series | Includes bibliographical references and index.
Identifiers: LCCN 2020001886 | ISBN 9781574417883 (cloth) | ISBN 9781574418002 (ebook)
Subjects: LCSH: Goodson, Barry L., 1949- | Sheriffs--Texas--Parker County--Biography. | Law enforcement--Texas--Parker County--Biography. | Crime--Texas--Parker County--History--20th century. | Criminal investigation--Texas--Parker County--History--20th century.
Classification: LCC HV7911.G655 A3 2020 | DDC 363.28/2092 [B]--dc23

LC record available at https://lccn.loc.gov/2020001886

Country Cop is Number 11 in the North Texas Crime and Criminal Justice Series

The electronic edition of this book was made possible by the support of the Vick Family Foundation.

Table of Contents

List of Photos

PREFACE

"*To thine own self be true.*" Polonius's words of advice in parting with his son in Shakespeare's *Hamlet* troubled my mind as a young man searching for a fitting career path. Life is merely a fleeting moment in the pages of time, and our commitment to ourselves remains a challenge to us all. As my teenage years disappeared, I watched friends choose their path in life based on their insight and heartfelt desires. They each knew, without a doubt, that they were destined to achieve their chosen career. For some reason, I lacked such insight or confidence in my destiny.

I suppose being a young man in the late 1960s served to be the catalyst toward my future career. Marine Corps leadership recognized the talents and gifts hidden within my psyche and vainly attempted to encourage me to accept an invitation to attend the Naval Academy, in contrast to the path leading to participation in the Viet Nam War. Something compelled me to accept my destiny as a combat Marine among the 1,000s of other young men caught up in the throes of war on distant shores. My focus on a career path was set aside as the reality of personal mortality engulfed my thoughts.

Life has a way of reminding us of who we are, our past, our programming, if you will. After I had been in combat for three months, the

Marine Corps presented a second opportunity, albeit happenstance. In the mid-1960s, Marine Corps Command developed an in-country special ops group as an effort to defeat the communist forces at their own game. This unit became known as the CAP Marines.

My heart ached as I witnessed the daily destruction of the homes and crops of the local farmers within our operational area. My thoughts returned to my grandfather and the years I spent as a child trying to help him nurture his crops and livestock to provide food and shelter for his loved ones.

Each time an American tank drove across a rice paddy or artillery or bombs devastated a village or farm, I questioned what I would do if such acts occurred on our farm in Texas. I had no doubt that my grandfather would have taken up arms against anyone responsible for such wanton destruction. A fellow Marine with a farming background as well shared his thoughts about joining the CAP Marines based on the understanding that we would live among the villagers and farmers and help them defeat their enemies and follow their chosen lifestyle. I joined the cause without questioning the probability of my demise. I wanted to help, not participate in the death and destruction of the people we were supposed to be helping.

I thrived as a CAP Marine because of my inherent desire to aid and protect the indigenous populations in the jungles of Viet Nam. Unknowingly, although it would be another twenty years, I had also found my calling in life. In contrast to being a combat Marine in an infantry unit as a machine gunner facing insurmountable odds and worrying that each step could bring death, my focus turned toward protecting the villagers and farmers with only a handful of other Marines possessing the same commitment: 24/7s. My survival became a moot point. My only desire was to ensure the safety of the farmer who wanted nothing more than to provide for his family.

I returned to my home in Texas proud of my contributions to the Vietnamese people I had grown to trust and love, proud of the fact that

I had done my part to help them not only survive but also live their life as they chose.

Upon returning to Texas, I entered Texas Christian University as an art major, based on my natural abilities to bring life to a piece of paper. I longed for a career path that would cater to my artistic nature and provide the solitude one attains from personal commitment through artwork.

I soon discovered that being a combat veteran of the Viet Nam War created a void between myself and the other art students who possessed a more carefree approach to life. They fostered none of the horrific memories of warfare; in fact they protested the very idea of combat as a plague against humanity.

I changed my major to business and managed to blend well with other students who only wanted to complete their degree path and move forward with a lucrative career in business. Soon my path led me to join a local engineering firm as a sales engineer, which provided the opportunity to rely on my artistic and design capabilities as well. However, I soon discovered that I lacked the necessary personality to be a successful salesperson. I struggled through nine years and a divorce before choosing a slightly different route with another engineering firm involved in designing and building surface facilities for mining operations throughout the United States. I enjoyed this career even though the haunting reality that I lacked sales skills remained in the background. My skills as a designer coupled with my presentation skills enabled me to be successful even though I still felt that something was missing in my life.

One career path after another appeared and vanished over the next twenty years before I found myself in 1989 standing before a friend, Chip Shumaker, Chief Deputy of the Parker County Sheriff's Office. I was a frustrated businessman looking for something more fulfilling in life. My visit with Chip focused on our plan for a future scuba diving adventure. During the conversation, Chip asked me if I would be interested in altering my career path once again. I immediately assured him that I had no intention of being a law enforcement officer because the salary alone offered no enticement. Also, I assured him that I could not entertain the idea of carrying a weapon with intent to harm another human being again. The Viet Nam War left formidable scars on my soul. The idea of taking another human life once again was unfathomable.

Chip saw something in me that I failed to recognize: an inherent trait that remained hidden, at least from me. He assured me that I possessed a strong desire to defend the defenseless, to help others move forward with their lives despite the odds against them. My stories about my exploits with the CAP Marines assured Chip that I would be able to transfer those skill sets to a career in law enforcement. I had to agree that I was miserable as a businessperson and longed for something more in life than the pursuit of money. I knew I could handle anything Parker County offenders chose to toss my direction. However, because of my combat training and experience, I questioned my ability to refrain from overreacting to outside stimuli. Would I indeed be able to make that transition without unduly harming another?

Life has a way of providing a gentle shove occasionally to ensure we accept an opportunity regardless of the perceived challenges accompanying that opportunity. My business and income had evolved to the point of relying heavily on one client, who suddenly filed bankruptcy, which negated that company's commitment to paying for services completed. My new wife, Cindy, and I were faced with a challenge to search for another career to satisfy the immediate needs of our growing family. We had two young children. The bankruptcy left us owing suppliers more money than our meager savings could cover. Once again, a career change was needed.

A few months later, Chip invited me to his office once again, this time to discuss his desire to bring me on board. Cindy and I spent countless hours and days discussing the pros and cons of dropping a lucrative career path in favor of carrying a weapon in defense of others, once again. I researched other local law enforcement opportunities, keeping my desire to help others in mind. City and state law enforcement officers are dutifully bound to enforce traffic codes and burdened with other similar duties that impose rules and regulations on the average American. Traffic control is a much-needed service. However, I knew that if I committed my life to service in law enforcement, protecting others against oppression or harm must take priority. Chip assured me that Sheriff Ben Whiteman's primary goal was to defeat heinous crime within the county, not to ignore traffic offenses or other menial duties, but to focus more toward protecting the citizenry of the county. Sheriff Whiteman and Chip's focus on fighting crime finally motivated me to choose the Parker County Sheriff's Office over any other agency. The security offered by Parker County in respect to insurance and retirement provided sufficient cause to consider Chip's offer seriously. In April of 1989, I signed on as a jailer with the Parker County Sheriff's Office with an assignment to work the night shift.

Even though one of the responsibilities of a County Sheriff is to provide care, custody, and control of alleged and convicted offenders in the country jail, I hesitate to refer to myself as one with career experience as a corrections officer. I served as a Parker County Corrections Officer only during the time that it took to complete my training with the Tarrant County Law Enforcement Training Center, which was about six months. Upon completion of TCLEOSE training and subsequent certification as a Texas law enforcement officer, Sheriff Ben Whiteman and Deputy Chip Shumaker chose to promote me to the position of deputy sheriff, which led to the beginning of my career as a patrol officer with the Parker County Sheriff's Office.

Motivation to share my career experiences as a patrol officer with the Parker County Sheriff's Office stemmed from the then-Manager Editor of UNT Press, Charlotte Wright, during the publication of my first book, CAP MOT. She assured me that many books relating the services provided by city, state, and federal agencies existed, but rural law enforcement lacked accurate representation in the world of academics. The purpose of this writing is to share personal experiences one may expect to encounter in a career as a deputy sheriff; a career that forces officers to face any challenge, any offender, alone, with no backup officer within miles.

After twenty years of moving through various career paths in the business world and starting a family in my late thirties, I finally rediscovered my true calling in life. Serving as a CAP Marine revealed my destiny to serve as a protector of the community in which I lived. I knew that if I served as a law enforcement officer, my primary concentration would be to ensure that other citizens remained free from any level of oppression and to live their life as they chose; to thine own self, be true.

Country Cop

Chapter One

Civil Process

When the average person considers law enforcement, he or she typically thinks about the allegedly wild adventures one may find in the life of the patrol officer. Thankfully, the general duties of the patrol officer actually have more to do with building a rapport with residents and businesses within his or her jurisdiction in order to provide the Intel and connections needed to complete his or her duties and serve the needs of the community safely. However, one of the lesser known, but equally important, responsibilities of the sheriff deputy is to provide civil process services for the county. The typical patrol deputy perceives such services as a burden serving only to thwart his or her efforts to combat crime. This motivates most sheriffs to create a separate department to handle the Civil Process.[1]

I worked aggressively, as a pro-active patrol deputy always searching for that one person imposing harm on another. I perceived myself as a crime fighter focusing on rendering the bullies of the county harmless. I maintained a log of the known, repeat offenders in our county and ensured that I was aware that a parolee's efforts to become a contributing citizen upon release from prison or jail were genuine. Eventually, in a cooperative effort between the offender's parole or probation officer, I was able to encourage previous repeat offenders to remain focused on a better lifestyle that would improve relations within their family and with the other members of the community.

Regardless of my focus, Sheriff Ben Whiteman and Chief Deputy Chip Shumaker recognized my leadership and organizational skills, which led to the sheriff requiring my transfer to head the civil process department. As a result, I soon found myself focusing my efforts on protecting citizens in our county based on civil wrongs against them in contrast to those heinous offenders I sought to remove from society. Thanks to Sheriff Whiteman, I soon carried a new certification of advanced civil process service from training through the State of Texas.

I felt sure that this opportunity was another step up the ladder and the additional training would empower me to not only diversify my service for the county but also increase rank more rapidly. I accepted the challenge, which thrilled my wife because serving in civil process placed me on permanent day shift with only a few requirements to work on weekends or after the usual 8-5 schedule. Family life blossomed.[2]

Ironically, the training revealed how little I knew about civil process and the significant role it played in the courts and with the citizens of Parker County. Criminal laws intertwined with the civil process to a more substantial degree than I ever imagined, especially the divorce decrees, Writs of Attachment, and Emergency Protective Orders. I soon found myself being challenged more, intellectually, with an entirely different set of laws applicable to the family code, mental health, and safety laws. Over the next several years, I discovered how essential the duties of the civil process service are to protect the rights of the average citizen in our county, and I accepted that responsibility with all sincerity.

One of the more important laws relating to civil process rests with the Texas Homestead Act.[3] Such deliveries of court papers can be one of the more challenging and dangerous situations a deputy faces because most people abhor lawsuits and some resort to violence to avoid the civil process. However, the duty can be pleasurable as well, if the officer recognizes that it is his or her responsibility to protect the rights of the person receiving the court summons as well as to ensure the court order is served properly to the designated person. Some exceptions to this rule are allowed.

The courts prefer that the papers be hand-delivered to the defendant in the case but will accept alternate service after the officer has completed three attempts to serve the papers in person. One alternative is to directly attach the papers to the gate or front door of the property, writing upon the paper's exterior that such service was rendered complete and advising dispatch of the time and date the papers were left at that address. Such notation is left on the court papers as well, and the officer keeps a log of the time and date of the completed service along with the name of the person receiving the court papers.

One should note that an officer cannot place the papers inside or attached to the defendant's mailbox, which may appear not to make sense. However, federal laws prohibit anyone but the resident and the postal employee from accessing the inside of a personal or business mailbox. Such action is considered a federal offense with penalties. However, one other alternative remains available as well. If upon the officer's third attempt he discovers anyone at the home who is a resident and at least seventeen years old, the officer may leave the court papers with that person, once again advising dispatch that such service is complete. Additionally, the officer should identify the individual by name and date of birth to be able to assure a court of law that a legal-age person received the service.

One form of service includes the Writs of Sequestration.[4] Courts may issue a Writ against specific property or assets of individuals or corporations. Other types of writs include the Writ of Attachment and the Writ of Execution.

In the state of Texas, the seizure of property can include anything so designated by the court with exception of homestead property.[5]

The Writ of Attachment and Writ of Execution are court documents, both of which are used to seize property determined in a court of law as a judgment by the court, which awards that property to the plaintiff. However, generally, the Writ of Attachment pertains to the seizing of a person.[6]

The Writ of Execution typically pertains to specific personal property such as motor vehicles, trailers, manufactured homes, and other similar types of property, which quite often are seized by default of contract against the defendant.[7]

The more common court papers in our jurisdiction were the Writs of Execution. Service to the community is paramount, especially to those who remain defenseless against any form of oppression or coercion, even from those who employ the legal system in their favor.

Texas law requires that the sheriff of the county must complete all vehicle and other property seizures based on the defendant's failure to fulfill contractual obligations. The sheriff of the county must seize this property under direction and empowerment from the courts. The reason for this law is to protect not only the person in possession of the property but also the person receiving the returned property.[8]

However, more significant issues arise from the illegal repossession of a vehicle, the most apparent of which is theft of personal property remaining inside that vehicle. Defendants retain the right to possession of those items, regardless of the value. Therefore, when the deputy arrives, he or she must inventory the vehicle with the defendant, allowing that person to provide proof that the additions made to the vehicle were after he or she took possession, under contract from the dealer or previous owner. However, if the person cannot provide proof of ownership of items found in or on the vehicle that could be rightfully considered part of the original condition of the vehicle, the deputy is required to leave that property in place and complete a report. The report identifies the equipment or part in question. Photographs provide proof to the courts that the item does exist and remains questionable in respect to actual ownership. Based on the preponderance of the evidence, the judge then decides who should receive that item. The car dealer or original title holder of the vehicle has no right to any aftermarket property installed or any personal item stored within the vehicle.[9]

Another concern with illegal repossessions rests with the fact that the person repossessing the vehicle may have to enter private property or even enter a private garage to gain access, both of which are criminal offenses (criminal trespass and burglary of a building). Therefore, numerous criminal issues can arise from a private individual given false papers from a creditor granting repossession of a vehicle.

Unfortunately, most sheriff offices and courts are side-stepped by unscrupulous banks and other creditors or car dealers, especially those who sell a vehicle based on a weekly payment plan. Such contracts are typically written to favor the original owner with no grace period or only one or two days before the contract empowers the original owner to repossess the vehicle. Quite often, such contracts are issued by unscrupulous car dealers who sell older vehicles that are worth less than $5,000.[10]

During my tenure on patrol, I received a call for service on midnight shift alleging that a wrecker service had shown up at a person's home to repossess the homeowner's vehicle. However, while in the process, the wrecker driver attempted to burglarize the homeowner's private business located on the same property, which introduces another reason why the Texas legislature determined that repossessions must proceed through the county sheriff's office.

I arrived at the scene with the homeowner holding the suspect at gunpoint. Ironically, the business the suspect had attempted to enter was a gunsmith shop, and the owner was in possession of numerous weapons inside his home as well as inside the shop, most of which belonged to customers. The gunsmith was well-known in the county, especially by all law enforcement officers. Therefore, there was little reason to assume the homeowner was attempting to thwart the repossession of his truck by falsely accusing the suspect of burglarizing his business. The wrecker driver was indeed in possession of a possible burglary tool: a pry bar, found in his hands, upon my arrival. Additionally, the entrance door to the shop did show recent damage from being pried open.

I photographed the damaged entrance door and took possession of the pry bar as evidence. Forensic study of the pry bar would allow matching of the tooling on the pry bar with the marks on the shop's door as well as possibly providing latent fingerprint identification of the offender. Such action provided sufficient evidence to develop probable cause that the suspect did intentionally attempt to commit the act of burglary of a building.

Since the act did not occur in plain view and no stolen property could be recovered from the suspect's vehicle, I was unable to affect an arrest. I asked dispatch to check the criminal history of the suspect and hold it for the report. I released the suspect based on personal recognizance, assuring him that the homeowner did prefer burglary charges against him.[11] However, I did validate that the offender was in possession of the official paperwork issued by the requesting agency, which, illegal or not, did verify the offender's presence at the victim's residence. This information was seized and accompanied my report. I provided the complainant with a witness form complete with case number and date and asked him to complete the form to the best of his ability and return it, along with any photos taken during the attempted crime, to the sheriff's office the next day. The case number on the document assured that clerical staff routed the statement to the correct investigator.

As I cleared the scene, dispatch advised that the suspect possessed an extensive criminal history for burglary, which assured me that he was probably on parole as well. The fact that the offender possessed the audacity to include his wife and children at the scene of the crime as well infuriated me, especially since firearms were involved. The case report included this information to ensure that the judge, upon conviction of the offender, would be aware that the offender risked the lives of his family, especially his children.

Therefore, even though most Texas courts may turn a blind eye to businesses relying on illegal repossession services to side-track the more expensive route required by law, one may readily see how such actions can place the person committing the offense in jeopardy of committing a crime. Additionally, the act incriminates the person empowering the illegal act in the first place (banker or car dealer). Pursuing repossessions through illegal means incriminates that person and company as an accessory before the fact. Since offenders recognize certain occupations that empower their livelihood through criminal actions, it becomes the duty of every law enforcement officer to ensure the protection of the rights of all citizens, even if the act appears to be legal.

In another case, I received a Writ of Execution against a private property owned by an elderly, retired gentleman who had chosen to live his remaining years on the Brazos River, which traced gracefully through the western part of Parker County. The Writ revealed that a Dallas County judge owned the property adjacent to the senior gentleman's property. The judge knowingly generated the Writ of Execution for personal gains, leading one to question the credibility of his action even though the law offered no right to interfere.

The judge's case rested on the fact that the man's roofline extended over the county utility easement, which violated the county laws. However, Parker County officials chose not to file an injunction against him. This violation is not to be confused with an infringement of the property line, which remains centered in the county easement.[12] The Writ of Execution ordered the seizure of the man's property and offering that land and home for sale on the county courthouse steps during the next available Sheriff's Auction in Parker County, based on the findings of that judge's court in Dallas. The idea that any judge chose to force an elderly man out of his home, a home he had worked so hard to create, maintain, and now rightfully expect a life of leisure on the Brazos River for his remaining years was unsettling. Regardless, the Writ of Execution was legal. I was required to proceed with the process under Texas laws.

Before proceeding with the service, I reviewed the Texas Homestead Act once again and then drove out to pay the man a visit. His place was far from the majestic presentation offered by the judge's summer cottage on the property next door, but the old man's property was neatly groomed and well maintained offering a covered wrap-around deck allowing one to traverse the entire perimeter of the home unencumbered by inclement weather. I knocked on the door. A man, about seventy-five-years-old, answered the door. He was cordial, which assured me that he had no idea what was about to happen to his home and way of life. He opened the door and extended his hand, saying, "Good morning, Officer. What can I do for you?" He waved a cordial entry into his home.

Instead of immediately advising the elderly gentleman of the Writ of Execution, I asked him if he was the sole owner of the property. He answered, "Yes sir, free and clear, my retirement home." I looked down at the Writ and then asked the man another question and hoped he had the right answer. "Sir, have you ever filed for a homestead exemption with the county?" He shook his head, "No sir. Never saw much need for it. I don't owe anybody any money, why?" I told him that I had papers alleging that his roofline encroached on the defined county easement for the property and that I was ordered to seize his property and put it up for sale. However, in the same breath, I assured him that since I did not find him at home on that date that I would have to return later to deliver the papers to him. The man was immediately taken aback as he slumped back into his chair. Fear and anger showed in his entire countenance. I could not blame him. Gradually, my words sunk in as he considered his next response. He agreed that he was not home when I knocked on the door on that date but did not understand what I was trying to do on his behalf.

I explained the Texas Homestead Act to the elderly gentleman and encouraged him to drive, immediately, to the county appraiser's office and complete the filing requirements for the homestead exemption. I told him that I would return the next day and legally serve the papers, but that the homestead exemption would protect him from losing his property to his neighbor, who was already prepared to pick up the property in the next Sheriff's Auction.[13]

The senior man (the defendant) was visibly upset as he told me how his neighbor had attempted to coerce him to sell his property to him in the recent past. A tear rolled down the old man's cheek as he told me the story. I ensured that he understood what the homestead exemption would do for him and told him, once again, that I would return to serve the papers the next afternoon at 4:00 pm. I left the old man to determine, on his own, what he should do next. I had told him exactly where the Parker County Tax Assessment office was located and assured him that the county staff at that location could help him file his papers for the homestead and encouraged him to call his nearest relative or friend who could assist him with the process. I could not legally accompany the man to the tax office. However, my duty was, first and foremost, to protect the citizens of Parker County from those who could and would use the system against any citizen. Therefore, I felt more than justified in my actions to stand in the gap for this elderly gentleman who wanted nothing more than the freedom to drop a fishing line in his nurtured honey-hole every day to catch his next meal, his haven against the outside world.

As promised, I drove to the defendant's home the next day. The man met me at the door with a glass of iced tea and shook my hand as he handed the drink to me, which was more than appreciated. We sat in the rocking chairs of his covered back porch. I produced the papers. "Sir, I am required to deliver this Writ of Execution to you. Please understand the purpose of this Writ of Execution requires that I seize your property based on the court order from the court mentioned in the Writ. I must enforce this Writ unless you can show me just-cause why such action is invalid." The man smiled, reached into his coat pocket and handed me a certified copy of the Texas Homestead Exemption provided by the Parker County Appraisal District Office located in Weatherford, Texas.

I took another sip of the tea while I perused the document. I folded it up and handed it back to the man saying, "Sir this document shows that you do have a legal exemption from seizure based on the Texas Homestead Act. Therefore, I will return the papers to the court and advise the court that you provided proof of the Texas Homestead Exemption."[14]

The old man smiled, saying nothing as we sat there finishing our cold iced tea, watching an occasional fish jump from the water, reaching in vain for the dragonfly hovering above. I finished the tea and said, "Sir, I love the home you have made for yourself. It is quiet and offers just the right solitude for a man to finish out his years. I wish you the best." I stood up and handed him my empty glass. "Thanks for the tea. I bet your wife taught you how to make it," I said as I turned to go. "You are right, son," he said, as he shoved his hand forward to grasp mine, "and thank you, Officer Goodson."

Standing beside his rocking chair on the covered porch, the old man waved goodbye as I drove away. I knew I saved an innocent, elderly gentleman from coercion that would have destroyed what remaining years of peace he had left. With his wife gone, he had nothing left in the world except for the memories the two of them had shared over the years on the Brazos River.

Not every writ allowed the freedom to provide citizens protection from oppression from those who would use the law against them. However, I remained in power to ensure that those citizens who could not fight the oppression were provided sufficient time to develop a defense before being forced out of their home or to relinquish their property.

In a similar incident, I received another Writ of Execution from a court in another county requiring the seizure of a double-wide mobile home from a private property just north of the county seat. The owner of the property was a young mother of two small children, one baby and the other a toddler still in diapers. Their mother was in her twenties. Her husband had died just a few days before I arrived to deliver the Writ, which ordered the immediate seizure and delivery of the manufactured home to the mortgage company. As I drove into the driveway, I noticed black plastic covering the entire ridgeline of the peak of the roof of the home, which was strange since the home was brand-new. Before knocking on the door, I walked around the house to observe the condition of the home.

A double-wide mobile home ships in two sections, which are assembled on the homesite. By all appearances, the construction crew poorly assembled the two sections leaving visible cracks from the ridge at the peak of the roof down each opposing outer wall. I assumed that a crack existed along the top as well, which confirmed the need for the black plastic. I took Polaroid photos and returned to the front door. A young woman answered the door with a baby in her arms. My presence imposed immediate stress as the mother almost collapsed to the floor in the doorway. I opened the door and helped her make it to a nearby chair, ensuring she did not harm the baby in any way.

She knew why I was there. Between her continual sobbing, I pieced together her side of the story, substantiated by the evidence I photographed from the exterior and now the interior of the home. She assured me that she filed numerous complaints with the company that had built her home, but she lacked the finances and the willpower to fight them because of the recent death of her husband, who typically handled such matters.

Unfortunately, a foreclosure on a home negates the power of the Texas Homestead Act. Therefore, the situation forced me to serve the papers to her immediately. However, it remained in my power to designate the time of eviction of the residents of the home, which could be legally extended up to thirty days to ensure the person in possession of the property had plenty of time to secure an attorney and/or find a new place to live. I assured the lady that I would provide the full thirty days to settle the matter before she would be forced to move out. Her stress level substantially decreased as we talked. I told her that my report to the courts would include my observations and photos of not only the pathetic construction but also the damage caused to the interior of the home because of the recent rains.

Leaving the woman to proceed with her efforts to secure a new residence, I filed the report. As with most of the writs I serve, I never heard from the homeowner or the courts again. However, the builder who had refused to repair the home did call to share his concern that he could not have immediate possession of the property. I reminded him that the laws concerning seizure also apply to the safety and security of the homeowners and that even though I legally seized the property, the homeowner could be given up to thirty days to rectify the situation or seek another place to stay. The builder expressed his displeasure, assuring me that Sheriff Whiteman would hear about my failure to allow immediate retrieval of his property. I assured him that he was welcome to pursue any legal remedy he felt entitled to and encouraged him to make that phone call to Sheriff Whiteman.

One of the more imposing writs of service is known as a Writ of Attachment.[15] This writ equates to seizing a person or persons and delivering them to the court issuing the writ. Additionally, this type of writ may order the seizure of specific property awarded to the plaintiff in a civil lawsuit based on a civil remedy. However, every Writ of Attachment handled by our office during my tenure related to the seizure of individuals.

One specific case that caused my hesitation to serve the papers stemmed from a case filed by a mother in another Dallas County Court, which issued a Writ of Attachment to seize two children, a girl about six years old and a boy a couple of years older. The red flag that warned me that something was amiss was the fact that the service of the writ was against the grandparents of the children. I had never received a Writ of Attachment ordering the seizure of children from a grandparent. It was more typical for the writ to order temporary custody to the grandparents because of the feud between parents, who were overwhelmed in a court battle over the custody of their children during divorce proceedings.

I drove to the location, which was in one of the older neighborhoods in Weatherford, a beautiful country town of approximately 30,000 residents nestled almost in the center of the county, with immediate access to Interstate I-20 and Highway 80/180 connecting Weatherford to the east and west. FM 51 bisected Weatherford, running north and south.

As I drove down the road approaching the grandparents' home, my suspicions increased since the homes in that area offered well-groomed lawns, relatively new vehicles in the driveways, and no evidence of crime concerns other than occasional signs warning offenders that private security services provide some level of burglary protection. I located the grandparents' home, which revealed the same positive traits of the rest of the homes in that community. The absence of cars in the driveway assured me that no one was home, or the owner stored the cars in the attached, two-car garage. The latter proved to be the fact as an elderly gentleman in his late sixties answered the door and immediately ordered me to leave his property as he attempted to shut the door. I gently forced him to allow me to enter his home as he began to tell me that he was not going to allow me to take his grandchildren back to that drug addict daughter of his and assured me it would only happen over his dead body.

I searched my mind for the proper level of verbal judo to apply to assure the man that he had to comply with the law, just as his wife stepped around the corner of the hallway and wrapped her arms around the belligerent man. As soon as she did, he collapsed into a chair beside him and burst into tears. I waited patiently as his wife soothed the tortured soul of her beloved husband. She turned to me with tears rolling down her cheeks and asked, "Can we share our side of the story before you take our grandchildren?" I told her that my intention and presence was to ensure the safety of their grandchildren and that if she had facts that she felt showed that the children were endangered then, yes, I needed to know. However, I needed assurance that the children were presently safe and secure and needed to have them brought before me immediately.

She turned toward a door in the hallway, saying, "They are hiding in that closet," pointing to the door. I asked her to have the children come out of the closet and to assure them that my intention was only to ensure their safety and welfare, but I had to witness to the courts that they were indeed safe. Her husband tried to protest, but she intervened once again and walked to the closet, slowly opened the closet door to reveal two, small children sitting on the closet floor hugging each other in desperation and fear. Their eyes locked onto mine as they both screamed out, "No...please leave us alone." Both were crying as well, apparently afraid of what they felt was about to happen in their lives.

The grandmother brought the children before me, and I asked her to provide visual proof that the children suffered from no harm. The grandmother assured me that I would see old bruises on their arms and legs, but equally assured me that the bruises came from someone else, not from them. I looked over the exposed skin of the children and made a note of the bruises, which indeed were already in the process of fading into history. I asked each child, separately, what caused the bruises and they assured me the bruises were from assaults from their mother and her boyfriend who were in Dallas. I asked no more questions and asked the children to go sit by their grandparents.

They both snuggled next to their grandfather's feet in the hope of protection from being taken away by the man with a badge and a gun. I never wore my uniform when serving any form of a writ to ensure that I would not appear threatening. Regardless, the ominous presence of the badge and holstered weapon imposed an unmistakable air of authority.

The grandmother began to tell her story with confirmation nods from her husband and the children. She told of the horrors the children had faced as their mother, the grandparents' daughter, forced them to live in a drug dealer's house in Dallas. Grandmother assured me that the house was full of rats and human waste as well as every imaginable piece of trash that would turn the stomach of any rational human being.

Her description repainted a picture I had witnessed too many times during my years on patrol. Indeed, such a setting was no place for a child and did indeed endanger their lives solely from the filth and disease present in the dwelling, not to mention the probability of being caught in the crossfire between drug dealers or their mules, or worse, being forced to serve as drug mules themselves.[17] Additionally, children in a drug-infested home were subject to the whims of those offenders who entered the home, which endangered both children as victims of sexual, physical, and emotional abuse.

It was quite common for drug dealer parents to force their children to deliver drugs. The purpose for using children rests with the absence of any harsh penalties imposed by the courts against the children, and the children typically chose to protect their parents by not revealing the fact that their parents forced them to deliver the drugs.[18]

Therefore, the grandmother painted a very realistic picture. I asked for the daughter's full name and date of birth and excused myself, momentarily, while I contacted dispatch to verify that the mother was indeed a drug addict or drug dealer based on previous arrests and convictions. Dispatch called me back a few minutes later and confirmed that the daughter did possess an extensive drug dealing history in Dallas County and that she did show a residence in Dallas County at that time but had just been released on parole and had no outstanding warrants at that time.

The grandmother had provided the same information before I called dispatch. She told me that they went over to pick up the children for a weekend visit about thirty days ago, shortly after their daughter was released on parole only to discover the daughter had already returned to her life as a drug addict and drug dealer. She told me that she found her grandchildren sitting on a filthy couch watching a small TV in a back room of the house. She admitted that they lost their composure and took the children without their daughter's permission out of fear for the health and welfare of their grandchildren. She also confirmed that their daughter had called numerous times demanding the return of her children and assuring them that she would keep them safe from the drug scene.

The grandfather interjected once again, "I do not want my grandchildren to return to such a dangerous environment," he stated. "It is bad enough that I have already lost my daughter to drugs." Tears welled up in his eyes again.

I asked to borrow their phone once again and called District Court Judge Mullin's office of the 43rd District Court in our county. His secretary answered the phone. Because of my time in service on patrol and civil process, the judge's secretary knew me well. I told her that I had encountered an issue enforcing a Writ of Attachment and briefly told her why. She asked me to hold on and then returned asking that I leave the children with the grandparents and immediately drive to the courthouse for a meeting with Judge Mullin. I assured her I would be there shortly, hung up the phone and turned to the grandparents.

I looked at both grandparents and issued a stern warning:

> I have set a meeting with the Honorable Jim Mullin who is the judge over our 43rd District Court. He is waiting for me at this moment. I will return immediately following that meeting to share his decision with you. However, if you attempt to secret the children away or leave your home for any reason before I return, I will ask him to provide a warrant for your arrest and the seizure of your grandchildren with an order for immediate placement in foster care.

The grandparents looked at me for a second and then asked what I intended to do. I told them that I was going to try to save their grandchildren's lives by asking the judge to override the Writ of Attachment from the court in Dallas County. However, I assured them that everything depended on the honesty of the report they had just provided to me and the relationship Judge Mullin had with the judge in Dallas. They promised they would comply with my lawful order and I left the children in their custody, temporarily, and headed for the meeting with Judge Mullin.

As I entered the judge's chambers, his secretary waved me on, saying, "He is waiting for you in his office." I thanked her and entered the judge's office extending my hand and my appreciation for the immediate meeting. We shook hands, and he invited me to have a seat and share my story with him. I handed him the Writ of Attachment and told him the story I had received from the grandparents, the present condition of the children, the excellent home the grandparents had prepared for the children, and the evidence I had uncovered through dispatch's efforts in the confirmation of the daughter's criminal history.

Judge Mullin spent a few moments reviewing the information and evidence I presented to him and stopped to reaffirm that the children were presently physically unharmed. I assured him that the grandparents' home was neat and tidy and located in a friendly neighborhood. I also shared the fact that the children sought shelter and comfort around their sobbing grandfather. Judge Mullin pushed the documents aside and called his secretary into his office. He asked her to make copies of all the documentation and to see if she could contact the Dallas judge. She buzzed his office a few minutes later, and Judge Mullin picked up the phone with a hand held out to ensure I remained silent.

He shared his concerns with the Dallas judge and asked if the judge would allow a change of venue in the interest of the children. The Dallas judge reviewed his files, and they continued a conversation for several minutes. Suddenly, Judge Mullin thanked the Dallas judge for his time and told him he looked forward to receiving the case shortly. He turned to me, smiled, and said, "The Dallas judge is transferring the case to my court, and the children will remain in the custody of the grandparents pending verification by our Child Protective Services personnel." He asked his secretary to contact the grandparents on the phone and ask them to remain at home until a CPS worker could arrive and complete an interview to ensure the children would be safe remaining in their custody until Judge Mullin determined the final decision in the case.

I asked Judge Mullin what he wanted me to do about the Writ of Attachment and he extended his hand reaching for the document. "You are now relieved of that duty, Corporal Goodson," he said, as he took the document and shoved it into a case file that his secretary had already prepared. I shook his hand and thanked him for his compassion for the children and the grandparents. As I departed his office, he patted me on the shoulder saying, "No, Barry. You are the one who has shown compassion and wisdom in the way you handled this case. Thanks for giving me the chance to rectify the situation." I shook his hand once again and parted saying, "You are welcome, Your Honor."

As I drove back to the grandparents' home, I marveled over the way laws can intervene in any person's life and the role we all play toward ensuring protection of the rights of all persons . I smiled as I pulled into the grandparents' driveway.

The grandparents were sitting outside watching the children play in the front yard. I stepped from the patrol vehicle and walked toward the grandparents. The grandfather almost leaped from his lawn chair as he stood to shake my hand. This time happy tears were rolling down his cheeks. "Thanks," he said, "thank you so much." I made sure that he had received a phone call from the judge's secretary and his wife assured me they had. I told them that they would probably not see me again and wished them the best in their quest to secure the safety and welfare not only of their grandchildren but also the future of their daughter. I returned to my patrol car and let dispatch know I was back on duty, leaving the grandparents and two happy grandchildren behind to continue their lives with relative freedom from any form of oppression.

When dealing with Writs of Attachment, one must attempt to remain objective and base all procedures strictly on the facts before them. Quite often many of the facts in a given situation were well known to me and even involved me as the witness for the state based on my previous service as a patrol officer. One case involved a Writ of Attachment for a mental commitment for a twenty-four-hour evaluation of a lady who lived in Hudson Oaks, right across the street from Weatherford Lake on the eastern side of the county seat.

My first contact with the lady in question was as a rookie officer. I will refer to her as Linda to protect her privacy. Dispatch contacted me by radio and asked me to contact the office for historical information concerning the call that was about to be dispatched to me. I called dispatch, and they informed me that Linda had called concerned about the aliens attacking her house again. I thought the dispatcher was referring to illegal aliens from another country. It turned out that Linda had a mental condition. However, local MHMR (Mental Health and Mental Retardation) services evaluated her as harmless and allowed to live on her own with a sixteen-year-old daughter. However, until the moment I was dispatched to visit Linda, she had remained harmless.

Earlier that evening, Linda had decided that she would deal with the aliens from outer space by firing a revolver through the ceiling of her home in hopes that the bullets would force the alien ship to flee or crash into the pasture adjacent to her home. The neighbors had called the Parker County Sheriff's Office (PCSO) complaining about the bullets whizzing over their heads as they sat in their front yard, which assured me that Linda was firing her weapon through the walls as well. I approached the front door of the home with caution and rang the doorbell, standing to one side to benefit from the protection of the multiple wall stud construction offered by building openings. I had good reason to believe she would mistake me as an alien as well, which prompted the defensive posture.

The door opened about six inches and a woman, whom I assumed to be Linda, stood behind the door. She said nothing. I introduced myself and provided her with the opportunity to view my law enforcement credentials. She opened the door and stepped out on the porch, cautiously. She shaded her eyes against the afternoon sun and asked, "Are they gone?" Since I possessed a written history of the calls made to Linda's home, I knew she was asking about the aliens. I decided the best way to handle the situation was to accompany her search for them.

I stepped past her and walked out into the yard and shaded my eyes to look to the heavens as well and remarked, "I see nothing of them, Linda. I guess they indeed have fled the area. They probably intercepted the message from my dispatcher." Linda perked up with the idea that I bought into her story. "So, you believe me?" She asked. I nodded my head and said, "Yes Ma'am. However, based on my experience with these alien craft a pistol or rifle slug cannot harm their craft. I have no doubt they toyed with you to encourage you to waste all your ammunition, right?" My purpose for the question was to determine if she indeed had no more ammunition, which would prevent her from firing the weapon again, at least for that evening. She glanced to the sky once again and confirmed that she had indeed exhausted her present supply of ammo.

She stated, "Well, tell me, officer, if they are afraid to stick around when you arrive what do you do to make them afraid of you?" I toyed with an appropriate response and noticed a garden hose lying on the ground, coiled neatly by the side of the house. I asked her if she ever saw the aliens when it was raining, especially during a thunderstorm. She studied for a minute, searching her memory. I was banking on the fact that she never paid attention to the weather during her brief encounter produced by her mind at random moments in her life. According to the record, the encounters seemed to occur during certain days of each month, within the same week, each month. Finally, she looked at me and said, "No, Officer, does that mean something?"

I replied, "Yes, Ma'am, it does. What the aliens are attempting to conceal from those who encounter them is the fact that they construct spacecraft from a special polymer that is impervious to bullets. Water, for some reason, melts the outer shell of their crafts as if it were acid." She bought the tale as she confirmed the idea by shaking her head. I seized the opportunity and continued. "They flee when I arrive because they know that I can use your water hose to run them off. You have good water pressure, right?" She nodded, and I said, "That's excellent, Linda, you can sneak outside when you hear them hovering overhead and turn that water on full blast. You will be amazed at how quickly they will flee and will probably finally leave you alone. Just make sure you have one of those high-pressure water nozzles to ensure the water reaches high enough to endanger their spacecraft." She agreed.

As I turned to leave, I assured her once again not to waste money buying more ammunition. It would only show the aliens that she was weak and knew nothing about how to handle their threats against her and her home. As I started to walk away, she grabbed my hand and led me to a line of shrubbery in front of her home. She reached down and broke a twig off one of the bushes and showed me how the bark was in an elevated position, which is typical of that specific shrubbery. She said, "Look what they have done to my shrubbery, Officer." I studied for a moment and stated, "Yes, ma'am. That does appear to be radiation damage. Make sure you keep that hose handy." I assured her I would request extra patrol on her behalf to ensure the aliens left her alone, at least on my shift. This decision served more toward additional protection for the neighbors. I returned to the vehicle and drove around the block to the complainant's home and met with them briefly to ensure they were aware of the method I had employed to convince Linda to stop firing her weapon.

I did indeed add Linda to the list for extra patrol in hopes that an occasional drive-by from an officer would decrease the attacks her mind portrayed during those given weeks. I returned to PCSO and completed a report including the temporary solution I proposed to ensure Linda no longer fired her weapon. Additionally, I proposed that the county judge consider a mental commitment based on the severe repercussions that could arise if she decided to fire the weapon at someone knocking on her door, believing that person to be an alien bent on attacking her.

With the report filed, I returned to regular duties and soon put Linda in the past, at least until the next call dispatching me to investigate Linda once again. I found myself standing on Linda's front doorstep numerous times over the next year as she continued her inner battles with her alleged aliens, quite often assuring dispatch that she was being held down in her bed and raped by the aliens. We investigated each call to assure the courts that nothing was assaulting Linda and continued to build a case for over a year.

One day, I received a call from dispatch advising that the County Judge had confirmed my request for a mental commitment hearing based on the numerous case filings relating to the dangerous condition of her mental illness, which confirmed that she might endanger herself or others. He had, indeed, issued a Writ of Attachment for her immediate seizure. Dispatch warned that she had just received a phone call from the neighbors as well, warning that they had heard gunshots coming from Linda's house again. I asked dispatch to send assisting units to meet me at Linda's home as well, more to assure I had witnesses when Linda was taken into custody than anything else.

I knew she would react violently to our presence because she would feel that I had violated her trust. I arrived at the scene first and waited for the backup units to arrive. Dispatch assumed it wise to recruit plenty of help as six law enforcement cruisers approached the home from different directions, parking along the roadside. Some were Texas DPS Troopers and others were local city police as well as other sheriff deputies. I gathered them together and assured them that we could be facing a highly volatile situation because all the signs warned that Linda was armed and dangerous, sharing the information concerning shots fired from her home earlier that day. I told them to let me enter the home first in hopes that Linda would cooperate with me. I doubted that she would since there was no hope of hiding all the patrol vehicles. The reason for our presence would be obvious.

I rang the doorbell as the other officers remained out of view off to the side. Suddenly, the door swung wide open revealing Linda completely nude, which was typical of her mental instability as well. She laughed and immediately ran toward another part of the house. I yelled, "Let's go, men," and attempted to follow her retreat. I was concerned that she would be searching for a firearm. We entered the house cautiously. As if to confirm my suspicions, I noticed a rifle lying against the living room wall near the door. I motioned for one of the officers to secure that weapon and take it outside. He did. The rest of us continued forward.

It was my first time to enter Linda's home, and I was a bit taken aback by the condition of the home's interior. Stacks of newspapers or clothing, reaching almost to the ceiling, covered every flat surface in the home, including the floor, kitchen counters, coffee tables, beds, and dressers, assuring me that Linda possessed a hoarder mentality as well. Traversing the piles of clothing and papers imposed a new danger based on the probability that she would be waiting on the opposite side of the next stack. I moved forward as quietly as possible. Suddenly, one of the stacks crashed to the floor in front of me as we entered the master bedroom. Linda burst from behind the pile. Fortunately, she had no weapon, but I could see the pistol lying on the nightstand by her bed, which was also covered in piles of clothing and papers, leaving just enough room to place the pistol within reach while she slept.

Diving forward, I caught her by the ankle, causing her to fall to the floor just shy of the nightstand. I tried to pull her toward me, but she began kicking wildly, screaming out, "RAPE! RAPE!" The other officers moved forward to help restrain the naked woman. Linda continued to scream and struggle until one of the officers managed to place her wrists in handcuffs behind her back. Her countenance completely changed with the click of the cuffs on her wrists. She looked at us, smiled and said, "Take a good look, boys. Take me. You know you want it." I grabbed a sheet from the bed and ordered the men to wrap her in the sheet immediately. They readily complied, picked her up, and began negotiating a path toward the front door as they carried her to another deputy's patrol vehicle where they placed her, kicking and screaming in the backseat of the car.

Along with one other officer, I completed a search of the interior and secured the home to make sure that Linda's sixteen-year-old daughter was not present or harmed. The house was empty. I found some clothes lying on the floor that I assumed were the ones Linda had on before she opened the door and took those with me to enable a female jailer to assist her with putting the clothes back on once we had her booked into the jail. The judge would not want to see Linda presented before him in the typical jailhouse, white uniform required of all the inmates.

With the house locked and secured, and Linda scowling at me from the backseat of the other Deputy's patrol vehicle, still sufficiently covered by the white bedsheet, I contacted dispatch, advising that I was heading straight for the jail to serve as a backup for the other officer. I asked her to notify the county judge that the subject was in custody.

The other officer keyed up his mike as soon as I finished my message and provided dispatch with his starting mileage, which would serve as evidence that the officer proceeded directly to the jail without stopping or diverting along the way. He would provide the ending mileage to dispatch as soon as he arrived at the jail, which was known as Station 10. We both checked out at the jail and carried Linda inside, along with assistance from female jailers. As soon as the corrections officers dressed Linda, they placed her in a holding cell to await the county judge.

A few days later I was notified that I was required to attend the mental commitment hearing held in the County Court of Parker County. The County Judge, Mark Riley, would hear the case presented by the county attorney. The hearing moved forward as I expected as Linda's attorney cross-examined me as the state's witness. He did not question any of the case histories, which he knew were fact. Instead, he asked me if I had ever assured his client that I too saw the alien crafts hovering above her home and if I told her that water would destroy their ship.

I confirmed his questions. Fortunately, he followed with a question that would assure the judge that I did not deserve a mental commitment hearing as well. "Officer Goodson, were you being honest with my client?" I answered, "No sir, I was not. I used that strategy as a ploy to convince Linda to stop shooting her firearm negligently into the ceiling and walls of her home."

Instantly, Linda became enraged, as I expected she would. She tried to run forward to attack me while I was on the stand. Her attorney stepped in front of her as he struggled to restrain her. The court bailiff moved in to assist, and the two of them took her out of the courtroom. A few seconds later her attorney re-entered the courtroom and asked if he could approach the bench. Judge Riley complied and asked the prosecuting attorney to join them in a brief conference. Suddenly, Judge Riley turned toward me and stated, "You are dismissed, Officer Goodson." I said, "Thank you, Your Honor," and returned to my place in the courtroom. Both attorneys returned to their tables, and Judge Riley hit his gavel on his benchtop and stated, loudly, "Case Dismissed." The bailiff yelled out, "All Rise." I was perplexed but knew all too well the workings of the court. It appeared the Defense introduced information that encouraged the judge to dismiss the case.

I later discovered that the prosecution had failed to provide the required public announcement of the hearing of the case before the County Court on that day, which stands as legal grounds for dismissal. To the county attorney and Judge Riley, it merely meant an easy way out of a lengthy hearing, which immediately lessened the county attorney's caseload as well as the judge's caseload. To me, it meant that a dangerous woman was set free to purchase more firearms and threaten the lives of her neighbors since no court order would be forthcoming to ensure otherwise. It meant that a year's worth of research and filed reports were now worthless because the judge dismissed the case based on a legal premise, which was his only option. I could only hope that Linda's family would recognize the need to proceed with some level of psychological therapy to help Linda cope with the mental episodes in a more productive manner.

I learned early in my career to never take such court actions personally. The legalities and roles played by all those involved in a hearing or a trial in any court remain entirely out of the control of anyone but the judge and jury. He or she bases decisions on specific rules, regulations, and case laws that set precedents on the actions in all future cases. Additionally, it remains the defense attorney's duty to ensure his client receives every opportunity to benefit from any weak areas in the filing of a case. Lead officers always review each officer's field report to ensure all reports are legally sound. Administrative review ensures that the reports violate no grammar, spelling, or legal regulations and that an officer's actions violate no offender's rights. The report review serves to ensure that a weak report does not empower that defense attorney to ask for a mistrial or dismissal based on any loophole that would favor his or her client. I have silently watched many felonious offenders walk free from a courtroom, but thankfully not because of improper case filings or violations against the offender's rights stemming from the Parker County Sheriff's Office.

People do not always file mental hearing cases with good intentions. All too often, I encountered a Writ of Attachment ordering the seizing of an older adult who, according to my observations, was in more control of his or her mental stability than many of the people I arrested. One such case involved an elderly gentleman whose personal wealth was close to one million dollars, including his home, which was a beautiful four-bedroom home in a gated community on the east side of Weatherford.

His daughter, a resident of another county, had filed for and received a mental commitment order from Judge Mark Riley based on the alleged domestic violence that occurred between the daughter and her father during an altercation the night before I received the Writ of Attachment. The Writ alleged that the man was mentally unstable and possibly a danger to himself and others. The Writ stated that the man was to be seized and taken before the court for a mental hearing to determine if he should be committed to a mental health institution for a twenty-four-hour mental health evaluation.

When I arrived at the home, I rang the doorbell, and the elderly gentleman answered the door. It was still relatively early in the morning, and I fully expected the retired gentleman to answer the door in his robe. However, he was nicely dressed in slacks and a sports shirt and neatly groomed as if preparing to leave for the office. I showed the man the Writ of Attachment and told him that he would have to accompany me to the courthouse for the hearing. I explained the meaning and purpose of the writ and his composure changed instantly as his body stiffened in response to the charges. He did not respond, nor did I ask him to respond to the allegations. That was not my duty.

He requested that I not handcuff him, and I assured him that I saw no need to fear that he was a danger to himself or others. However, I asked him to empty his pockets on the table near the entrance to his home to assure me that he was not carrying any weapon. He readily complied and remained cordial throughout the entire situation. I allowed the man to sit in the front passenger seat of my vehicle to provide some level of trust and comfort in his behalf. Moments later I turned him over to the bailiff for the hearing.

About an hour later, I received a call from the court to return and pick up the elderly gentleman for transport to a mental health facility on the south side of Ft. Worth for a twenty-four-hour evaluation. I had just finished writing the report concerning transporting him to the courthouse. Therefore, I was only minutes away. I returned to the courtroom and received custody of the man from the court bailiff.

The elderly gentleman had the appearance of complete dejection. He no longer walked entirely erect with the pride he had shown earlier. His head hung low as I escorted him to the patrol car. Once again, I assured him handcuffs were not required. I sat him in the passenger seat next to me and headed east on Ft. Worth Highway in the direction of the Ft. Worth hospital. The man cried quietly for a moment and then wiped his eyes. His gaze seemed transfixed as his eyes looked forward, but seeing nothing, as we proceeded down Ft. Worth Highway. He decided to share his thoughts, "My daughter is after my wealth." He stopped for a moment, wiping his eyes as more tears fell from his cheeks. He turned to me and said, "Officer, there is nothing wrong with me, mentally. My daughter came over last night and told me that it was time for me to move into a retirement home. She lives in East Texas and claims that she fears that I am going to suffer from falling or some other health issue and she will not be there to help. We did get into an argument last night, but only over the idea of me having to leave my home... our home."

He paused for a moment, then continued, "My wife, God rest her soul, died in our home and my daughter spent her high school years in that home, and now she claims that I suffered a mental breakdown last night and that I ransacked the house in fits of rage...me...her own father."

He remained quiet for a few moments and then looked over at me with a quizzical look on his face. "Officer, would you mind being a witness on my behalf?" he asked. I assured him that I would not make a good witness other than to assure the judge that I witnessed no hostilities during our brief time together. He waved his hand to assure me that was not his intent. He said, "No...no that is not what I meant. I know you cannot witness to my character since you do not know me. However, the alleged fit I threw last night was during the altercation with my daughter. After she left, I was so upset that I went straight to bed. Therefore, if I ransacked the place as she alleged, there would still be evidence of that today, correct?"

I thought for a moment and confirmed that I did pick him up at 8:00 am that morning. I assured him that he could have cleaned up the mess after his daughter left or earlier that morning before I arrived. He agreed but assured me that his daughter had claimed that he had broken lamps and other objects in the home forcing her to leave him in a fit of rage. He implored me to at least stop by the home to witness whether the house showed any evidence of violence in the home. I agreed to do so and advised dispatch that I would be making an unscheduled stop at the address of the man's home, which was right off Ft. Worth Highway (Highway 180/80), therefore, not a lengthy diversion.

The man politely waited for me to step from the patrol car and made no effort to open the passenger door until I walked to his side of the vehicle, which assured me he was doing everything he could to convince me that escape was not on his mind. I opened the door for him, and we walked past his well-manicured lawn to the front porch. The outside of the home offered no evidence of violence. He handed me his house key, and I unlocked the front door. He entered and immediately proceeded to shut down the burglar alarm system, which was behind the front door. He stepped aside and waved a hand with a quick statement, "Please look around and see if you see anything out of place or any evidence of broken lamps."

When I read the evidence section in the Writ of Attachment it clearly stated that the man broke a lamp in the living room leaving pieces of the lamp scattered on the carpeted floor. Additionally, the writ mentioned numerous other broken items previously neatly displayed on the fireplace mantle as well as pictures that had been ripped off the wall and thrown on the floor to shatter into pieces. I observed that the only lamp in the room was a beautiful, crystal lamp sitting on one of the end tables between the couch and a love seat. It was in perfect condition. I looked at the mantle expecting to see nothing but shattered pieces of glass. Instead, the mantle was not even scratched, which would be evidence of violence from glass objects being shattered on it. I observed that all the pictures hanging on the walls were in place and the wall paint showed no signs of damage, nor did any telltale shadows exist to reveal proof that a painting or picture had previously occupied that position on the wall.

I knelt to the carpet beside the fireplace and then near the area of the table lamp to inspect the depths of the carpet for broken pieces. No evidence of broken glass or any other objects could be found in the carpet even though it was apparent the carpet had not been vacuumed within the past day or two, judging from other small pieces of trash among the carpet fibers. I asked the man to follow me back outside to the patrol car. He readily complied.

I opened my trunk and retrieved the Polaroid camera I used to photograph evidence of a crime scene. I returned to the home and photographed the entire area mentioned in the writ, including close-up photos to assure the judge that the investigation revealed no evidence of violence.

I asked the man to turn his home alarm back on, and with the home secured, we continued our journey to the mental hospital in Ft. Worth. During the brief stop at the man's home, I had advised dispatch as soon as we stopped and as soon as we left to ensure we had a record of the time spent in the home. I assured the elderly gentleman that the judge would receive a copy of my report along with the photos showing the interior of the home. I dropped him off at the hospital, leaving him in the care, custody, and control of the hospital attendants and signed a release of the man to the hospital.

Unfortunately, as is typical in law enforcement, I never heard from the court or the elderly gentleman again. Rarely does an officer hear the outcome of a hearing or trial, even if he or she serves as a witness on behalf of the state or the victim. I assumed the elderly gentleman returned to his home with a court order advising the daughter to cease any efforts to force her father to be committed to a retirement home. Since I had received no further directions from the court, I assumed the case was dismissed based on the findings of the hospital and my written report.

Other cases involving Writs of Attachment prove to be not so convoluted. However, each case does indeed offer its own, unique facts and circumstances. During my years on patrol, especially on specific holidays such as Thanksgiving and Christmas, a lady I will call Sharon would turn a knife on herself, always cutting only the top side of her forearms and bicep area as well as the less vulnerable area of her legs to ensure that she never cut an artery. Her arms revealed so many scars from previous cuts that she had little visible hair in the area of the wounds. Scars covered the entire surface of her skin on her arms and legs. Once she was satisfied with the cuts, she would move about the house, rolling her body, legs, and arms against the walls, furniture, refrigerator, and any other flat surface to show evidence of her misery.

I transported her to the North Texas State Mental Hospital in Wichita Falls, Texas, so many times that they finally labeled her as a lost cause, unresponsive to treatment or care, and refused to accept her in their facility.[19] Until that moment, I was unaware that a state mental facility could refuse to accept the care, custody, and control of a person with a mental health condition.

During my last encounter with Sharon, I took the time to visit her in the hospital and asked her why she lived the life of a cutter.[20] Previous training concerning the mentally ill suggested that a person prone to self-mutilation typically does so because of internal guilt about an act. Sharon's mother died a year before she became a cutter in our county, or at least before PCSO became involved in the cutting episodes. Sharon's mom probably served as the only avenue of relief from mental anguish for Sharon. Her death left Sharon with no outlet for the mental pain, which encouraged her to turn to self-mutilation.

In our final conversation, Sharon shared an event that occurred when she was ten years old. She shared the fact that a relative had raped her, but she had been blamed for the rape by other members of the family who assured her that it was her fault for being a little whore. When we first met, Sharon was in her late forties. Therefore, she had been carrying that burden for over thirty years, with her mother being the only safety gate to her pent-up emotion. Because of the label she carried, Sharon never dated and never married, leaving only her mother to serve as her guide to some level of sanity in her life.

Sharon disappeared from her home shortly after she was dismissed from the hospital the last time, and we never received future calls to her home. I drove by her single-wide trailer a few months later and discovered it was empty. I could only pray that she found peace in her new location and hoped that maybe another relative moved her to his or her home to help her endure her tormented mind. I had assured her, during our last conversation, that the man who raped her held 100 percent of the blame and that he should be serving time for the harm he caused to her. I tried to get her to tell me the name of the man, but she refused, which is typical of those abused by relatives. They do not want to see the person they love, despite the damage done to them, harmed.

NSSI (Non-Suicidal Self-Injury) may entail even more destructive actions like breaking a bone, injury to limbs, eye injury, or auto-amputation. It is frequently linked to multiple probable health issues, both physical and psychiatric, and can occasionally result in more severe medical complications.[21]

Such is the life of an officer assigned the duties of civil process: to fade in and out of the lives of various citizens, hopefully with the ability to provide services that will empower that person to stand against wrongs. Additionally, an officer hopes to provide some guidance toward legal services that might help citizens move forward with their lives even when legally in the wrong. Quite often, people make the wrong decisions in reaction to the harm forced upon them, which only further empowers those bent on oppressing them.

A prime example of oppression relates to those labeled "Slum Lords," who are typically trailer park owners who forced tenants to sign a contract knowing that the tenant would never read the full contract. One may describe a slumlord as: "an unscrupulous landlord who milks a property without concern for tenants, neighborhoods or their own long-term interests. Slumlords overcharge for property in poor neighborhoods that are kept in ruin. Some indicators of property run by a slumlord include numerous police calls, and city and county code violations on the properties."[22]

One such Slum Lord in the northeastern part of Parker County who carried the note on trailers he sold had written into his contract that the buyer of the trailer was required to pay contract payments weekly. Failure to pay rent on-time forfeited that new owner's rights to all belongings inside the home as well as to any temporary improvements made to the single-wide trailer. His contracts offered no grace period. Therefore, he assured his tenants that they had no legal recourse.

He knew that most of the people buying the trailers were already living from paycheck to paycheck and that if he gave them the typical thirty-day grace period with a monthly payment that they would probably be able to scratch together sufficient funds. However, meeting a weekly payment requirement created more than a challenge for most tenants, who already struggled with finances. Just remembering that the payment was due proved challenging enough.

Unfortunately, such actions typically remain under the radar of law enforcement and other legal entities because the people accepting such contracts lack the experience and education to understand the illegal methods employed by such offenders. However, once a person involves law enforcement or any other legal entity, the acts of the offender are brought to the attention of the courts, which empowers the county to shut down illegal operations, such as slum lords (selling or renting property), car dealers, and used furniture suppliers. Quite often, the people involved in such situations are attempting to hide from the law as well, which further empowers those who would use such tactics against them. It is the duty of law enforcement officers, especially civil process officers, to remain alert to such red flags to ensure they can temporarily provide assistance that may help the citizen overcome the threatening situation.

Unfortunately, the State of Texas allows private citizens to assume the duties of civil process service as well, which lessens the probability that the citizens of the county will receive the adequate protection of their rights. With this knowledge in mind, I worked diligently to ensure that I was able to serve all civil process papers within the required time limits in order to defeat the existence of the private civil process server within Parker County. Ironically, I typically found myself responding to a call for service from a citizen who found themselves confronted with an unscrupulous, private, civil process server.

However, many attorneys retain private civil process servers on a regular basis, which defeats any efforts by county Civil Process Officers who do indeed believe in their duties to serve and protect the citizens within their jurisdiction. The only hope citizens have is that their attorney, should they choose to employ one, will be able to ensure the protection of homeowner rights once he or she accepts their case and stands in the gap on their behalf in a court of law. However, the fact that some cases result from frivolous lawsuits assures such professionals that a need does exist to increase the number of well-trained, civic-minded officers to ensure adequate consideration of the rights of all citizens. Officers must keep in mind that not all offenders are behind bars and some weave their evil deeds through the civil side of the laws.

Chapter Two

Patrol

Law enforcement patrol includes multiple facets of responsibility with convoluted circumstances requiring an officer to serve as a counselor, advisor, parent, friend, and quite often the only contact a citizen has with a local government. Therefore, one must assume that the impression each patrol officer makes creates the perception citizens hold concerning the entire criminal justice system, be it negative or positive, which imposes considerable responsibility. Therefore, officers must ensure that they are thoroughly knowledgeable of the criminal laws as well as the actions relating to those laws. Officers must also possess a strong working knowledge of the family code, mental health code, and civil laws. Officers should be able to provide advice concerning victims' rights to every victim they encounter as well as provide contact numbers of victims' services and victims' rights advocates.

During witness or victim interviews, officers must be fully aware of the application of the Miranda Warning based on the probability that a general conversation with a victim or witness may suddenly reveal that person is a suspect. In such instances, the officer must recognize the need to stop the questioning and provide the Miranda Warning to the suspect in a crime as well as a witness or a victim. To continue questioning that person or allowing that person to continue talking without being advised of his or her rights will jeopardize the case the officer is investigating. An officer should present the Miranda Warning as follows:

1. Before we ask you any questions, you must understand your rights.
2. You have the right to remain silent.
3. Anything you say can and will be used against you in a court of law.
4. You have the right to talk to a lawyer for advice before we ask you any question and you may have him or her with you during questioning.
5. If you cannot afford a lawyer, one will be appointed for you.
6. If you answer any questions now, without a lawyer present, you will still have the right to stop responding at any time.

Additionally, an officer must be thoroughly knowledgeable of the Res Gestae, which allows the use of an unsolicited, uncoerced outburst from a suspect during an initial confrontation or following the person's arrest, but before the officer has provided the Miranda Warning. Any evidence presented by a suspect under his or her own volition does not relate to the Miranda Warning and prosecution may use that evidence against the suspect during the subsequent trial.

The other side of the equation in law enforcement patrol efforts rests with the inherent dangers one faces, quite often unknown to the officer. Therefore, an officer must remain vigilant to ensure awareness of surroundings, always, without fault, which is an impossible feat, but noteworthy. Cognitive awareness remains relevant whether the officer is on or off duty.

One of the deadlier challenges an officer may face remains a building or residential search for a suspect. Searches are especially real when attempting to arrest a known felon who possesses an extensive history of aggravated assault against a law enforcement officer. Such offenders are known to prepare for law enforcement intrusion long before a warrant is even released. Such dangerous offenders will install warning devices and even video surveillance to help track law enforcement's approach to his business or home. Additionally, some offenders will set traps intended to either impend the officers' progress or to maim and kill an officer. The types of traps are as variable as one's imagination but can be something as simple as a fishing line with dangling treble fishhooks stretched between trees, porch posts, or in the hallways of the home. Other traps may be nothing more than an overhead acid bomb that pours acid on the unsuspecting victim.

A dangerous offender who is compelled to attack a law enforcement officer will rely on any method. He or she may also attempt to impede the search of his or her vehicle, property, or even his or her person for contraband, evidence to a previous crime, or concealed weapons. Therefore, the experience and skill-set an officer develops while dealing with the devious methods one can employ against another in combat can relate directly to their survival.

Another dangerous situation involved individuals who have mastered the use of high powered weaponry, such as sniper rifles. Such weapons allow an offender to strike out against any target with such penetration power that he or she can take out an officer driving in a car, or walking down a trail to get to the offender's home, or as soon as the officer parks his or her patrol car in the offender's driveway.

The inherent dangers law enforcement officers face daily cannot be made more apparent than the recent Dallas, Texas, shooting that occurred during an organized protest in downtown Dallas. In a comment concerning the blatant hate crime of the Capital Murder of Dallas Police, one author stated, "Along with the five officers who died, seven others were wounded Thursday night when sniper fire from what turned out to be a lone gunman turned a peaceful protest over recent police shootings into a scene of chaos and terror."[1]

Without a doubt, law enforcement officers on patrol, completing a prisoner transport, or providing security for a protest march must remain cognizant of their immediate environment, even when eating a meal, on or off duty.

Politicians and community leaders flounder in their efforts to address the drug, crime, and low-income issues that are prevalent not only in our impoverished communities but also in average communities in America. Officers are required to patrol high-crime areas by written policy and dispatch requirements in every jurisdiction of the United States. It is not an officer's option to patrol or not patrol high-crime areas. The prominence of crime in a community forces the presence of officers in that area more often than in other districts with less criminal activity. Service to high crime neighborhoods works from the age-old business principle of supply and demand. The higher the level of crime, the higher the need for a law enforcement presence. Law enforcement officers cannot ignore this principle. In the business world, if supply falls short of the demand, that business will cease to flourish as customers turn to alternative sources. This fact is relevant in our crime-ridden communities as well. Citizens in a high-crime community will turn to alternative sources for help if law enforcement cannot meet their immediate needs. Law enforcement's inability to protect citizens from harm leads to the creation of vigilante groups or the victim turning to a weapon to defend against harm. Violence begets violence. As communities become overwhelmed with violence, corruption, and other types of crime, they lose faith in law enforcement and blame officers for their plight. The situation becomes self-perpetuating despite the desires of all good citizenry. The only hope for recovery is for politicians to concentrate funding and efforts to help communities rise above poverty levels with programs that will encourage the defeat of crime in populated areas and increase the average income level of the family unit.

Serving and protecting citizenry remains a tall order as our criminal justice leadership searches for low-cost programs such as community policing and broken window philosophies to help bring some level of peace and tranquility to a troubled neighborhood. However, criminals operate a lot like the vermin in this world. They only show their faces when the sun sets or in some cases when law enforcement leaves the neighborhood. They thrive through intimidation of the good people of the community. In frustration, the good citizens strike out against the very people who are trying, often in vain, to provide the help the citizens need: law enforcement. The criminal element recognizes this as a golden opportunity to increase their power in an area by creating anti-law enforcement movements, giving rise to hatred and blame against the very people who have devoted their lives to protecting citizens.

With the criminal element controlling entire communities while simultaneously preying upon those same people, the fear continues to rise along with the blame against law enforcement, which in turn further empowers the criminal element. This cycle of violence will continue to evolve until our government makes an honest effort to provide the goods and services that will cater to the needs of the oppressed citizenry in our low-income communities. The efforts extended by law enforcement entities, although offered with good intentions, lack the personnel and funding to satisfy the demands of these communities, creating a more reactive atmosphere rather than the desired proactive.

The challenge of providing safety and security is especially relevant to county law enforcement who are required to cover a sizeable territory. It is paramount for county officers to anticipate the need for service in a high-crime area by ensuring that they patrol the area frequently rather than wait for a call. The adage, "the squeaky wheel gets the grease," prevails in law enforcement.

In Parker County, most of the high-crime areas fell in the regions bordering adjacent counties. Based on the actions of the known offenders in those locations, we surmised that the reason for the high crime areas along the county borders was that the offenders believed they could easily flee to the other county, out of our jurisdiction. If the law enforcement entities in adjacent counties failed to share offender information, the offenders relying on this strategy survived with relative immunity to prosecution. To unite against this strategy, we created the Tri-County Drug Task Force as well as a Tri-County Criminal Investigations Unit, which focused on drug trafficking and other offenses throughout the combined county enforcement effort. However, little effort was extended to unite patrol officers from adjoining counties or cities. Therefore, unless a patrol officer ventured out of his or her jurisdiction, the offenders working the borders remained unchecked.

I confirmed the suspicion of offenders crossing borders with a traffic stop during a midnight shift patrol in the northeastern, high-crime area of Parker County. On a cold morning around 2:00, the offender entered our county from the main road leading from Tarrant County.

By direction of Sheriff Whiteman, we were required to allow PCSO dispatchers to accompany us on various shifts to help dispatchers learn the territory. Sheriff Whiteman was on target with his strategy, because it provided officers the opportunity to build a better rapport with dispatchers and provided dispatchers critical insight that may serve to provide life-saving assistance.

The dispatcher accompanying me that night was Officer Wendy Duke who had been a dispatcher with Parker County a couple of years and today serves as a deputy marshal with the City of Fort Worth. Wendy was very dedicated to her service and welcomed the opportunity to ride-along with a patrol officer.

I chose South Cardinal Road, which runs parallel with the county line, and traverses north and south, just inside the county jurisdiction off FM 1542 (Reno Road).

The knoll I chose was only about fifty feet from the intersection with Reno Road on the northern junction of South Cardinal. The spot provided a clear view of FM 1542 all the way to the intersection with Boyd Road to the east and west, approximately one-quarter of a mile, and of South Cardinal as it crossed Reno Road. It was a perfect place to sit on a moonless night with the darkness providing sufficient cover even though our patrol vehicles were a high-gloss white. Anyone genuinely observant would notice the white Crown Victoria sitting quietly along the roadside, with nothing to reveal activity but the smoke created by condensation from the tailpipe. The only other action that would give away my presence stemmed from any accidental touching of the brake pedal.

I remained cognizant of that action as I shared my purpose for choosing the location with Officer Duke. Concern that drug dealers and other felony offenders would easily enter our county from Tarrant County by relying on the connections mentioned above remained paramount. This information helped Officer Duke understand where and why an officer may advise a temporary location for a Signal 51, which was the Parker County Signal Code for investigation at that time. Parker County served as the primary dispatch office for all emergency calls in the county. However, every emergency service in the county offered individual agency dispatch services as well. Regardless, every officer in the county relied on the same 10-Code and Signal Codes to ensure secrecy when communicating with dispatch. The use of codes kept seasoned offenders from knowing the location or actions of every officer, which was necessary because of two reasons. First, offenders relied on a public radio scanner to listen to law enforcement radio traffic to help them ensure that no law enforcement officer was in the area when he or she wanted to commit a crime. Secondly, the scanner helped the murderous offender keep tabs on the location of an officer, which empowered that offender to ambush an officer.

Presently, the Department of Homeland Security has resolved to end the use of 10-Codes and Signal Codes of the past to improve emergency communications between the city, county, state, and federal law enforcement.[2] However, one may question if returning to standard English conversation on the radio is practical as well. Will it not empower terrorists to continually monitor emergency services during a critical incident? Regardless, the use of codes is history.

It being a cold night, I was unsure of the probability of offender movement. However, cold nights could spur the need for drugs by drug addicts as well. Therefore, taking a few minutes out of a routine patrol to watch a given area can indeed provide excellent results.

Suddenly lights could be seen turning off Boyd Road onto Reno Road. The car was a dark color, four-door sedan, occupied by a single person. Since nightclubs in Texas are required to close at 2:00 am, the driver could be a lone patron returning to his or her home to sleep off the liquor he or she had consumed that evening. Additionally, the driver could be merely a late-night employee returning home from a long shift at the nearby hospital or other twenty-four-hour operation. Therefore, moving on the vehicle could not be justified just because of the time of night. My peripheral caught movement from the opposite direction just as Officer Duke said, "There is a second vehicle coming from the west, on FM 1542." My eyes followed her pointing finger as a light-color pickup truck continued over the hill in the distance.

The four-door sedan continued to the South Cardinal junction and turned south off FM 1542. The car completed a U-turn just past the stop sign and pulled up about fifty feet south of the stop sign where the driver stopped his vehicle. His brake lights lit up the dark of the night despite the glare from the streetlight above his car. The driver of the pickup truck slowed at the same intersection, turned right and stopped adjacent to the driver's side of the vehicle. Thankfully, the position of both cars being just south of the stop sign provided an excellent view of each driver because of the radiant light produced by the corner streetlight. It was evident that we were witnessing some level of suspicious activity.

I decided to not wait for drugs, weapons, or other contraband to exchange hands and quickly applied the brake to place the patrol car in drive. Suddenly, the driver of the pickup sped southward down South Cardinal, away from Reno Road. The driver of the sedan ran the stop sign and sped eastward back toward the allegedly protective border between Parker and Tarrant Counties. With the driver providing probable cause for the stop (failure to stop at stop sign), I immediately initiated a traffic stop while I advised dispatch of the license plate number as well as the color and description of the sedan. I anticipated that the driver would continue to flee to lose me in the adjacent county, but instead, he pulled over immediately, which warned me that he had either decided to bluff his way out of the situation or was ready for a fight.

I turned the radio over to Officer Duke and stopped my patrol car off-center from the offender's vehicle to ensure that if he stepped from his car and began firing a weapon, my patrol vehicle would provide some level of protection as well as response time to develop a more appropriate approach to a deadly situation. I activated my takedown floodlights that lit up the interior of the offender's car. The driver remained motionless, which offered another red flag assuring me that he was ready for my approach.

Frequently, during a traffic stop, drivers will continuously check the rearview mirror or turn their head to see if the officer is approaching as they proceed to hunt for the proof of insurance and driver's license. The takedown lights deterred that strategy because they were too bright to allow an offender to see an officer as he or she steps from the vehicle. In many such situations, I would make my way around the back of the offender's car and approach from the passenger side, which may catch the offender off guard. For some reason, I felt that type of approach would not be the right choice.

I stepped from the patrol car and began my approach to the driver's side of the car. As I approached the rear of the vehicle, I pushed down on the trunk to ensure it remained latched, which is a sound strategy to avert any effort by the offender to release the trunk latch to allow a second offender to attack the officer from inside the trunk while the officer is concentrating on the driver. Additionally, offenders will use the trip latch for the trunk or even the gas lid on the vehicle to provide a momentary diversion, distracting the officer long enough to allow the offender to initiate an attack.

This offender did not rely on any of these tactics. However, as I approached the driver's door, I noticed that the driver's window was already down. Since the ambient temperature was about 20-degrees Fahrenheit, lowering his window before I stood beside his door was impractical, something a reasonable, prudent person would not do. Another red flag raised its ugly head. I decided to stop shy of the driver's door, leaving my body behind the driver's reach. Suddenly, before I could even attempt to verbally justify the traffic stop, the man bent forward, reaching toward the floorboard beneath his feet. I reacted instantly, by grabbing him by the shoulder and upper chest area with my right hand, aggressively shoving him against the upper part of the driver's seat, holding him as he squirmed to free himself from my grasp, continually pushing forward in an attempt to lunge toward the floorboard. He could have grabbed my hand or arm at that point and attempted to twist free. However, his focus remained on whatever lay in wait on the floorboard by his feet.

Fortunately, the sedan did not have the typical door post with the window providing the only seal against the rubber gasket lining the doorway. The absence of the door framework typically encasing the window enabled me to retain my grasp of the offender while I opened the unlocked door with my free, left hand. As I opened the door, I tightened my grip on the offender and forced him from the vehicle immediately onto the pavement, where we momentarily struggled until I managed to secure him with handcuffs. I lifted him to a standing position and forced him to walk towards my patrol vehicle. Officer Duke, being a certified officer as well as a dispatcher, was armed and ready standing alongside the passenger side out of the patrol car, prepared to assist if the need arose. I bent the offender over the hood of the patrol vehicle and completed a more thorough search to ensure he was not hiding any weapons or contraband that could harm Officer Duke or me.

With the man adequately secured with handcuffs behind his back, I placed him in the rear seat of the patrol car and asked Officer Duke to keep an eye on him as I returned to the car to determine why the offender had attempted to reach the floorboard during my approach. Lying on the floorboard of the offender's car, right in front of the driver's seat, was a .380, semi-automatic pistol, cocked, unlocked, and ready to fire. I am unsure if he dropped the weapon accidentally as I approached, or if he kept it there within easy reach to ensure that he would be able to shoot anyone, including an officer, who got in his way. Regardless, his intent was indeed to bring deadly force against me, which meant that Officer Duke's life was in danger as well.

If I had chosen to approach from the passenger's side, it may have empowered the driver to reach his weapon before I could recognize the danger and react with equally deadly force. However, from that position, looking through a glass window into the darkness of the vehicle interior would have impaired my ability even to see that the man was wielding a gun before he was able to fire. Additionally, if I recognized the weapon, such action would have required me to side-step to enable me to assume a proper stance to return fire. I secured the semi-automatic pistol, ensuring that I did not destroy any latent fingerprints on the weapon. I then contacted dispatch and verified ownership of the gun by serial number. Moments later, dispatch reported that the gun had been stolen out of Atlanta, Georgia.

During the vehicle search incident to arrest, I discovered numerous fur coats and other fur garments still boasting the Neiman Marcus sales tag. I had to assume those garments were stolen from either the Dallas or Ft. Worth locations. I completed an inventory of the furs and released the vehicle, which was confirmed to be owned by the offender, to the rotation wrecker service. Officer Duke and I delivered the offender to the jail and booked him in on multiple charges, including Criminal Attempt Capital Murder of a Peace Officer. The subsequent search of the vehicle by other officers on my squad while I was booking him into the Parker County Jail revealed about $7,000 worth of methamphetamines as well.

I was glad and sorry that Officer Duke was with me that night. We always know that a deadly encounter can erupt at any moment from any given situation. However, had I made the wrong decisions that night, Officer Duke and I would have, at the very least, engaged in a gun battle, and possibly endangered Officer Duke's life and my life. Fortunately, the traffic stop ended up with a favorable ending. I shudder to consider the alternative.

During that night, I was the only patrol unit working the northern sector of the county, which includes everything north of Interstate I-20. Additionally, the time of night dictated that none of the smaller community police agencies could offer assistance if a violent situation arose. Most small-town police agencies shut down all services at night with 911 calls directed to the Chief of Police. Azle was the nearest town and only had one officer on duty that night. I spoke to him earlier. The Azle written policy dictated that since he was the lone officer on duty he had to restrict his patrol to within one mile of Highway 199, which bisected the city. He would not have been able to assist us.

Additionally, the only Texas DPS unit on duty that night had already arrested a DWI offender and returned to the Parker County Jail to complete the intoxication review. Therefore, he would have been over thirty minutes away, unable to make the scene before the gun battle ended. Thus, Officer Duke and I were on our own.

A civilian ride-along or the accompaniment of a reserve officer is rare because most people remain concerned about the dangers. The career naturally offers extreme dangers which remain an imminent threat. One civilian, however, fell outside the realm of the average citizen. As a combat veteran of the Viet Nam War, Colonel Larry Beale was equally prepared to expect and properly respond to any given scenario that may arise during a ride-along. We met shortly after the publication of my other book, *CAP MOT*, in 1997. Unknown to me, he was the U.S. Army officer who was responsible for dispatching helicopter gunships to rescue my CAP Unit during the Viet Nam War on the night of TET

1969. He read the book and immediately drove to the sheriff's office to let me know that he was the soldier I wrote about but could not identify. Dispatch contacted me one evening to advise that a complainant was waiting for me in the lobby. A patrol sergeant had the duty to meet with complainants, regardless of location on patrol at the time.

I asked dispatch to advise the complainant that I would arrive at the office in about twenty minutes because I was in the northeastern part of the county. She assured me he would wait. A few minutes later I checked out at the station and walked into the visitors' side of the sheriff's office. A man, about fifty years old, saw me walking in and almost ran across the room with his hand outstretched. He asked, "Sergeant Goodson?" I returned his smile and assured him that he had the right man. "Well, I want to shake your hand," he quipped. He grabbed my hand in a firm death grip and introduced himself as retired Colonel Larry Beale of the U.S. Army. I asked him what I could do for him. He assured me that his mission was to inform me that I had told the story exactly the way it happened. I stated, "Well, Colonel, we are not about to lie on a police report." He laughed and said, "Police report, I am not here to report a crime, I am talking about your book... the night of Tet '69!"

His words set me back momentarily. My mind had to change gears from talking with a complainant to talking to the man responsible for saving my life and the lives of every Marine and Vietnamese soldier in my CAP Unit that fateful night, a small unit of eight Marines known as CAP124. During the heat of the battle, we were exhausting all our ammo and had to switch our rifles to single fire to conserve it, which signaled to our enemy that it was time to prepare for a charge on our position. The NVA (North Vietnamese Army) surrounded our defensive perimeter. I had already lost one man and had one man wounded. I was in the middle of calling on the radio for help from CAP Command and was engrossed in an argument with command, who remained convinced that we were not actually in a battle for our lives. Colonel Larry Beale filled that gap in history. I did not know the identity of the other voice that suddenly came on the radio advising that AH-1 Huey Cobra Gunships and a UH-1 Huey Gunship loaded with ammo had been ordered to help us out. Those gunships saved our lives as the NVA started their charge. Now this man, our unknown savior, was standing in the Parker County Sheriff's Office, shaking my hand.

Dispatch interrupted our reunion, of sorts, to advise that I needed to break for a domestic violence call in progress. A man was beating his wife severely. I turned to Colonel Beale and assured him I would hunt him up the next day, and he said, "What about riding out with you now?" I quipped, "Hell yeah, come on!"

Larry and I became very close friends from the moment of the handshake. I owed him my life. He became my partner in fighting crime from that moment forward, riding along with me almost every night except when he traveled as a consultant for the U.S. Military. It turned out that he was a bit of a hero to the U.S. Army as well since he created a wheel-type device known as the Beale Wheel that guided the proper aiming of guns on American tanks.[3]

Inclement weather always provides supreme challenges for patrol officers. One evening, Larry was riding along and the night had been relatively quiet with the exception of a couple of domestic violence calls. However, dispatch advised that a massive thunderstorm was heading our way around 8:00 that night.

The storm hit with ferocity as tornadoes accompanied the marble-size hail crashing against the glass of the patrol car. I was about halfway between Weatherford and Springtown, heading north on FM 51. The storm was prohibiting much progress, but I knew we would have immediate needs in the Springtown area, which prompted my decision to head north. We began to worry that the vehicle window glass would fail against the onslaught of the relentless hail.

The female dispatcher contacted me through a garbled connection. Her words were barely decipherable as she advised that a tornado was sucking a man and his pickup truck up from the ground on Veal Station Road. I was only about a half-mile from the Veal Station intersection, but I dared not increase my speed because of the pounding hail. The winds against us were at least sixty mph and carried debris that joined the thunderstorm. Part of a roof flew by the passenger side of the patrol car, causing Larry almost to flee to the driver's side. I turned right onto Veal Station Road, continuing my effort to reach the man trapped in the tornado. My mind raced with thoughts concerning how to rescue a man and a pickup truck in the clutches of a storm. About a half-mile later, the radio static activated again. Dispatch advised that the tornado had dropped the man and his truck on the side of the road and he could drive clear to safety. She cleared me from the call and asked me to head to Springtown where another tornado was taking out plate glass windows on all the stores. As I turned to head toward to Springtown, the hail stopped, and the rain and winds dropped almost entirely.

I turned north on FM 51 with Springtown only about five miles away. Regardless, driving was still hazardous as the engorged ditches on the side of the road forced debris onto the highway in front of us. As I negotiated a safe path through the rubble, I noticed a car in the bar ditch ahead. A man clutching his wife and two children was standing on top of their vehicle, which was engulfed in storm waters, rushing like a river. There appeared to be no injuries. I stopped alongside their car. Larry and I endured the rain and raging waters to help the man and his family from their stranded vehicle. Ensuring that none of them were injured, I placed them in the rear seat of the patrol car, handed them two blankets I kept in the trunk, and then continued my trek toward Springtown. As I turned onto Highway 199 off FM 51, the small town appeared to be a ghost town. There was no electricity anywhere. Glass, portions of roofs, broken tree limbs, and other debris littered the highway. The canopy cover over the pump stations at one of the convenience stores was completely missing. The glass in the front of all the stores was scattered across the parking lots. People were huddled in groups far back into the interior of the stores, praying the storm was over. After verifying that the local police officers had control of the situation and the man and his family found shelter in one store that remained unharmed by the storm, I turned my thoughts to my own family as I headed my vehicle south on Old Springtown Road. Our home lay hidden underneath massive live oaks trees on a hilltop toward the end of Mill Road, which was in the direct path of the tornado that had dropped down on Veal Station Road. I could not let my mind accept the dread and concern I felt for my family. I had asked dispatch to check on my wife and children when she first contacted me about the man caught in the tornado. She advised that she could not make contact.

Mill Road runs through five ninety-degree turns before one could drive straight into our driveway through the tangent of the sixth curve. As we approached my home, I could see that the roof of our barn was gone, and the walls were sagging outward at the top, which assured me that the structure was damaged. I shined my spotlight on the house. Most of the wooden shake shingles were gone, but the windows appeared to be intact. I hit my siren to see if my wife and children would respond. A beam of light radiated from the interior. Moments later I confirmed they were all safe and scared, but unharmed. I hated having to leave them alone during such a violent storm, right in its path, but knew I had no choice. Larry assured me he could do without Texas thunderstorms.

One of my more memorable encounters with another combat Viet Nam veteran during law enforcement came with a call for service to investigate shots fired in a small, rural community just east of Springtown, Texas, and right off Highway 199. Dispatch advised that his neighbor was shooting at him and his wife.

One never knows what to expect in shots fired calls. Usually, the call reveals nothing more than people exercising their legal right to practice shooting their weapons innocently and safely on their property. County ordinances for rural areas allow one to fire a gun as long as no residence is within one mile of the weapon. However, if that person has created a protective berm or some other form of barrier to ensure the spent rounds stay within the target area, then a closer neighbor may fire his or her weapon with care to assure no bullets endanger humans or domestic animals. This requirement does not infringe on legal hunters or residents' rights to protect domestic animals and family from attacks from any predator. However, occasionally, an officer may encounter violent situations requiring immediate attention. In this instance, however, the case relates to the scenarios mentioned above.

I drove to the complainant's home first to ensure he and his family were safe and secure. I lowered my windows as I approached the scene to listen for the telltale sound of gunfire. The silence of the night echoed back, interrupted only by the cars passing on Highway 199 behind me. The complainant's home was off the main road about 100 yards, nestled behind a large grove of beautiful, massive oak trees. As I pulled to a stop, I continued to listen for gunfire...nothing. I assumed the complainant was inside and checked out with dispatch and advised that there was no present concern for gunfire. I looked to the left as I stepped from the car, observing that I could not see the neighbor's house, the alleged offender in the case.

I rang the doorbell, and a woman answered the door. She invited me inside where a man was sitting in the living room watching television. He did not even bother turning off the TV as he stood to greet me. I listened to his story relating to having an argument with his neighbor who became enraged and fired a rifle toward the complainant's home. I asked him where the dispute took place and he told me that he and the neighbor had met on the roadway between their homes, argued briefly and then separated, returning to their own homes. He assured me that the suspect then stepped out of his house, firing his weapon toward the complainant's home. I reduced his story to writing, thanked him for his time and assured him I would deal with the neighbor. He immediately returned to his television show as his wife showed me to the front door. She was very cordial and assured me that she did not feel threatened by the neighbors in any way. She was just concerned that her husband would end up in a physical confrontation with the neighbor.

I left the complainant's property, driving to the suspect's property, which was realistically not next door, but the second property over from the complainant's. The property between the two homes was heavily wooded with massive oak trees reaching fifteen to twenty feet into the air, which were engulfed in the undergrowth as well. The probability of a bullet penetrating the wooded area remained very remote. I was beginning to doubt the validity of the neighbor's complaint, especially since watching television remained his priority instead of sharing a valid concern about the safety of his family.

The suspect neighbor's house was set back off the roadway as well. I drove the short distance to the home, which was a beautiful, yellow-framed, two-story country home, nestled among the mighty oak trees, a classic country setting. I advised dispatch that I would be out of the car with the suspect and assured her that all was well. I observed a man about my age, sitting in a chair on the front porch, smoking a cigarette. As I pulled my patrol car to a stop, he stood up and began walking toward me. There was no weapon in sight. He smiled and extended his hand. He assured me that he knew why I was there but hoped that he could share his side of the story before I made any decision concerning right or wrong. I assured him that was entirely my purpose for a visit, to gather facts.

He introduced himself as Jerry Walden. I could not help noticing his Viet Nam Veteran cap, set securely on the top of his head, obviously worn with pride. I side-stepped the inquiry, momentarily, to validate his service in Viet Nam. Jerry pulled the cap off his head for a moment, studying it as if searching to ensure all the pins and patches were still in place. I recognized the 1000-yard stare. I knew his mind was taking him back to the jungles of Viet Nam. He stared at the cap for a moment and then looked up at me and said, "Yes, sir. I am a combat veteran of the Viet Nam War. I served as an Air Force Commando and helped drop supplies and ammo to the Marines in Khe Sanh." His eyes returned to his cap, which he stroked to ensure it was properly aligned and then returned it to its rightful place on his head. I smiled and extended my hand again, offering my gratitude for this devotion to duty. "Thank you for your service, Jerry." He asked, "How about you? You appear to have that military look as well." I laughed and shared a brief history of my life as a CAP Marine. We exchanged handshakes again as he invited me to go inside his home where he could introduce me to his wife.

Moments later, we were sitting at his kitchen table sharing a cup of coffee. I returned to the business at hand and asked him to share his side of the story. Jerry told me a chilling story relating how the complainant repeatedly killed any neighborhood dog, cat, or any other animals that strayed not only onto his land but even walked down the road. He provided names and numbers of other neighbors who had endured the arrogant wrath from the same neighbor, a man allegedly consumed by animal abuse.

By county and state law, a person has the right to defend against an attack from any animal, to the point of death, if that animal invades his or her private property and poses a threat to his or her safety, the safety of others, or the safety of his or her livestock or family pets. The purpose of the law was to provide citizens with the right to defend themselves against packs of wild dogs roaming the backcountry and other animals that were prone to attacking anyone, especially children. However, unless the animal is an immediate threat, the person is required to contact authorities for assistance with the stray animal. Jerry's neighbor appeared to choose animals as target practice. Separately, Jerry's wife confirmed his story and shared a concern that the man was seen shooting his weapon across the roadway, where the homes were only a few feet from the roadway.

I thanked Jerry and his wife, Carol, for their time and their honesty and thanked Jerry once again for his service. I thanked Carol for her hospitality and wished them the best in life. I left their home assuring them that I was only going to write an incident report advising that Jerry committed no real offense. Additionally, I promised Jerry that I would have a conversation with the complainant concerning the laws governing animal abuse. Jerry and Carol had assured me that he did go outside with a rifle and fired the weapon in the air to release his frustration, which may have related to Jerry's PTSD issues. I assured him that his action was the wrong choice because of the possibility of the stray bullet dropping from the sky and harming another person or animal. I assured him that the proper approach would be to call the PCSO and ask for assistance with a suspect who was committed to animal abuse. The offender admitted that he had not considered the path of the stray bullet and commented how he should know better since he was a combat veteran, familiar with the dangers of stray rounds.

I shared a case I had worked in the past where a man in a trailer park in Willow Park, Texas, a small community about fifteen miles east of Weatherford and split by Interstate I-20, had stepped outside and fired his rifle in the air, thinking nothing of the bullet's path. The round, unknown to the man, dropped from the sky, lodging in the neck of a man watching his son participate in a football practice in a vacant field adjacent to the trailer park. The man died instantly. The subsequent investigation led to the arrest of the man in the trailer park. The courts charged the man with involuntary manslaughter, which ruined his life and his career. The offender's family was devastated as well, but the little football player lost his father forever.

Jerry and I ended up becoming lifelong friends, and even though we are more than a thousand miles apart today, we still share thoughts, concerns, and memories of our time in Viet Nam through phone calls, text messages, and emails. Our families are friends for life as well. Jerry is a success story of a Viet Nam combat veteran who chose to rise above the challenges of PTSD and become a successful Master Electrician as well as a father of numerous children, stepchildren, and grandchildren. He serves as a community leader as well as the leader of the local chapter of the Sons of the Confederacy, which contrary to some, is a proud reflection of a part of American history; so is Jerry Walden, a proud, American Veteran.

Being a solitary officer in the county was quite common during the 1990s. For example, on one evening, Corporal Dale Pilcher and I were the only officers covering the midnight shift, which can be entirely void of known criminal activity, but as proven in the events mentioned above, can equally offer some of the more challenging, life-threatening experiences. Per written policy, regardless of limited personnel, we had to split the county into two halves with each deputy patrolling his or her respective section. I took the north end, while Corporal Pilcher covered the southern sector.

Shortly after midnight, I received a radio call from Dale on our car-to-car channel. The signal was very weak, almost undecipherable. It appeared he was relying on his handheld in a remote section of his area. I immediately started heading south to provide what assistance I could, knowing that anything taking place would be over by the time I arrived. Either Dale would take command of the situation or the offender would overwhelm him.

As I struggled to understand the weak transmission, Dale advised that he had initiated a traffic stop on a possible drunk driver who proved to be at least twice his size and that the man was assuring Dale that he was not returning to prison. I felt confident that Dale could handle the intoxicated suspect, but asked dispatch to close the channel and to search for any other city or state officer who may be closer to Dale's location.

The highways were void of traffic, which enabled me to proceed quickly without endangering myself or any civilians. Regardless, I activated my overhead lights, leaving the siren to use when I had to drive through Weatherford, which indeed would still have a few citizens lingering on the streets. I never heard any more from Dale, which caused even more significant concern. Dispatch had not been able to find another officer nearby. Therefore, I was Dale's only hope.

About thirty minutes later I arrived at the scene. Dale had parked his patrol car according to training, with the front-end offset from the rear of the vehicle to protect him from an offender who exitted their car with a deadly weapon. I could not see Dale or anyone else in the general area of the two vehicles. I parked my patrol vehicle just short of and off to the left of Dale's, which effectively blocked the entire roadway, and searched for signs of him or the offender.

Suddenly, I noticed Dale's patrol vehicle rock as if someone was moving inside. I was shocked to see a large man sitting, uncomfortably, in the back seat of the patrol car, apparently already in custody. Dale's head popped up behind the suspect's vehicle where he was possibly completing a search incident to the arrest. Incident to arrest searches are standard procedure to ensure the recovery and identification of all property and to provide a historical record of all personal belongings discovered at the time of the arrest. Of course, any further evidence found during the search incident to arrest served as admissible evidence against that suspect as well.

Dale walked toward me as I shut down my overheads, leaving only the warning lights flashing to warn approaching vehicles of our presence. The probability of traffic on the remote country road during early morning hours was very slim, but keeping the warning lights on was good practice regardless. I observed Dale as he approached to see if he had suffered any wounds or signs of a struggle with the beast, now squirming away in the back seat of Dale's patrol vehicle.

I asked, "What happened? I tried to stay in touch, but received no answer, as did dispatch." Dale assured me that his radio lost reception, which was common in the remote locations in our county. I asked him how he managed to subdue the huge man, who appeared to be sobbing, confirmed when I observed him more closely. I waved my hand toward the man and asked, "What did you do to the man?" Dale laughed and said, "Nothing other than to appeal to his better side."

It turned out that Dale decided it may be to his advantage to attempt to reason with the man rather than to rely on a higher level of force, which he felt the man would endure, or resort to the use of deadly force. The man was close to seven feet in height and probably weighed close to four hundred pounds with arms the size of a gorilla.

Dale told me that he assured the man that as a struggling officer with a wife and two small children and that if he failed to arrest him, which was his assigned duty by Sheriff Ben Whiteman, then he would lose his job. Dereliction of duty would cost Dale his career and put his family in a dire situation with an economy that was already struggling. Dale said the man's threatening demeanor suddenly changed as the man began to cry and apologize for being such a brute. He agreed to the arrest and seated himself in the back seat of the patrol car without Dale having to raise a hand against him. I followed Dale back to the PCSO and helped him extract the intoxicated man, who was still sobbing, from his patrol vehicle. Dale had relied on solid training in the use of verbal judo as a first resort in the lawful use of force. I found that tactic to work quite often as well.

In addition to courthouse duties required of the day-shift patrol, I worked diligently with the Burglary Investigator to concentrate officers' patrol efforts on areas with high burglary rates. We worked from a list of known offenders who were on parole as a starting point and visited each one to ensure they were home and to identify the latest vehicle or vehicles in their possession. However, that strategy only proved useful if the offender used his or her car. Quite often, they would call upon a partner from an adjoining county. Therefore, day patrol became a game of cat and mouse as we each attempted to predict each other's moves.

One of the more common criminal strategies was for the offender to listen to law enforcement radio traffic through a scanner to get to know the officers' locations. We all used 10-codes, but offenders learned the codes, making them ineffective and limiting their usefulness to informing dispatch where we were and why we were there. However, we developed a system for each major area in the county as well as one for each business. Additionally, we changed the system at least once a month and provided dispatch with an updated copy.

As I close my review of the responsibilities of patrol officers, I would be remiss to not mention an essential function of patrol: the familiar image of the officer or other emergency personnel retrieving a cat from the tree for the little girl in the neighborhood. Such opportunities to contribute what some may assume to be in a minor way are rightly an honorable use of the law enforcement officer's time.

Numerous citizens in the county lack the physical or mental capacity or understanding of circumstances to overcome the most perplexing and fearful challenges. Those citizens include a few of the elderly, mentally challenged, and single parents in a community. Many elderly citizens live in forced loneliness created by the sudden departure of their spouse. Quite often they, especially widows, will develop an unnatural fear of the dark or a knock on the door regardless of the time of day. They have only one option to ensure the reassurance of their safety... the patrol officer.

We received a 911 call of a prowler around 9:00 pm, which is close to shift change, 11:00 pm. Most officers were already heading back to the station for the debriefing meeting to exchange information that may create issues for the arriving shift. I was entering Weatherford city limits when dispatch received the call. I heard the call dispatched to another officer who had just checked out at the station. I told dispatch I would take the call. Dispatch advised that the call came from a widow who recently lost her husband and that she lived on Ranger Highway, just outside the city limits on the west side of Weatherford. I was only minutes away.

I arrived at the widow's home only a few minutes later. The front-porch light was on. Out of habit, I turned my headlights off and stopped at the house next door so that the potential prowler might not become aware of my presence. Before I stepped out of the patrol car, I advised dispatch that I was at the scene and asked that she notify the complainant that I was going to be approaching the front of the house on foot. As I approached the house, I observed that the back-porch lights were on as well and noticed the lifting of a Venetian blind by someone inside in the living room, whom I assumed to be the complainant.

Anytime I approach a scene, I rarely, if ever, use a flashlight, for multiple reasons. First and foremost, a light beam immediately warns an offender not only that you are present, but also tells them exactly where you are, which could bring a bullet your direction before you are even aware of the offender's presence. During my time in combat, having lived in the jungle, I grew accustomed to relying on and cultivating my night vision and learned, quickly, not to look at any light, even the moon or stars, because the light immediately impairs your vision. Although I carried a flashlight, I rarely used it and shut my eyes for a few seconds before exiting the patrol car to ensure I maximized my night vision. Additionally, my weapon, a Colt .45, Series 80 Enhanced Model, offered Trijicon Night Sights to help me see a target regardless of the absence of light.[4]

I walked stealthily toward the front of the house, keeping to the shadows and checking the darkness surrounding the house for any sights or sounds before moving forward, which is another skill-set developed in combat. One's movement inevitably creates sound. When you are making noises, you cannot hear sounds produced by anything else, be it an enemy, animal, or nature. I knelt in the shadow of a nearby cedar tree and waited. The rumble of a car approaching from the south broke the silence. The wind rustled the leaves of the nearby trees and shrubbery and then moved on. The silence remained broken only by the approaching car. I quietly made my way to the dark side of the house and settled into the shadows adjacent to the corner of the home and waited for the car to pass. From my position, the car's headlights could not strike me to warn anyone of my presence.

I knew that the front of the house was void of human presence, which was confirmed by the front-porch light. I focused my attention toward the rear of the home and began strolling quietly toward the back corner. With exception to the offsetting of the front porch, the house was a basic rectangular shape covered with wood siding painted a basic white. The trim, based on the trim color revealed by the front porch lights, was a dark blue. As I continued walking toward the back of the house, I checked every window to ensure the screens were in place and the windows remained closed. They were.

Upon arriving at the corner of the northeast side of the home, I could see the back-porch light radiating across the backyard, filtering through the trees into the darkness beyond. Once again, I knelt for a moment to allow my ears to listen to the sounds of the night. A bug met his match in the bug zapper hanging above the back door. Suddenly, I heard a noise inside the house, from behind me. I turned and could see the blind in one of the rooms raise slightly as the complainant tried to keep up with my movements. I gave her an OK sign with my fingers and turned to check around the corner before moving into the light.

The darkness of the trees along the backside of the lot offered no sounds or visual signs of movement. The yard was unfenced, which made it easy to move around the house, but also made it easier for an offender to flee. Seeing nothing in the darkness at the back of the house, I risked lightly walking across the well-lit backyard, checking the windows and back door as I moved forward; nothing was amiss.

Since my body created a shadow that anyone hiding on the south side of the home could see, I decided to move forward quickly and rounded the corner of the house and knelt in the darkness as soon as I cleared the reflective glare from the backyard light. Because of the radiant glow from the front and rear lighting, the south side of the house did not offer the cover of darkness as did the north side. Hearing nothing, I stood up and made my way to the front of the home, once again, checking the windows as I moved forward. If an offender had indeed been in the complainant's yard, he or she had long since left.

From experience, I learned never to advise a complainant that they were wrong; no one was threatening their security. One must merely inform them that no evidence revealed the presence of an offender, no windows or doors suffered damage, and no footprints existed to leave evidence of the existence of anyone other than the officer. I contacted dispatch and advised them that the home was secure on the outside and to phone the complainant again and ask her to come to the front door.

I never risked knocking on the front door for multiple reasons. First, the offender could be hiding inside the house and could overcome the complainant before I had access to the interior of the home. Secondly, the complainant could be armed and mistake my knock as an effort to enter his or her home as an offender, which could lead to deadly consequences. I stood at the foot of the steps, in plain view by the porch light, and waited. I could see a face peering out the window next to the door. Slowly, the door opened, and the elderly lady invited me inside. I suggested that she allow me to search the interior of the home, and she readily complied. I asked her to remain in the living room and leave the lights on.

She complied, and I notified dispatch that I was completing a search of the interior to ensure further that no offender was present. I searched diligently from room to room, never assuming that any cubby hole, closet, or room was void of an offender. The search revealed no offender or evidence of forced entry from any opening in the house. I verified that the house had no skylights, which are also a relatively easy way to enter a person's home undetected. I returned to the living room and sat briefly on the couch with the elderly lady to ensure her fears had subsided and that she felt secure. I offered my condolences for the loss of her husband the past week and assured her that I would drive by every evening about the same time to check on her. She smiled at that idea and thanked me for being so diligent in my search. I left the complainant's home trying to imagine what it felt like being an older adult forced to suddenly live alone after relying on a spouse for so many years. Strength and trust come in numbers.

In the close of this chapter, the discussion should move toward a critical aspect of the responsibilities of not only the deputy sheriff but also any law enforcement officer. Officers must possess the training and expertise to recognize the mental illnesses that may confuse the average person and make the officer incorrectly assume that the victim is a violent offender or under the influence of some drug or alcohol. Quite often lack of knowledge can create a violent situation as well as potential harm or death to the alleged offender. Such diverse understanding should include a broad repertoire of all diseases and mental disorders. However, the primary ones are Alzheimer's, Dementia (both of which relate to elderly mental issues), PTSD (any person's survival of a traumatic event, including child abuse), Epilepsy, and Autism.

Chapter Three

Mental and Neurological Disorders

Physical and mental impairments force many people to appear or act in ways that lead an officer to believe that the person is an offender. The officer must recognize the symptoms of each malady to ensure he or she relies on proper methodology during an encounter. Three major neurological disorders that impair mental and physical control and arise in numerous law enforcement encounters are autism, Asperger's, and epilepsy.

The Autism Research Institute has created the following list of traits that may lead one to understand that a person suffers from an autism disorder. I will address some of these traits as they relate to law enforcement's encounters with people with autism disorders to emphasize how imperative it is that law enforcement officers be able to quickly recognize a neurological-disorder. I will also discuss accepted methods to ensure proper communication and handling of alleged offenders or even witnesses or victims of crime. Some of those traits applicable to law enforcement encounters are:

Social Interaction Traits

- Very little or no eye contact.
- Resistance to being held or touched
- Aversion to answering questions about themselves.
- Gives spontaneous comments which seem to have no connection to the current conversation.
- Prefers to be alone, aloof or overly friendly.[1]

Numerous factors force a person to avoid eye contact, one of the more common of which is guilt, while others result from cultural practices, shyness, and, of course, mental disorders. Many of us, as Americans, are taught from an early age to judge a person through eye contact. For example, most of my adult peers, especially my grandfather and my father, taught me as a young boy that I should greet every person with a smile, look them in the eye, and grasp their hand in a firm handshake, which immediately told that person that you were sincere in your greeting.

After being in combat in the Marine Corps, I believe I developed a sensitivity to my environment, which leads me to believe someone is watching from afar. As a law enforcement officer, training empowered me and other officers with knowledge relating to body language and other neural stimulators. We have been taught to perceive certain stages of body language that signal whether someone is about to resist arrest, attack us, flee, or attack another innocent victim.

For example, officers know from experience that if a person's eyes reveal sudden extreme concentration as well as tension in their body, they may be intending to commit an action putting someone else in danger. The same may apply to the change in someone's countenance from aggressive to resignation, which is especially true in an arrest but could also be an attempt to cover his actual intent to harm the officer or someone else.

The concern that lies with those who have autism is that the need not to make eye contact rests much deeper within the soul than one expects from cultural practices. This neural disorder creates a disconnect that imposes a strong desire in the victim to withdraw from any perceived threat, which may or may not be aggravated by the situation or the individual. Therefore, it remains paramount that the officer, if possible, gain prior knowledge from Child Protective Services, Adult Protectives Services, a therapist, or MHMR counselors before approaching anyone suffering from this disorder. Unfortunately, that is not always an option, especially with traffic stops.

Quite often an officer will initiate a traffic stop with no idea that the person he or she is about to encounter is a person with autism or Asperger's, much less how he or she should approach that person. That officer is trained to meet aggression with superior force and intellect so that the aggressive offender calms down or discovers the officer may resort to the lawful use of force that the officer knows will encourage compliance. This training may not work with a person with autism.

A prime example rests with those persons with autism or Asperger's who are prone to loud talking. Loud or abusive language does not justify an equally loud response or physical abuse from the officer. However, it should result in a higher state of awareness and a defensive posture from that officer, which will lead the officer to realize he may be dealing with someone with autism. In such situations, the officer's training and experience should teach him that verbal judo will be the best tool to resolve the perceived verbal assault. However, the officer must be ready to deal with violent threats expeditiously to ensure the safety of all those involved. Therefore, if the person escalates from loud behavior to aggressive actions, then elevated use of force, based on the use of force continuum, remains paramount. However, in some instances, the officer, made aware of the disorder either by the family, MHMR, or other associated services, might search for a more appropriate methodology to ensure a safe resolution to the conflict.

One evening, around dusk, I received a call from dispatch advising that a complainant, about ten miles north of Weatherford, was calling about problems with an autistic teenager. I pulled over and called dispatch to ensure I had all the facts before proceeding to the scene. Dispatch advised that the sixteen-year-old boy was making his way around the exterior of the house with a baseball bat and breaking windows, doors, and creating other damage to the home. The parents were hiding inside in fear of serious, bodily injury from their son, unable to gain control of his aggressive behavior. Dispatch advised that the boy was an MHMR patient and that the counselor was en route as well but would not make the scene until I arrived. The dispatcher advised that the boy was known to love to start fires as well. With the parents secured in a hiding spot inside the home the probability of the situation escalating to manslaughter through arson remained elevated.

No backup officers were near the location; therefore, I had to deal with the boy alone. I needed a decent strategy to employ against the emotional attack the boy was enduring. I was glad to hear the MHMR counselor would be present and anticipated getting advice from the counselor before acting. I did not use my siren or red and blues but sped to the scene as rapidly as the traffic would allow. Dispatch asked the parents to remain on the phone to ensure their safety.

I arrived at the scene about five minutes before MHMR and stopped my car about 100 yards shy of the residence. I advised dispatch that I could see the boy wielding the bat against the target of his rage. I tried to imagine what tormented his mind and soul, feeling that maybe I could relate to his disorder to some degree, based on my bouts with PTSD, which remains a futile comparison. A car approached, and the driver pulled in behind my patrol car, which assured me that help had arrived. The lady from MHMR, Kathy, and I had met numerous times in the past, and I always valued her assistance. She provided me with a brief review of the boy's history with MHMR as well as a list of triggers that would increase or decrease the escalation of the situation.

As Kathy reviewed David's case history, we could hear the loud banging of the bat and the shattering of glass. It dawned on me that the boy may be barefoot or otherwise cut from the falling shards of glass, which would only serve to aggravate his frustrations. I asked dispatch to put an ambulance on standby. During our conversation, Kathy briefly commented that the boy loved to watch law enforcement and cowboy movies and always rooted for the good guys. Picking up on that bit of information, I asked her if she felt that maybe I might be a calming force instead of one creating more issues. She thought for a moment and said, "Yeah, that might work. You dress the part of the wild west with the white 'silver belly' Stetson hat and the cowboy boots." I smiled at her comment.

The way we dressed was a requirement from the sheriff, who dictated we wear brown western slacks, a white or tan shirt, golden star, cowboy boots, and the silver belly hat. I found that playing the part did indeed create an instant acceptance with most of the good citizens in our rural areas. In this case, I thought it might be a lifesaver. Facing a teenager engulfed by rage while he wielded an aluminum bat was not desirable, and I preferred not to resort to a higher level of force than wrestling with the boy because of the possible traumatic impact resulting from using force. I decided the straightforward approach would work and walked toward the boy while whistling a well-known country song from my past, attempting to create the picture of a casual, non-threatening approach, one I felt sure he would recognize. The whistle was soft to ensure the sound was appropriately unobtrusive as I approached: "Happy trails to you..."

I sauntered toward the boy as if I was out for a stroll in the woods. When I was about twenty feet away from him, the boy stopped sounding the bat against the side of the house. The house appeared as if shrapnel from an artillery strike had hit it; even the nearby trees bore the marks of his wrath. I continued walking forward and whistling. The boy lowered the bat to his side and stood still watching my approach.

I stopped about ten feet away and said, "Howdy, David. Do you mind if we talk?" To assure him that I meant no harm, I dropped to a kneeling position, which left me open to a lunge attack from him. I knew I held the upper hand but hoped beyond hope that the boy's love for the country and cowboys, especially sheriffs from the past, would calm his racing mind and ease the pain and torment that one could only imagine haunted his mind.

His eyes momentarily moved from me to the ground and then back to me. I knew this was a good sign. I told him that I was passing through the backwoods keeping an eye out for bad guys and wanted to make sure that no one was hurting him in any way. The boy looked to the ground again and shook his head no. I waved my hand behind my back where only Kathy could see, motioning her to join us. I calmly stated, "David, I ran across a friend of yours and brought her with me. You remember Kathy, don't you?" I asked. His gaze followed my pointing finger as I turned to acknowledge Kathy as she approached. I looked back at David, who dropped the bat to the ground and ran toward Kathy, his haven in a world of confusion and violence.

He hugged Kathy only briefly, turned and pointed to me, then dropped his gaze to the ground as he turned back to Kathy. "He is a sheriff, Ms. Kathy." It appeared that he was trying to smile. I smiled back and contacted dispatch on my handheld, asking her to verify that the parents were okay and to advise them that MHMR had the situation well under control. David's parents came to the front door as Kathy and I walked with David back to the front yard. David yelled out, "Mom, Dad, look. A sheriff!" He pointed toward me again, this time his eyes focused on mine, and then gradually turned away. I stepped forward and shook their hands and told them in an equally loud voice what a bright boy they had and assured them that he might end up being a sheriff someday.

I asked Kathy if she felt comfortable with my leaving and she nodded. I looked at David and told him, "David, I have to continue my hunt for the bad guys now. Ms. Kathy will call me if you need me to come back. Maybe someday I can drop by and share a tea with you and your parents, but right now, I have bad guys I need to round up." I walked away from a scene of shattered glass, damaged house siding, and a boy with a troubled future.

During the 1990s, most people were still struggling even to understand autism and Asperger's, much less create therapy and medical treatments that would assure people like David of a more promising future. Thankfully, many professionals have taken up the challenge, which has led to significant breakthroughs in helping people who are victims of autism and Asperger's disorders live some semblance of a healthy life.

One of the more challenging aspects of autism or Autism Spectrum Disorders (ASD) is the need for a controlled sensory environment. TouchPoint Solutions suggests that sensory input provides uncontrolled responses causing avoidance and even violent reactions. [2]

The Touchpoint Solution offers a recent innovation designed like a wristwatch, which is "designed to interfere with the body's stress response by keeping it from entering the flight, fight, or freeze mode."[3]

TouchPoint Solutions assures users more opportunity to sleep during the night or remain calm during any encounter that may otherwise create a conflict or meltdown.

One benefit TouchPoint™ fails to mention is the fact that the device, if known by law enforcement personnel, may help identify the wearer as a person with ASD. Such recognition, based on the officer's knowledge of the malady's symptoms and stress stimuli as well as calming strategies, may empower that officer to de-escalate a potentially volatile situation.

According to the Center for Disease Control and Prevention, doctors treat ASD with a variety of medicines, but unfortunately, each pharmaceutical treatment varies with individual and produces different side effects. Drugs provide only a temporary solution and can indeed induce undue stress factors if they are improperly applied or the individual reacts poorly to side effects.[4]

During my tenure in law enforcement, I was friends with a Texas State Trooper, who was an excellent officer with a family that loved and supported his career with the Texas Department of Public Safety. He never talked about the fact that he was a victim of Asperger's, which is the allegedly milder form of ASD. I did not doubt that he benefited from various types of therapy but knew his doctor placed him on Prozac. One of the more severe side effects of the drug is known as overstimulation reaction, which can lead to suicidal thoughts and actions. I worked numerous suicides over the years from patients whose doctors had prescribed Prozac and from my experience and training, came to realize that the drug can create a feeling of euphoria leading the user to believe that he or she no longer needs it. Stopping regular use of the drug creates extreme depression from which it appears there is no return.[5]

My friend decided to stop taking his medication. He returned home for a meal with his family after an arduous day on patrol. He knew he needed a break from the stressors imposed by his duties. I heard him check out at his home on the radio. A short time later, I received a notice from dispatch to contact the office. I will never forget the message she had to deliver, which was equally difficult for her since we all knew and worked with him. My friend had finished his meal with his family, returned to his patrol car, and walked into the backyard and committed suicide with his duty shotgun. I can only imagine how devastating this was on his wife and his children. He had not shared his depressive state with any other officer; only he knew the pain he felt from the oppressive state created by the withdrawal from the drug, assuming that was the actual cause.

Therefore, pharmaceuticals are not always the answer to any neurological disorder, much less ASD or Asperger's. The risk of side effects from the drugs can be extremely devastating not only to people suffering from this disorder but also to those who love and care for their welfare.

Another typical reaction with ASD or Asperger's is resistance to touch or being held. This might lead to danger during an encounter with law enforcement when the officer is unaware that ASD or Asperger's is present. The resistance to touch is especially true when the person is in a public place, which already imposes extreme stress and causes overt reactions to external stimuli. The result can cause a violent struggle between the officer and the offender, a situation that may be avoided with proper officer training. Therefore, it is imperative that an officer approach every situation calmly to create a window of opportunity to evaluate the level of mental stability in the offender. Sometimes a subtler approach may be required or an MHMR or family representative should be dispatched to assist the officer.

In the early 1990s, a Parker County resident I will refer to as John suffered from Asperger's but had been able to control the issues through therapy and pharmaceuticals. Unfortunately, John was injured in an auto accident, which altered his entire perspective and aggravated his Asperger's. John was a rather large man, standing about 6-feet 5-inches and weighing around 240 pounds. Before the accident, John worked on his father's farm helping with all the daily chores. Before the crash, he was a peaceful man if people respected his condition. He would go out of his way to help another person.

The accident caused a violent side to arise in John, which resulted in the need to increase his medication. However, just as with my DPS friend, John would occasionally cease taking his medication, which left him in an uncontrollable violent state. During one altercation with his parents, who contacted 911, nine officers arrived at the scene to help bring John back under control and force him to take his medication. John physically heaved all nine officers out of the house, some through a window, before other officers arrived and successfully forced him into shackles and handcuffs.

Ironically, John liked me. I was unsure why. I thought it might be because I always talked to him before acting. During evening shift, on another cold January night, I received a call from dispatch asking me to assist a Springtown PD unit with John, who was creating a ruckus at one of the local restaurants. I arrived at the scene just in time to see John dancing in the middle of the restaurant floor with nothing on but his Wrangler jeans. He was spinning his massive body and arms in every direction without concern for anyone else. Patrons were huddled together in one corner of the restaurant in fear of the near-naked giant.

The Springtown officer met me outside. He said, "Thanks for coming. I have no idea how to deal with John, and I have heard stories about how he threw nine officers around like children. Dispatch told me that you might help because you know him." I assured the officer that I would try, but also knew that John's actions were highly unpredictable. I entered the restaurant and took a quick look around to see if anyone was injured. They all appeared to be okay.

I notified dispatch that I was about to meet with John and asked that she close the channel to emergency traffic only. John was still spinning in the center of the room with the jukebox playing one of his favorite country songs. He appeared oblivious to his surroundings. I stepped forward as John glanced my way. He immediately ceased dancing.

Stopping about ten feet in front of him, I said, "Hey, John. Are you enjoying your dance?" He smiled and said, "Don't you know it, Goodson." He gave it one more spin and then stopped facing me with a menacing look in his eyes. I knew better than to approach him inside the restaurant. The mayhem he could unleash would be tough to control. Pepper spray, historically, had no impact on him other than to increase his aggression. Technology leading to the development of Tasers was far in the future. I tried another route. "John, why don't we step outside, so we can talk? I don't want all these people to intrude on our conversation." He looked at me for a moment, smiled, grabbed his shirt and shoes, and headed for the door. I followed along behind him, watching for signs of violent changes that might lead him to turn on me. The Springtown officer followed behind me.

As we left the building, I walked straight over to the patrol car with my back to John, which I knew would lower his need for aggression, but also would leave me open to an attack from behind. The strategy worked.

I turned back towards him as we stood beside the patrol car. John stood ready for a fight. I looked at him a moment, his hands clenched in rage, and said, "John, what are you doing?"

He looked at me for a moment and then his eyes darted to the ground. He glanced back up and said, "Are we not going to fight?" I laughed and said, "I don't think so, John. I am not sure about you, but it is too damn cold out here for me to worry about fighting and I have no reason to fight you anyway." He looked confused and stated, "Well what are you here for?" I smiled back at him and said, "I heard this Springtown officer was giving you some grief and I thought I would give you a ride home and help you find your medicine." He laughed and asked, "You are not taking me to jail?" I laughed as well and said, "For dancing, not hardly? Besides, I like that song you were playing. Just get in the car, John. I am about to freeze to death, and I am sure you are too."

He smiled for a moment, looked me over to make his final decision, put his shirt on, opened the car door, and sat in the backseat. I assured him he was welcome to sit in the front, but he shook his head and said, "Just get me home, will ya?" As I drove toward his home just a few miles further west on Highway 199, I cleared the channel with dispatch and advised them that I was taking John home.

Silence returned from the radio for a moment; then she confirmed that the channel was open. I assumed she expected a call for help. I remained thankful that the strategy had paid off. I thanked John for letting me drive him home, and he assured me that it would have been a long, cold walk. John took his medicine as soon as we walked in the door and I spent a few minutes chatting with him and his parents to ensure he was going to be okay. I shook his hand and his parents' hands and left him to continue fighting his new battle brought about by the car accident.

His father followed me outside. "Officer Goodson, I want to thank you for being kind to John," he stated. I assured him that the kindness stemmed not from me, but from John. His father lowered his head and assured me that life had been a living hell since John's accident and that seeing him brought home instead of being hauled off to jail was a blessing. I assured him that jail was not a good place for John, to which he readily agreed. I told him that I was still unsure why John reacted so positively to my presence in contrast to other officers and John's father smiled and said, "Because he respects you. One of his friends told him that you were a combat veteran of the Viet Nam War, which made all the difference in the world to him." My thoughts turned to all those in the past who despised me because I was a Viet Nam veteran and now a solitary man suffering from extreme ASD issues in Springtown, Texas, was kind to me because I was a veteran of that war, an ironical twist.

Our dispatchers soon understood the bond of trust that John and I possessed, which elevated me to their contact person whenever John found himself in another delicate situation. A few years after the Springtown incident, the sheriff promoted me to the rank of Patrol Sergeant. The promotion moved me to the commander of the day shift.

One day, a DPS officer, another deputy, and I were concentrating patrols in the northeastern part of the county. Around 2:00 pm I received a call from dispatch advising that they needed my assistance in the jail. Simultaneously, she issued a call to every available officer to proceed to the jail to assist with a violent offender refusing transport to court.

She returned to our conversation and told me that John had been brought in by his parents to attend a District Court hearing. Because of his history of violence, the sheriff decided to put him in a holding cell. Being forced into a holding cell, especially a clear view cell with plexiglass windows, aggravated his disorder and encouraged John to act violently. Putting him in a cell instead of leaving him in the presence of his parents only created an avoidable scenario.

I arrived at the jail as soon as possible and while en route, asked dispatch to advise all the officers to stand down pending my arrival. As I entered through the second locked door of the jail, I observed about twenty officers filling the booking area; some were deputies while others were from DPS and other agencies. They all looked at me as the Jail

Sergeant walked to the cell occupied only by John and started to order the door opened.

John backed into a corner of the cell and locked eyes with me. His body began swaying dramatically in reaction to over-stimulation from the twenty men leering at him from the booking area. One of them yelled out, "Open the door. Let's get him!" I looked at the Jail Sergeant who was waiting for my command. I took one more look at John, turned to the crowd of officers and said, "Stand down." Those who knew John tried to argue that time was not on their side. I agreed, but said, "Let me try something first." They laughed. One officer said, "Your funeral, Sergeant."

I asked the Jail Sergeant to step aside as I reached forward and activated the buzzer beside the door, asking the Jail Controller to unlock the cell door. As I reached for the handle, I told all the other officers, again, to stand down and to only enter the cell if John jumped me. I opened the door and broke all rules concerning officer safety inside a cell, letting the door lock behind me. John looked up as he swayed back and forth. "Hey, Sergeant Goodson," he said, "Let them in. I'm... I'm ready. They want blood; I'll give them some." His concentration returned to his tormenters glaring at him from outside.

His eyes darted to and from the mob of officers, who were posing a significant threat to John, just from their body language alone. I turned back to John and said, "John, let's make fools out of those idiots out there. What do you say?" His swaying lessened and suddenly stopped. He glanced at the crowd, scowling at them like a caged animal. "You going to fight them with me?" he asked. I laughed and assured him that I had no intention of fighting anyone.

I shared my plan with him, which was to walk out of that cell, figuratively hand-in-hand, to my patrol car parked in the Sally Port. I assured him that agreeing to go with me, without any form of violence, would rob them of the opportunity to assault him and provide him with a victory because he was able to control their actions without brutality. I assured him that they were scared to death of him anyway and that they would probably be inwardly thankful that he decided not to hurt them. He looked at the angry men once again and laughed. "I guess that would be a bit of a show, huh?" he said. "Let's do it, but I don't want to wear those damn handcuffs. We go out of here as friends."

I assured John that was my exact thought, but that once we arrived at the courthouse, by the order from the judge, I could not take him to the courtroom unless he was in handcuffs. I assured him that I would not handcuff him until we arrived at the courthouse and that I would let him keep his hands in front of him, regardless. He thought for a minute and said, "I don't like cuffs." I laughed and said, "Hell, John, neither do I. Is it a deal?" I extended my hand in plain view of all the men crowded outside to see. John smiled, looked out the cell window and glared at the other officers as he shook my hand.

I told him, to prove we were friends, I would go out first, leaving my back to him, which would perplex the other officers even further. John liked the idea and yelled out, "Lead out Sergeant." The controller was listening to the conversation and asked, "Unlock the door Sergeant?" I assured him we were ready, and John followed me out of the cell and then moved up alongside me, ensuring he placed me between him and the officers who remained prepared to attack, wondering why I would allow John to exit without handcuffs.

I told the Jail Sergeant that I would take John to the hearing and asked the controller to release both Sally Port doors simultaneously to ensure our path was unimpeded. I dismissed the other officers as I pushed the first door open, John following right behind me, grinning from ear to ear. Once we were in the Sally Port, he reacted like a giddy child, laughing and yelling out, "We won! We showed them!" I agreed and asked him to go ahead and sit up front with me.

This time he complied, knowing that it reinforced my statement that we were friends. We entered the courthouse without any incident, and I remained with John until the judge released him to his parents. He was slowly winning a victory over his issues with ASD. No doubt his therapist had employed the right methods to ensure John's recovery. I wished him and his family the best. We shook hands and parted. I never had another call to assist with John and never heard of any further arrests. I eventually lost track of him as my efforts were forced to pursue true offenders in our county. I trust John continued a road of mastery of his issues and became a contribution to his family and community once again.

ASD and Asperger's are only a few of the neurological and mental disorders assailing offenders, witnesses, and crime victims. Several of our offenders were not offenders by nature, but like John, suffered from neurological disorders. Epilepsy, for instance, sometimes leaves a driver of a vehicle appearing as if he or she is overwhelmed by drugs or alcohol. This unresponsive appearance might lead an officer to develop false probable cause under the assumption that the victim is publicly intoxicated. Or sometimes a similar problem occurs when encountering a person in a parked vehicle who appears to be asleep but turns out to be drunk. Additionally, these occurrences make the person a target for true offenders who might assault them or steal their car during their seizure.

The following story stems from a Parker County case file as well as personal interaction with the alleged offender in this situation.

On one fateful day, Roger, a local citizen of Weatherford, set up his daily vigil outside the 7/11 convenience store on South Main Street. Roger spent every morning in front of the store providing simple services on behalf of the store manager, such as cleaning up trash that thoughtless customers tossed as they hurried away without even a "Howdy" to Roger. However, he did not mind, because he was friendly to everyone and never perceived anything as a threat even though many of the neighborhood children and even adults would tease and bully him.

The 7/11 manager was a kind man who understood and knew Roger well. Roger was intellectually challenged and had the mental capacity and attitude of someone about nine years old or less. He was always happy and responded to occasional scolding and bullying by lowering his head and swaying his body until the scolding ended. He would immediately look up, smiling and thanking the person for helping straighten him out.

On this day, an out-of-town salesman stopped at the 7/11 to grab a drink and a candy bar to help him stay alert while he finished his drive westward. The man stepped out of his car, placed his briefcase on top of his car, removed a notebook, and walked to the pay phone in front of the store and made a couple of calls.[6]

Instead of returning to the car, he shoved his notebook into his pocket and entered the store. Roger watched him walk into the store and attempted to remind him that his briefcase was still lying wide-open on top of his car. Roger had witnessed too many things stolen from the store as well as from patrons' cars and decided that he would close the case and hold it until the man returned. He felt sure that the man would give him a candy bar and a drink in reward for his troubles, just for protecting his briefcase.

Unfortunately, the man saw Roger pick up the briefcase and grabbed the phone sitting on the counter and called 911 before the manager realized what transpired. A Weatherford PD officer arrived within a couple of minutes and grabbed Roger by the arm and led him inside the store. All the city officers knew Roger and could surmise why he had picked up the briefcase. Roger attempted to assure the man that he was only securing his property, hoping for a small reward. Instead, the man insisted that the officer arrest Roger and valued the contents at less than $500. The officer had no choice but to comply with the man's request since the officer did see Roger in possession of the briefcase when he arrived. I can only imagine how embarrassing that must have been for the manager and the officer.

I was just a young officer still attending the academy while working in the Parker County Jail as a corrections officer. This alleged crime occurred before the sheriff and Chief Deputy Shumaker hired me. By the time I arrived for duty in the jail, Roger had been sitting in the holding cell by the booking desk for over six months, which was well past the typical sentencing for a Class B Misdemeanor, which carried a possible sentence of six months or less. His mother could not afford bond, nor could she understand why her son was in jail. He had never harmed a soul.

When I reported to midnight shift for duty on my first night, I noticed a man curled up in the fetal position in the far corner of the cell, seemingly in fear of his life. He was sobbing profusely. Fortunately, my academy studies taught me that a corrections facility must keep an intellectually challenged person separate from other offenders and he or she must be afforded constant care by MHMR representatives. I pulled Roger's file and read the charges against him, which told the actual story.

I reviewed the case with Jail Sergeant Alice Youngblood, and asked permission to file a report with the sheriff. She readily agreed, and I completed a two-page statement advising the sheriff that the man had been in jail for over six months and that the officer's report assured the courts that he had committed a false arrest because he knew Roger was innocent.

The sheriff called me into his office the next morning as I was about to leave for class at the Tarrant County Law Enforcement Academy, about an hour drive from the Parker County Sheriff's Office. I usually arrived just before classes began at 8:00. I knocked on the sheriff's door, and he waved for me to enter. I had met Sheriff Whiteman when he swore me in, but saw him no further since that day because of being assigned, by request, to the midnight shift so I could attend the academy from 8:00 am-4:00 pm daily. He thanked me for sending the report and assured me that he would contact the court that morning. Sheriff Whiteman asked me to ensure that Roger's needs were taken care of and that his anxieties were relieved.

The next evening, as soon as I arrived to start my duty on the midnight shift, I walked straight to the holding cell and hit the button. Roger was still curled up in the corner, sobbing. I asked another jailer to hold the cell door while I approached him and knelt down and placed my hand on his shoulder, reassuring him that the sheriff had assigned me the task of taking care of him. I invited him to step out of the cell and to follow me to a private room where we could talk. He perked up instantly and said, "I... I can get out of the cell?" I assured him that he could. I helped him stand, and we walked to the interview room adjacent to the booking desk.

Roger reeked of body odors. I asked him when he showered last and he told me that I was the first one to open the cell door other than the corrections officer handing him the food for his meals. I told Roger I would let him shower as soon as we finished talking. He smiled and said, "I will do a good job, I promise." I assured him that I had no doubt and asked Roger what I could do to make his stay at least bearable until the sheriff arranged for his release with the courts. I told him that the sheriff was dropping the charges for the crime and that he would soon be a free man again.

Roger told me that if he could get out of his cell and help clean the place like the other inmates in the orange suits, that would delight him. I promised him that I could only speak for my shift, but I guaranteed he could work outside of his cell throughout my entire shift. He jumped for joy! "Can I wear the orange suit the trustees wear?" He asked. I laughed and said, "Yes, as soon as you shower." He jumped up with the eagerness of a child begging to begin his new adventure.

I took him to the showers and ordered one of the trustees to bring a set of orange fatigues for Roger as soon as he finished showering. I chose one of the trustees who had proven to be trustworthy and asked him to watch over Roger, ensuring that he understood that Roger was intellectually challenged and that he had the mental understanding of a child. The trustee welcomed the opportunity to do more than his present assignment of cleaning and laundry detail. I assured him that I felt Roger could and would handle any task assigned. Roger did not let me down.

Soon Roger came out of the shower room, fully dressed and ready to accept his new adventure. A few moments later he was feverishly attending to shoving the white fatigues of the real offenders into the commercial washing machine in the laundry room adjacent to the jail's kitchen. The entrusted trustee kept Roger busy and treated him with the utmost respect. Each time I started my shift, Roger waved wildly from the jail cell and pranced eagerly in his cell as I asked the controller to open the cell door. Roger remained so enthralled with his freedom and his chores that he soon left the other trustees with little or nothing to do until their shift ended.

During a final shift before the sheriff arrived with the good news, the jail, with Roger's constant cleaning efforts, clearly showed the fruits of his struggles, with exception of the dark mass in the cracks of the tile floors. I told Roger that he was welcome to mill around with the other trustees, but that we had nothing left for him to clean. He pointed to the filth in the cracks to which we had all grown accustomed and said, "Can I clean that?"

I looked at the filthy crevices for a moment recalling how I had been forced to clean similar cracks during boot camp at Marine Corps Recruit Depot in San Diego. I remembered that even though it was very laborious, it gave me an opportunity to be away from the demanding voices of my tormentors… the USMC Drill Instructors. I laughed at the memory, patted Roger on the shoulder and said, "Let me see if I can find a toothbrush." Moments later I provided Roger with a scrub brush and a toothbrush. Before the shift was over, the floors developed a shine that I doubted had existed since they were new. Not only did Roger clean the cracks, but he added another coat of polish, sliding the floor buffer across the floors with glee.

The next evening a document from the sheriff awaited my arrival. It was a Parker County Court Order granting Roger a full pardon for his alleged crime and providing him complete freedom, along with $500 for his contribution to helping clean up the jail. The court document ordered the official release at 8:00 am the next morning. The sheriff arranged with the academy to allow my late arrival to ensure I had time to share the news and take part in Roger's return to freedom. I pulled Roger out of his cell and showed him the papers. His reaction shocked me. "I don't want to leave, Officer Goodson," he stated, as his gaze dropped to the floor. "I like my job." I smiled and promised him that the sheriff reserved that job for actual offenders and that he was not an offender and never had been; it was all a mistake.

Tears fell from his cheeks as he pleaded to be allowed to stay. I comforted him, offering assurance that I would address his request with Sheriff Whiteman. As the end of the shift arrived, Roger stood ready in the clothes he wore when arrested. The trustee who worked with him had washed and pressed his clothes as thanks for the help. I promised him he could meet with the sheriff before he left as a free man. It was an easy promise because Sheriff Whiteman had left a note asking me to bring Roger to his office before we released him.

As we entered the sheriff's office, Roger looked in awe at all the paraphernalia the sheriff had collected over the years. Sheriff Whiteman stepped forward just as Roger realized his grandmother was in the room. He jumped for joy and hugged her, yelling out, "I'm sorry, grandma. I'll be a good boy." The sheriff handed Roger a letter that officially provided a pardon from him as the sheriff, which was nothing more than a formality to accompany the court orders. However, he knew it would mean a lot to Roger and his grandmother.

Sheriff Whiteman apologized for the arrest and the issues Roger had to endure during his time in jail and extended his hand as an offer of goodwill. Roger shook the sheriff's hand while his grandmother took his picture. As he turned to go, Roger turned to me and thanked me for being kind to him and reminded me that he wanted to work for the sheriff. I told him we would talk it over, but that I felt the 7/11 would be happier if he asked them for a job. His grandmother had already told me that the manager wanted to pay Roger to clean up around the store as his step toward goodwill.

The next notice I received concerning Roger was a news release in the *Weatherford Democrat* about his release from an unfounded arrest and how the manager awarded him with a job with the 7/11. I never saw Roger much after that because the sheriff placed me on evening shift patrol as soon as I graduated from the academy and I spent my evenings learning how to negotiate the roads in our county, most of which county officials never named; instead, each road received a rarely posted number. This practice left one relying on only a county roadmap. Six months later, the sheriff swore me in as a full-time deputy, releasing me for full-time patrol on the evening shift.

Roger soon became history with the 7/11, however, because his grandmother died and courts awarded custody to the state because of no existing relatives. I could only hope that this final transition would somehow be another adventure that Roger would embrace with joy, even though his grandmother was gone.

Throughout their careers, officers face seemingly insurmountable challenges as people like Roger, John, and David enter and leave their lives. One can only hope that such people today are treated with the utmost respect and with the knowledge and skill sets required. Sadly, a Department of Justice Statistician's report by Doris James and Lauren Glaze states the following statistics of the percentage of inmates who suffer from some level of a mental health issue: "State prisons: 73% of females and 55% of males; Federal prisons: 61% of females and 44% of males; local jails: 75% of females and 63% of males." Additionally, a second report from the same source notes that 61 percent of those mentally challenged offenders committed violent crimes.[7]

E. Fuller Torrey, M.D., in his 2011 report, confirmed significant new problems across the U.S. concerning mental health issues since the federally mandated withdrawal of funding for psychological health institutes nationwide. Many psychiatric patients have been forced into homelessness as our country has turned its back on some of our needier citizens.[8]

As the mental facilities continue to close across America, jails and prisons have become the psychiatric facilities for our mentally challenged, even for citizens not previously perceived as offenders. Now many such citizens find themselves forced to steal food and clothing because they cannot hold down any semblance of employment without help. Dr. Torrey tells us that the "three largest de facto inpatient facilities in this country are the county jails in Los Angeles, Chicago, and New York, and there is not a single county in which the public hospital has as many mentally ill individuals as the county jail has."[9]

According to the Florida National University, "Forensic psychology plays an important role in determining why a person committed a crime, and whether or not they can be charged for it."[10] One must wonder why we do not witness increased use of the mental health analysis services offered by forensic psychologists. Such services include a psychological analysis of each alleged offender shortly after they are arrested to ensure they understand the Miranda Warning and charges filed against them.

If over 50 percent of our offenders are known to suffer from at least one mental health issue, would it not be prudent to assume that many others, yet to be diagnosed, exist in prison as well? With that logical assumption, one may also surmise that a more significant percentage of our offenders are mentally challenged during the commission of their crimes.

Additionally, we can surmise that witnesses and victims may also suffer more than we realize from some level of mental challenge. Therefore, are the courts and law enforcement failing in proper investigative procedures by ignoring the rights of those mentally challenged witnesses and crime victims? How can we guarantee the protection of the rights of all parties involved in a case without employing the services of a forensic psychologist to ensure each person understands their involvement in a criminal case and the role they will be required to play throughout the investigation as well as the trial?

Some elderly find themselves increasingly challenged as various debilitating diseases creep into their lives, such as Dementia or Alzheimer's. For example, one elderly lady, Suzie, like Linda in the previous chapter, relied on a firearm to defend herself against perceived enemies. However, she offered more challenges because she fired the weapon through the doorway unless the visitor assured her that he or she did not intend to cause her harm. Fortunately, she never injured anyone or herself.

The neighbors repeatedly called 911 because of stray bullets and Suzie called 911 because of her fear of the demons rising against her. When I responded to her home, I turned on all emergency lights as well as my siren so Suzie could identify me as a law enforcement officer. Suzie perceived the presence of evil spirits or ghosts that descended upon her from any opening regardless of size and regardless of the time of day. Therefore, she kept the house bolted shut, day and night.

However, any open outlet, as well as the television and the radio or stereo, served as avenues for attack from the demonic spirits as well. Following repeat visits, I decided that a solution to her problem may rest with the ability to plug up the entrance areas she identified. As I mentioned, electronic equipment served as outlets as well, but only when those devices were turned off. Therefore, I purchased a handful of childproof outlet covers and assured Suzie that they had been prayed over and blessed as blockage devices. I helped her insert each one in every open outlet in her home and provided extras for her use when she finished watching television or listening to the stereo or radio. I instructed her to unplug those devices, lay the cord away from the outlet and insert the blessed, anti-demonic devices to ensure nothing could exit those outlets. The idea turned out to be a real Godsend because calls from Suzie or her neighbors ceased. I drove by a few times and visited with her to ensure she was okay, and she appeared to be a different person.

Suzie even returned to her previous love of gardening and planting flowers in her flower beds that had overgrown with weeds because she had previously been afraid to venture outside. Her home soon became a home of beauty and tranquility all because of a handful of plastic, childproof, electrical inserts.

The physical affliction of epilepsy remains a challenge for citizens as well. This malady leaves a victim momentarily paralyzed, sometimes following violent seizures, which may occur without warning. The paralysis is temporary but may last for hours. If a seizure occurs while the victim is driving and the driver is fortunate enough to pull over, he or she may appear to be intoxicated or a drug addict suffering from paralysis created by the alcohol or drug. Unless the officer pulling over to check on the driver is aware of such conditions, he or she may assume the victim is intoxicated and place the person under arrest for DWI (Driving While Intoxicated) or PI (Public Intoxication). Therefore, knowledge of this disease is required as well since the situation may impose a false arrest as well as possibly inflict physical injury as the officer arrests the victim.

Traffic stops can be the most dangerous action an officer takes, since there are so many unknown variables. Proper training and expertise empowers officers to recognize mental and neurological disorder symptoms to ensure the safety not only of the officer but also of the driver.

Chapter Four

Traffic Stops

Even though probable cause, which is required for all traffic stops, remains as variable as the depth of the penal, family, and traffic codes, there are only two types of traffic stops. The more common is primarily an investigative traffic stop based entirely on a violation of traffic laws or any other infraction in plain view of the patrol officer. Even though all stops are considered potentially dangerous, the investigative traffic stop does not carry with it the elevated need for the use of force. The average traffic stop only carries an increased awareness that the stop may require an instant decision to escalate from verbal commands to the next level in the use of force continuum. The use of force continuum allows the use of one level of force above that of the offender, ranging from the officer's presence to deadly force based on the immediate threat against an officer or another person at the scene.

Sometimes, the use of force continuum develops as an officer witnesses a crime in progress. The felony traffic stop, the second form of traffic stop, develops from the probable cause that a felonious crime has been or is about to be committed. Regardless, any traffic stop, as revealed by the stop mentioned in Chapter Two: Patrol, can immediately evolve into a felony stop.

All law enforcement officers, regardless of assigned duties, must be prepared to complete a traffic stop to ensure the safety of others. Therefore, the only difference that may arise between city police traffic stops and county or state trooper traffic stops is the proximity of a backup unit. However, that is variable as well. Even though city police cover a much smaller jurisdiction than county officers or state troopers, they do not receive fewer or less-dangerous calls for service, nor do they always have a backup unit immediately available.

Law enforcement officers are trained to remain in control of the timing and location of a traffic stop to ensure that they are near a backup unit before initiating the stop. However, even though an officer is in control of when he or she activates the emergency lighting to initiate the stop, this does not dictate when exactly the offender will comply.

There remains a slight difference in the reasons a deputy sheriff will initiate a traffic stop in contrast to city officers or state troopers. By directive from the sheriff, deputies only initiate traffic stops to ensure the safety of the driver, passengers, and other vehicles on the roadway. However, the primary motivation for a deputy to stop a vehicle is to search for wanted felons who focus on harming citizens in the county. Regardless of the motivation, probable cause (traffic code violation) must exist before any officer can initiate a traffic stop. City officers and state troopers have an assigned duty, dictated by written policy and enforced by their administration to participate in a given level of traffic control. Therefore, most, if not all, city and state trooper vehicles include radar equipment to provide probable cause for initiating a traffic stop. Statistically, one may assume that city officers and state troopers spend more time working traffic, which includes securing school zones, running radar to cover proven, dangerous areas on state highways and local roadways, and checking vehicles to ensure that they comply with state traffic codes.

On the surface, such traffic control concentration could lead an officer to become somewhat lax in his or her attention to dangers. However, the inherent dangers one must expect from any traffic stop demand that an officer remain suspicious of the driver's or passenger's intentions. The less experience an officer has with such dangerous encounters or the lack of proper training and discipline within the law enforcement agency can and will jeopardize an officer's safety.

One may consider the following cases as representative of improper and proper actions during a traffic stop. These cases include assaults against a Texas DPS trooper and a South Texas constable during two separate, unrelated, traffic stops. As mentioned, state troopers spend their entire shift working the highways and roadways of their assigned jurisdiction, which may cover a significant portion of a county or even multiple counties. Quite often officers work without partners, which makes them dependent on a backup unit that may be miles away, while the incident unfolding at the scene is over in a matter of seconds, which makes traffic stops one of the most dangerous encounters for an officer.

The first scenario deals with Texas Constable Darrell Lunsford, who was a rather large man, standing about 6-feet 7-inches. He was referred to by his friends and relatives as a gentle giant who used force only when absolutely required. Like most constables, he rarely conducted traffic stops. A constable's primary duty is to serve civil process in assisting the sheriff as well as serve as court bailiff for the Justice of Peace in his jurisdiction. Quite often the papers he or she serves deal with residents in his or her precinct.

This scenario remains vivid in the memories of all Texas officers serving as law enforcement officers in Texas in 1991. Constable Lunsford initiated a traffic stop on a suspect vehicle in Nacogdoches County, Texas, on a cold night in January of 1991. Fortunately, Constable Lunsford activated his dash-mounted camera. Otherwise, the world would not have witnessed the brutal attacks against him by the three Hispanic offenders who stepped out of the car to join the suspect driver during his encounter with Constable Lunsford.

The offenders exiting the suspect vehicle should have served as a significant warning to Constable Lunsford, but before we judge, we must remember that constables do not typically conduct traffic stops. Therefore, in his defense, he may have lacked the training and experience to recognize the red flags of danger. Constable Lunsford correctly checked out with dispatch as he initiated the stop and a Texas DPS trooper began heading his way but was still miles from the scene. Additionally, a deputy sheriff drove by during the initial stages of the encounter and witnessing nothing amiss, continued down the highway. Moments later, the scene changed. However, had the deputy witnessed multiple people getting out of the vehicle the deputy may have surmised that something was wrong, which would have prompted him to return and assist with the stop.[1]

As a rule, patrol leaders train officers to assist any officer engaged in a traffic stop, even if everything appears fine, just because of the probability that a situation can turn threatening within an instant. Within seconds an officer may die because of the lack of a backup unit.

As the YouTube video reveals, the three offenders, seemingly being very cooperative, surround Constable Lunsford as he turns his back on each of them while he bends over to search the contents of the trunk. He discovers marijuana hidden in the trunk, and as he communicates his findings through his handheld, the men begin to maneuver to take advantage of the constable. He towers over them in the video, but one dives for his legs while the other two men lunge for his upper body, wrestling the constable to the ground as he struggles in vain to access his weapon and break free from their assault. As they continue to wrestle, the constable falls to the right side of the offender's vehicle, which puts him out of camera range. However, the report stated that one of the offenders stabbed the constable with a screwdriver while the others took his weapon away and shot him with his own weapon.[2] Such a scenario is a prime example of how rapidly a situation can turn deadly on America's roadways.

In a later, unrelated event in the early 1990s, Texas State Trooper Andy Lopez, Jr., stopped a vehicle in south Texas on a moonless night for a traffic violation, with the memory of the murder of Constable Lunsford still fresh in his mind. Like the situation above, Trooper Lopez encountered numerous Hispanic men. As the trooper engaged the driver, he grew cautious because of the body language of the occupants and the evasive answers from the driver. The trooper moved to the front side of the driver's door to ensure he had a plain view of all occupants. Based on the suspicious actions of the driver and the occupants, the trooper suspected they were transporting drugs, which is common in that area. He asked for permission to search the trunk. The driver hesitated and then complied with the request. The driver activated the trunk release inside the vehicle as the trooper walked to the back of the car, unfortunately momentarily turning his back on the occupants, with his focus trained on the sound of the trunk opening.[3]

Multiple scenarios were probably racing through Trooper Lopez's mind at that moment. During traffic stop training, all officers are warned about and practice numerous scenarios regarding the ability of the driver or front passenger to activate the trunk release, which could enable someone hidden in the trunk to attack the officer. As the trooper approached the rear of the vehicle, the driver remained in his seat as the passenger in the right front seat stepped out and approached the trooper from the opposite side. The officer advised him to remain in the vehicle, but he continued toward him. As the trooper reached the open trunk, he smelled the odor of marijuana just as the passenger stepped around the rear of the vehicle. The other two passengers stepped from the vehicle as well and attempted to surround the officer. The first offender (right, front passenger) turned his back to the trooper momentarily, and attempted to pull a pistol from under his shirt. The trooper saw the movement and yelled "gun" and immediately shoved the offender against the car, which provided the distance and time for Trooper Lopez to draw and fire his weapon. The offender fired his weapon as Trooper Lopez continued to maneuver into the divided section of the highway, effectively using the cover of darkness to engage the offender with the firearm. Relying on the night sights to center his weapon on the body mass of the offender, the trooper fired multiple shots. The offender died at the scene from multiple gunshot wounds.[4]

During the engagement, one can hear the officer repeatedly providing dispatch with information to assure all officers of the danger he has encountered as well as his success in dealing with the offenders. Trooper Lopez survived the encounter, and the surviving offenders were convicted and remain in prison today.[5] However, if the officer had not been alert, and had not ensured his safety by installing Trijicon Night Sights on his weapon, he may not have survived the encounter.[6]

Night sights provide a permanent glow in the dark, which can give an officer's position away. From the front of the officer's weapon, however, the glow cannot be seen; only the officer can see it. The debate arises when searching an area where the offender could be off to the side or behind the searching officer.

In contrast, many officers welcome the use of a flashlight or laser beam to aid in sighting in on the target. I support the use of a laser because the beam is hard to see from directly in front of the weapon unless in a foggy or smoke-filled area. Flashlights, however, are dangerous. An offender can not only see the officer from any position but also can use the flashlight beam to serve as his or her target.

Richard Johnson, who is a veteran law enforcement officer, aptly counters the debate against night sights for weaponry in his statement, "If you train to do something, you are more likely to do it under stress. The more frequent and realistic the training, the more likely the shooter will use the sights."[7] I carried a Colt Model 1911 Series 80 Enhanced .45 semi-automatic pistol during my tenure in law enforcement and indeed did rely on Trijicon sights to enhance my aim not only at night but during the day as well.

Both actual events described above include officers making mistakes during a traffic stop. The first rule of engagement in a traffic stop is never to allow the driver, or other occupants, to step out of the vehicle without your knowledge and permission. In both these scenarios, offenders exit the vehicle without permission, and the officers soon find themselves dealing with multiple offenders from all directions, which severely alters one's ability to focus on threats as they unfold.

In the assault against Constable Lunsford, he realized his mistake and began backing up in hopes of gaining proper distance between him and the offenders, but unfortunately, his effort came far too late. In the scenario with Trooper Lopez, he managed to focus on the only real threat, momentarily, which was the man attempting to draw the weapon. However, the other men were close enough to have tackled the trooper, which could have drastically affected the outcome.[8]

In the late 1990s, several years after the two dangerous encounters mentioned above, I initiated a traffic stop based on the minor traffic offense of a failed taillight. Multiple Hispanics occupied the vehicle, which did not raise a red flag, but their actions did. They were all looking back as I pulled my patrol vehicle to a stop, offset and about twenty feet behind their vehicle. Based on their exaggerated actions, I flipped the switch on the takedown lights and pointed the spotlight toward the rearview mirror on the driver's side to hinder their ability to watch my approach. I decided to approach straight toward the driver's side. Abruptly, all four doors opened, and all six occupants began piling out of the car, walking toward me. The scenario involving both the officers above as well as personal experiences in combat assured me that these men intended to subdue me unless I reacted immediately.

Without warning, all the lights on the patrol car turned off, including the headlights, leaving me in instant darkness. Being unsure of the reason for the blackout, I knew that concern would have to wait. The darkness revealed the dark silhouettes of the men as they began to spread out behind their vehicle. I stopped my approach, ignoring the light issue and focused on the six men. I immediately drew my weapon and ordered the men back into the car. They all stopped where they were. I issued a final warning, assuring them that I would begin shooting if they did not comply. Focusing on the moves of six people at one time requires one not to concentrate on one person's specific movements, but instead to pick up abnormal movements from the panoramic view.

As if on command, all the lights on the patrol car reactivated, lighting up the darkness before me and blinding the men who reacted predictably with their hands raised before their eyes. None of the men showed any signs of an immediate threat. However, holding my weapon firm, not pointing at any specific individual, I remained ready. The men stood still for a moment and then the driver said something unintelligible from my distance, which motivated all the men to return to the car. The driver remained near the rear of his car.

Instead of approaching his vehicle, I ordered the driver to my position, leading him to stop alongside the front, driver's side of the patrol vehicle, which positioned both of us out of the view of the other occupants because of the intense lighting. I forced the driver to turn facing the car and told him to lie against the fender and spread his legs behind him to allow me to complete a frisk for weapons or contraband. He assured me that he had none but complied with my request. The search revealed nothing, lowering the level of anxiety significantly. I asked him for his driver's license, and he complied without protest. Relying on the handheld radio, I contacted dispatch and advised her of the situation with the light issue and asked her to route a backup unit in my direction. During the wait for the backup unit, I waited for dispatch to complete a search for warrants against the driver and to verify ownership of the vehicle. I maintained a vigilant awareness of the other occupants. None were trying to exit their vehicle.

The backup unit, a Springtown PD Officer, arrived. The returns came clearing the vehicle and the driver. I asked the Springtown officer to watch the driver while I approached the other occupants in the suspect vehicle. To do so, I moved around the back of my patrol car and walked into the bar ditch so the occupants could not see my approach.

I closed the distance rapidly and knocked on the rear passenger window, startling all the occupants who were still trying to see what happened to the driver. I shined my flashlight into the car, rapidly moving the beam from one occupant to another to ensure no weapons were visible. The passenger by the right rear door lowered his window while I asked him for his ID and asked all other passengers to hand their IDs to him. With the IDs in hand, I returned to the darkness and made my way back to my vehicle. Dispatch assured me that no warrants or criminal history stemmed from her search of the records. Therefore, I decided to release them without asking to search the trunk. Based on his cooperation and the cooperation of his friends, I chose not to write a citation for the traffic offense as well.

If either an occupant or the driver had a criminal history, I would have asked for permission to complete the search. However, the absence of any evidence in plain view did not warrant such actions. Regardless, the encounter was indeed one of intense stress, partly enhanced by the knowledge that officers in the past had lost their lives in very similar situations.

These examples reveal how a traffic stop for a minor infraction can instantaneously turn into a felony traffic encounter. Therefore, elaborating on the need for an officer to be aware of the differences between the two kinds stops remains a moot point. Throughout my career, I rarely enjoyed the pleasure of a backup unit during traffic stops, had numerous stops immediately become felony pursuits or felony traffic stops, and rarely had the opportunity to choose when and where the offender would pull over.

I initiated one stop in a business district along Highway 80/180, assuming the driver would pull over at the next available roadside location. Instead, he continued until he decided to pull into a business's parking lot. During the stop, the store manager came out and asked me to move the stop down the road, because it was bad for his business. I assured him that he was interfering with a legal traffic stop and subsequent investigation and that he should return to his store. He started to argue, and I told him that I would question the integrity of his store and his clientele if he genuinely thought that a law enforcement officer performing his or her duties would indeed interfere with his business. With that, he decided it was more prudent to return to his store. The infraction was a minor one, and the driver had no warrants and no record. Therefore, I completed the stop within a matter of minutes and gave the driver a warning to encourage him to repair the issue on his vehicle.

Traffic citations relate to one noteworthy difference in the duties of the sheriff deputy versus those of state troopers and city police. A deputy's primary focus on patrol is to prevent felony offenders from committing crimes and ensure that those with existing warrants are taken into custody and transported to the county jail.

State troopers and city police carry the same burden but are required by policy to write citations for any infraction unless they can justify a written warning. This is not to diminish the duties of any law enforcement officer, but to focus attention on the fact that the primary focus of the duties of the sheriff, carried out by his or her deputies, is to ensure the safety of the citizens of the entire county, which in our case covered over 1,000 square miles. Therefore, it remains prudent for deputy sheriffs to not encumber their primary duties with a focus on unnecessary traffic stops or write citations that would eventually require a day in court, effectively removing a much-needed officer from patrol. It remains paramount to leave traffic issues to the other agencies, which keeps our officers out of minor court cases concerning fines contested by the average, hard-working citizen. Deputies should focus on suspicious vehicles, foot traffic, and activity we discover by patrolling the backroads.

Quite often, felony criminals rely on a phone call ploy to dispatch to create a false report that requires the assigned officer to leave the offender's area to answer the call. These fake calls usually inform dispatch that loose cattle are blocking the highway in a remote, western part of the county. By listening to a police scanner, criminals may easily tell how many officers are patrolling a given part of the county. Once they are sure that only one or two units are in their area, they make the fake calls. When I was Patrol Sergeant, I would contact dispatch by phone as well as the officer receiving the dispatch and reassign the call to me to ensure the officer could remain in his or her area. It was not surprising to see an increase in such calls when an officer arrived in high crime areas, mainly when drug dealers were ready to disburse the latest batch.

We knew most of the drug mule delivery vehicles and officers forced to leave a typical drug area found a place to pull over outside the drug dealer's location to await the known cars to exit the area. Once the officer recognized the drug mule, he or she checked dispatch to verify existing warrants for that person. Each of these known offenders typically had a White Warrant[9] or some other felony warrant that would give our officers automatic probable cause to initiate a traffic stop, possibly resulting in the discovery of drugs and leading to further delivery charges, encouraging parole officers to convince a judge to send the offender back to prison. We primarily focused our efforts toward busting the dealers and drug mules in contrast to searching the highways and major thoroughfares for possible users/addicts. UNODC (United Nations Office on Drugs and Crime) brings true awareness of the heinous crimes committed against human trafficking victims not only around the world but also in local areas such as Parker County, in their report relating to human trafficking victims forced to serve as drug mules, thereby serving a dual purpose: selling drugs and selling the victim as a sex or labor slave.[10]

Parker County established a Tri-County Drug Task Force with three surrounding counties to strategically crack down on drug manufacturing and delivery within each county because of the known fact that we shared the same offenders. The Tri-County Task Force was composed of numerous undercover officers who posed as buyers throughout each county. The routine effort expended by task force officers required about one year to bring a case to a close. The undercover officer committed many buys from the offender throughout the year to ensure sufficient evidence accumulated to develop a solid case history before filing the case with the District Court.

Time constraints are the primary reason patrol officers focus drug interdiction efforts on the main thoroughfares passing through the county. Watching known locations of drug manufacturers and dealers enables patrol officers to get to know the backroads the drug mules typically depend on. However, once the general routes are known, the probability that the patrol officer would be set up to observe a drug delivery in progress increases exponentially. Other than highway and backroad interdiction efforts, patrol officers lack the time or opportunity to develop long-term involvement in developing a drug case.

Some patrol officers develop criminal informants who live among a drug-related community. However, most of the time, the discovery of drugs by a patrol officer stems from a general traffic stop or during domestic violence investigations. Such was the case with one of my largest drug busts. Dispatch received a 911 hang-up call from the popular drug area known as Briar Oaks. Per written policy, all 911 calls must be verified by an officer on the scene to ensure the safety of the individual making that call, even if the victim immediately disconnects the call. I received the dispatch and started driving toward Briar Oaks. I was only a few minutes from the entrance to that location. As I turned on the roadway at the Briar Oaks main entrance, I noticed a car approaching. The driver of the car flashed the bright lights on and off. Thinking the driver may be the victim involved in the 911 call, I activated my red and blues and completed a 180-degree turn to encourage the driver to pull over. I noticed the driver and one passenger in plain view were men. I notified dispatch of the license plate number and location of the stop, advising that I felt it might be related to the 911 call. I should note here that the headlights prevent other vehicles from seeing insignia or overhead lights on an officer's vehicle; the drive told me later he thought I was a friend of his.

The driver pulled over. As I walked forward, I noticed the driver and the passenger were actively engaged in exaggerated action requiring them to bend over, evoking memories of my encounter with the drug offender who attempted to kill me during the previously described stop in Reno. I shined my flashlight toward the two men to ensure I was fully aware of all activities in plain view and approached with caution. The driver's window was down, but being summertime, this was not alarming. However, sitting in the passenger's lap was a large rectangular bundle approximately twelve inches high by about two feet square. The men were frantically ripping a green leafy substance from the shrink-wrapped bundle and attempting to shove it under the seat.

I laughed and told the men to cease their efforts to hide such a massive amount of marijuana. The driver turned to me and assured me that the bundle was nothing more than grass clippings he was taking to the community trash dump. I asked him to step out of the car and ordered the other man to remain in the car. The bundle of marijuana was hampering his efforts to exit anyway. I quickly completed a pat down of the offender and placed him in handcuffs while I notified dispatch, by handheld radio, that I needed a backup unit as soon as possible, as well as the next rotation wrecker to take custody of the vehicle as well. I placed the driver face down on the roadside and then removed the burden of the green leafy substance from the other gentleman. I repeated the pat-down method and handcuffed the second offender and placed him on the ground with his friend. Dispatch assured me that the driver had a White Warrant out for his immediate arrest, but that the other man did not have any warrants. Regardless, I arrested both men for possession of marijuana with the intent to deliver a controlled substance. I turned the vehicle over to the assisting officer and transported the two offenders to the Parker County Jail. Unfortunately, the District Attorney negated the charge against the driver, with the drugs providing evidence that the

White Warrant justified returning the offender to prison to finish his previous sentence. The other offender soon joined him with a sentence for possession with intent to deliver.

Today, the special task force is known as Weatherford-Parker County Special Crimes Unit (SCU), which is a combined effort by officers from the Weatherford Police Department and the Parker County Sheriff's Office. One of my good friends, Tim Oglesby, just retired from a position in the SCU.[11] Tim started with the PCSO as a dispatcher during the 1990s and soon was assigned to patrol to begin his lifelong career in law enforcement. Every law enforcement officer has a personal dislike for specific crimes, and with Tim, that was drugs. I remember when he first approached me years ago with a request to work drug interdiction primarily on the interstate and state highways that crisscrossed Parker County. I readily agreed, reminding him that he must break free for violence-related calls.

However, despite the SCU Task Force and patrol efforts, drug manufacturing and delivery remain a prominent issue in Parker County today. The local newspaper, the *Weatherford Star-Telegram*, regularly posts numerous arrests. The extent of the problem is demonstrated by a recent report by Reporter Mitch: "More than four pounds of meth, 31 pounds of a date-rape drug, $14,000 and guns have been seized in Parker County after authorities were tipped off by Weatherford students."[12] Production and delivery of illicit drugs in Parker County falls back on the theory that offenders work the county borders to evade detection by opposing jurisdictions. The significant demand for drugs from Dallas and Tarrant Counties ensures a steady market that encourages continued expansion of drug efforts in the surrounding counties, including Parker County. Therefore, it remains paramount that the SCU continues its efforts.

Another issue that arises in typical traffic stops, especially during evening and midnight shift operations, is driving while intoxicated, also known as DWI or DUI (driving under the influence). The difference in the two rests with the fact that a DWI relates strictly to the alcohol content level discovered in the offender's body at the time of arrest, whereas a DUI relates to drug influence, which can stem from illicit drugs or abuse of over-the-counter drugs.[13]

As with drug addict offenders, I encouraged my officers to rely on city police and state troopers whenever possible and practical to complete a stop on DWI/DUI offenders, for two reasons. First, this is a primary function of traffic control by these agencies. Second, once again, sheriff's deputies, by policy, must focus their patrol efforts on major crimes within the county. Parker County Deputies conducted numerous stops of DWI offenders but chose to turn the offense over to the state troopers or city police whenever possible to ensure our officers were available for domestic violence calls and other calls for service that typically dominated an evening shift.

Most DWI/DUI arrests fell into my lap, unlike those one must follow for a mile or so to develop probable cause for the stop. Usually, an officer waits for probable cause provided by the offender swerving across lane markers without using a turn signal or any other violation that would lead an officer to believe the driver was DWI.

The Brazos River runs through western and southern Parker County with numerous crossings underneath I-20 and local highway bridges. Many of these locations are choice areas for drug and alcohol parties as well as robberies of local fishermen who choose the quiet of the late evening to enjoy the peaceful sounds of the river and fish. Many citizens gained most of their food from the river and frequented the easy access quite often. They too consumed a bit of alcohol or imbibed an occasional marijuana joint while enjoying watching the cork bobbing slowly with the ebb of the river current.

One of those areas was about ten miles south of I-20 on Dennis Road, which was also known as FM 1189. Local drug offenders typically occupied the area under the bridge; therefore, when working the southern area, I always stopped by for a visit to ensure everyone was safe.

One night, I parked my patrol car on the roadside adjacent to the parking area created by the local county precinct. The light from a riverside campfire bounced against the trees and undergrowth along the riverbed. I turned the handheld radio to silent and quietly approached the campfire. Within minutes I was standing in the shadow of the tree line within a few feet of the men and women consuming their evening alcohol and exchanging stories about their daily lives, enjoying the cool, spring night air. I waited long enough to determine that the men and women were violating no significant laws or local ordinances and decided I would join them for a moment to pick their brains concerning crime in the area.

I walked forward and sat down on a large log already occupied by one of the women. All of them were focusing on another friend who was fighting a fish on the end of his line. I sat silent for a moment and finally notified them of my presence, "Good evening, ladies and gentlemen," I said. They were all sufficiently intoxicated, which delayed their reaction to my presence. I thought the woman sitting beside me was going to faint as she grabbed her chest in fear. I honestly thought they would see me walking casually into their midst or at least hear the scuffle of my boots as I sat down to join them. I suppose I underestimated my sneakiness.

One of the men yelled out, "Oh my god, it's a cop!" He pointed at me as if no one else knew I was there. I stood up to ensure each person was aware that I was a law enforcement officer as the woman beside me regained her composure, assuring me that she almost suffered a heart attack. I informed them that I just dropped by to make sure they were safe. I recognized a few of them as locals who lived along the river and within walking distance of their favorite fishing hole that they baited with leftovers and dog food to ensure all the excellent fish remained in the area. They each regained their composure as I moved through the circle shaking their hands and encouraging them to continue their party and making sure that none of them were considering driving home. I had not seen any cars in the parking lot; therefore, I assumed they all had followed the foot trails from their respective homes.

They confirmed such by passing forward their IDs verifying that they were indeed local. I talked to them briefly, sharing concerns about crimes reported in the area, one of which was the robbery of a neighbor of theirs while he was fishing about this same time of night, which contributed to my motivation to join them on the beach that night. They were aware of the crime but could offer no clues as to who committed the crime. I handed my calling card to each one and asked them to contact me if they did see any suspicious vehicles or people in the area.

I left them alone and returned to my patrol car, fired up the engine and made my way north to Interstate 20. It was approximately 2:00 am. Just as I entered the interstate, a car turned off the adjacent frontage road running parallel with and about fifty feet above the eastbound lanes of the Interstate. I watched as the driver drove straight down the steep incline of the embankment leading down to the highway. The car bounced with every rock and hole it contacted along the descent onto the interstate and bent the front license plate as it negotiated the change from the steep incline to the level area of the emergency parking area alongside the Interstate. The driver, utterly unaware of my presence, continued straight across the two lanes of the highway and continued forward until his intoxicated mind assured him that he was about to enter the median.

He turned hard to the right, causing his vehicle to lurch severely against the asphalt producing a screeching sound as the tires begged for mercy. Satisfied with his entry and direction, the driver proceeded in the left-hand lane at approximately twenty miles per hour, providing an opportunity for a late-night trucker obeying the seventy miles per hour speed limit to collide with the intoxicated driver's vehicle. I followed him for about a mile as he wandered from one lane to the next as I chatted with a nearby DPS unit, Trooper Roger Smith, who readily agreed to head my direction. He asked that I initiate the traffic stop if the driver would comply.

I activated my red and blues, following behind the twenty-mile-per-hour vehicle, waiting for the man to respond, ensuring that I maintained at least fifty feet between my vehicle and his, anticipating a knee-jerk reaction when the overhead lights finally reached the conscious side of his brain. Suddenly, as predicted, the driver steered drastically toward the shoulder to the right, slamming his brakes on with the vehicle barely inside the emergency shoulder area of the interstate.

I pulled up behind him and advised dispatch that I would be out with a possible DWI at the given mile marker location and made sure that Trooper Smith monitored my location. To ensure the driver's and other motorists' safety, I approached the vehicle with the intention of removing the driver from the vehicle and ensuring the vehicle was completely secure as well.

The driver lowered his window and said, "I'm glad you are here. Is this Highway 35 West?" As I helped him out of the car, I asked him where he was headed. He told me he lived in Denton, Texas, and thought he was probably just a few miles from his home. I assured him that he was about sixty miles shy of his destination, depending on the route he took. Additionally, I shared the fact that he was on Interstate 20, about thirty miles west of I-35.

As the driver leaned against his vehicle for support, he started to argue that I could not possibly be correct because he just left a party in south Ft. Worth, and that there was no way he could be in Parker County. About that time, Trooper Smith arrived and took over the DWI investigation. I promised the trooper that I would provide him with a probable cause affidavit to validate the traffic stop and leave it in his box at the PCSO. I helped him complete the arrest and subsequent inventory of the vehicle to facilitate the impound and waited until the wrecker arrived before returning to my duties. Trooper Smith headed east to complete the final phase of the DWI investigation facilitated by the equipment in the Intoxication Interrogation Room inside the Parker County Jail.

I did not envy Trooper Smith's job. Writing a DWI report and completing the interview and toxicity analysis in the jail typically required two to four hours, which is why I always tried to turn the situation over to DPS or City officers. Working a DWI/DUI arrest took precious time away from patrolling high crime areas. Additionally, the task prevented proper, timely response to domestic violence calls or providing backup to such calls for service. It was paramount that county officers remain free to respond to these inevitable calls from dispatch.

During another evening, I was heading north on FM 730, which connects Weatherford with Azle, a city that shares borders with Tarrant and Parker County. It was a dark, moonless night during the middle of our midnight shift, approximately 3:00 am. I chose this route because it served as home to numerous churches offering easy access for burglars as well as relative seclusion on a dark night.

The road was virtually empty, offering no lights in the distance to warn of oncoming traffic from any direction, with the exception of to the east. Just as my vehicle crested a steep hill, a car lurched forward from one of the many country dirt roads connecting the various farms, ranches, and remote homesites to FM 730. The car was an older model Ford four-door driven by one male. Instead of negotiating a natural turn onto FM 730, the driver continued across the farm road to the steep decline of the bar ditch on the opposite side, spun out momentarily in the loose gravel on the shoulder of the road, causing rocks and debris to hit my patrol car, and almost sliding into the ravine below. As the driver regained some semblance of control, he continued north on FM 730 in the southbound lane, making no effort to move back into the northbound lane.

I searched ahead for the sign of any headlights; none could be seen radiating above the top of the next hill as the driver continued north in the southbound lane. If lights had been present, I would have faced the decision to initiate a pit-stop maneuver to force the intoxicated driver to the side of the road. However, such action would probably endanger the intoxicated driver and the approaching vehicle. Just in case I missed the dim lights from an approaching vehicle and contrary to standard procedure, which requires that an officer follow a suspect DWI vehicle for at least a mile to validate probable cause, I decided to proceed with an attempt to complete the traffic stop. I activated my red and blues and tapped the siren as I continued following the weaving vehicle; the driver remained oblivious to my presence. Then he swerved across the highway back onto the northbound side, continuing to the opposite shoulder where his tires showered my patrol car with gravel once again. He finally negotiated his way back to the correct lane and started to accelerate to the posted speed. I followed him for about two miles, continually tapping the siren before he finally responded by pulling the car to a stop along the narrow shoulder on the northbound side. FM 730 is widely known as the Highway of Death to residents and law enforcement in Parker County because the road design placed the roadway substantially higher than the bar ditches and ravines dropping sharply off on each side. The road offers no shoulder, making pulling to the side of the road treacherous, at best, even when sober.

As I approached the vehicle, I could see the man leaning heavily against the steering wheel. He appeared to be sobbing, his shoulders bouncing with every uncontrolled motion. I tapped on the window with my flashlight as he gained momentary composure while lowering the window. Before I could tell him why I pulled him over he stammered out, "Please officer, can you follow me home? I live about a mile down the road. This will be my third DWI, which means I will go to prison."

He began crying again. He was correct if he did already have two DWI convictions on his record. The Three Strikes Out law required that the officer file the third offense as a Felony DWI, which could send the offender to prison. However, the third DWI/DUI usually led to felony probation.[14] Ignoring his plea, I removed him from the vehicle and subjected him to a field sobriety test, which he failed without question. All the DPS officers were off duty or already testing their DWI arrests. Therefore, I transported the suspect to the Parker County Jail and began processing him per state law.

Some DWI cases offer somewhat comical results even though each case also offers a brief view into the sad life of those who choose to endanger their lives and the lives of others through their behavior. Heading north on Jaybird Lane (FM 2257), my focus was on the high-crime area of Briar Oaks in the northeastern sector of the county. Additionally, this area served as the source of the majority of Parker County's domestic violence calls. FM 730 created the eastern border of our county in that area. However, with cooperation between Parker County and the numerous small-town law enforcement agencies, including Azle Police Department, we never hesitated to cross that border in search of a wanted felon.

About five miles north of Highway 199, Jaybird Lane swerves slightly to the left and then makes a hard turn back to the right as it continues its route eastward. This area was so well known for the dangers it imposes to the average driver, to say nothing about those under the influence, that the county had posted numerous signs warning approaching traffic of the dangerous curve. Earlier that evening, a thunderstorm had moved across northern Parker County dropping torrential rain as it progressed. The owner of the property adjacent to the hard curve grew tired of mending his fences along the roadside, much less fighting the swampy conditions created by the low area immediately off the tangent of the curve. Thunderstorms left a temporary, shallow pond in the area that generated the local mosquito population and served as a home for the various native bull and tree frogs. A Google satellite view provides an idea why the curve is such a challenge to all citizens, much less the random DWI/DUI.

As I approached the hard turn from the south, on that evening, I could see the taillights of a vehicle that appeared to have stopped just as it entered the curve. I drove forward slowly relying on caution since the area was indeed a dangerous area occupied by known offenders who loathed Parker County Deputies. I remained ever-vigilant to ensure I did not innocently drive or walk into any form of ambush. Most death threats against Parker County deputies originated from the northeastern sector of the county.

As I entered the curve, I focused the beam from my spotlight forward to gain a better view of the vehicle, which had slid through the tangent of the curve and remained helplessly entrenched in the muck of the shallow puddle created by the thunderstorm. The vehicle was a greyish-blue, old Nissan pickup with a full-bed construction rack that was home to numerous ladders and various sizes of electrical conduit, revealing the probability that the driver, or owner at least, was an electrician.

I advised dispatch that I was out with a single-vehicle accident and asked her to notify the north DPS Trooper. I focused the spotlight on the interior of the vehicle as I completed radio traffic with dispatch. The light revealed a man slumped over the steering wheel. He did not appear to be moving or breathing.

I contacted dispatch again and advised her that a driver was still in the vehicle and appeared to have succumbed to the crash. She advised that Trooper Bill King was en route, but that he was several miles away. I advised her that I would proceed with the investigation to ensure the safety of the driver.

I moved my patrol vehicle off the road on a high section of the rain-soaked roadside, just out of the way of oncoming traffic from any of the three directions and activated the overhead red and blues as well as the takedown lights. Stepping from the vehicle, I trudged through the mud and water with my boots sinking ankle deep in the muck. The truck had settled with the body of the truck resting on the top of the water; the front tires were about halfway underwater assuring me that a hole had stopped further progress of the sliding vehicle. The driver remained slumped over the steering wheel, offering no proof of life, and my flashlight revealed no visible signs of bleeding or other injuries. I tapped on the window and received no reaction. I checked the door, which was unlocked, and gradually opened it to gain access to the driver.

Placing two fingers along the side of his neck, I checked for a pulse. The driver reacted violently, flailing his arms to ward off his would-be attacker. I stepped back a moment to allow him a chance to regain composure and let reality seep into his troubled mind. He looked up as I visually searched the seat and floorboard around him for any weapons or contraband, my eyes following the dancing beam from the flashlight. The only object visible was a near-empty fifth of Jack Daniel's Whiskey, lying next to his left foot adjacent to the driver's door.

I laughed as the man struggled to free himself from the seatbelt. "Had a drink or two," I quipped, pointing to the former bottle of whiskey at his feet. He managed to get free of the seatbelt and attempted to lunge at me as he exited the vehicle, yelling, "I'll kick your ass!" I spun him around and held him against the truck as he struggled to regain freedom.

He stopped struggling and stated, "You need to leave while you still can, mister." I chuckled and asked, "Why is that?" He looked around at his water-bound vehicle and said, "You are not allowed to see this craft. This aircraft is a test vehicle for the United States Air Force, and I have been conducting a test flight over Eagle Mountain Lake." I laughed again, which only served to further infuriate the alleged UFO pilot.

He waved his hand at the body of the old truck and stated, "The untrained eye sees only a Nissan pickup truck. With a unique lens in my eyeglasses, the actual picture appears. It is a top-secret, polymer structure designed to disappear with a flip of the switch."

A cam recorder seemed appropriate for the moment. State and city administrators issued video dash cams to DPS Troopers and city police, which would have provided comedic relief to any viewer. I asked the man for identification, and he refused based on the Air Force ruling of a need to know basis, and I did not qualify for the right to need to know. About that time Trooper King arrived. He activated his red and blues as well and joined us in the mud puddle. He had no idea he had just jeopardized his life by viewing the latest top-secret weapon and test pilot from the U.S. Air Force.

The man immediately turned his wrath against this new invader, which proved to be his fatal mistake as Trooper King assisted him with a shiny pair of stainless steel handcuffs, also made in the USA. We assisted the test pilot into the rear of Trooper King's patrol vehicle where the suspect would be able to secretly contact the test center through the two-way radio implanted within one of his molars. I assisted Bill with the search of the vehicle incident to the arrest and discovered no further contraband or secret documents meant for his eyes only. I cleared the scene with a comical memory of the USAF test pilot that strayed from his approved flight pattern to the mud puddle in Parker County, USA.

Intoxicated drivers do occasionally provide officers with comical outcomes. However, most are nothing more than bad situations going to worse. One DWI stop in Springtown reveals how people turn into disgusting drunks. This stop involved a young woman from Poolville, which is one of the few areas still offering vast, open terrain owned by generations of ranchers and farmers, some being distant relatives of notorious outlaws and cattle barons of the west. Some of the ranches cover thousands of acres with huge herds of livestock with herds of deer and other wildlife sharing the acreage. This lady boasted just such heritage.

I had just started midnight shift on a Friday evening, which offers officers a life of boredom occasionally interrupted by sudden events that can only occur in the late-night hours between 11:00 pm and 7:00 am. I was traveling westbound about a mile east of Springtown city limits on State Highway 199. My thoughts turned, momentarily, to my wife and children who were enjoying their sleep in our home nestled on a hill approximately five miles south of my position.

About 100 yards ahead, I observed a new Ford pickup swerving from one lane to the next as I followed behind in the westbound lane. Technically, I was well within Springtown's city limits. Traffic in Springtown is usually relatively quiet around midnight, with the exception of weekends. The local fast food restaurants were still open, offering food and drinks to those returning home from work, those continuing their late-night journey westward, and those who decided to call it a night before the alcohol consumed them. Highway 199 divided the city, bordered by clusters of small shopping center strip malls.

Most were closed, but the parking lot and the roadway were cluttered with numerous teenagers enjoying a moment of freedom from home. No Springtown officer was in view. I decided it would be a wise decision to stop the intoxicated driver before he or she entered the city proper and hit the crowd of teenagers or other innocent citizens. I advised dispatch that I was going to be out on Highway 199 West approximately one-half mile from the shopping area as I activated my red and blues, providing the dispatcher with the license plate number of the suspect vehicle.

The driver pulled over almost instantly, leaving the curious teenagers to peer in our direction as they wondered what poor teenager was being harassed by law enforcement once again. I approached the vehicle, which was a new Ford F-350 Diesel Dually 4x4 boasting Parker County Farm Tags, a beautiful vehicle. I verified the license plate with dispatch, who confirmed that the returns showed the truck belonged to a rancher in Poolville, Texas. However, some of our more heinous drug manufacturers and dealers set up camp wherever they could find a few acres nestled between the massive ranches in that area. Otherwise, crime virtually did not invade that peaceful community.

As I approached, the driver's door opened and a pretty woman, about thirty years old, slipped out of the seat as her legs stretched for the ground several feet below. If she could have managed to stand fully erect, she would have been about 5-feet 10-inches tall. Regardless, because the massive truck was a 4-wheel drive, she had to hold onto the steering wheel to guide her descent to the automatic running boards that extended out from under the truck as she opened the door.

The young woman leaned against the driver's seat as she stepped from the running board to the pavement. She rested in that position momentarily, looked at me, and giggled, saying, "I'm drunk." She attempted to stand up and then opted to support herself against the bed of the pickup as she negotiated her way to the rear of the truck.

"Ma'am, I stopped you based on your inability to maintain a single marked lane," I stated as I delivered the required probable cause announcement to the driver. She laughed and said, "Hell, I can't even see the marked lane." I assured her that I would put her through a series of tests to confirm she was intoxicated, and she looked at me in momentary silence, presumably attempting to digest the information. She shook her head and said, "No, I have to pee." She held her hand out in protest as I started to assure her that could wait. She suddenly stood fully supported on her own with her eyes seemingly focused on an object in the distance and repeated, "I have to pee."

Abruptly, her pants became saturated with the liquid flowing down her legs. I could hear the urine slowly filling her beautiful cowboy boots of hand-tooled leather. Rapidly, she had transformed from a beautiful young lady to nothing more than another filthy drunk headed for the Parker County Jail. I decided against any further efforts to subject her to any roadside tests for intoxication, placed her in handcuffs, and leaned her against my patrol car while I secured a blanket from my trunk. I placed the folded blanket in the back seat and helped her seat herself on it in hopes that she would not have the urge again until we made it to the jail, which was about thirty minutes away.

I advised dispatch that I had one white female in custody for DWI and provided my starting mileage, which is standard procedure when a male officer transports any female. A Springtown officer arrived just in time to help with the seizure of the vehicle by the next rotation wrecker. Soon, we arrived at what we referred to as Station 10 (the Sheriff's Office and Jail) where I removed the intoxicated woman from the rear seat, along with the blanket, and escorted her inside the jail. The female jailers came forward and escorted her to the front of the booking desk and allowed her to stand with support from the grab rail installed on the front of the booking desk. Sergeant Youngblood, a veteran corrections officer with the county, asked the woman for her name.

The woman looked at her and stated, "I have to pee." The Sergeant quipped, "You will have a chance to pee when we put you in the cell." I quickly stated, "Sergeant, you might want to comply with her request." Just as the last word passed through my lips, we could all hear little splashes echoing inside the woman's boots as the already filled boots accepted the pee trickling down her pants legs.

I laughed as the Sergeant glared at me as if I had released a curse on her. She stood up and looked over the desk at the floor beneath the offender's boots and yelled out, "Trustee!" I laughed as I headed for the exit, assuring her I had to complete paperwork. Since I rarely worked DWI arrests, I lacked the Intoxilyzer certification required to operate that equipment. Therefore, the jail no longer required my presence. Sergeant Youngblood yelled out, "Leave, you coward!" I laughed and waved goodbye as the trustee returned with a mop.

As this chapter relates, patrolling the byways and highways of any county or parish, depending on each state's designation, offer all officers the leisure to drive through the county with occasional stops to build a rapport with local citizenry and gain information relating to crime in their area. However, quite often, the career offers moments of extreme danger coupled with a bit of humor relating to the miseries of others.

Returning from a call to investigate an alarm in Aledo, an affluent area in the southeastern part of the county, I noticed a couple arguing in the front seats of the car next to me. Without warning, the driver delivered a closed fist to the face of the woman, forcing her head against the passenger's window.

Infuriated by the offense happening before my very eyes, I activated the red and blues and hit the siren to get the driver's immediate attention. He looked at me as I waved a command for him to pull to the side of the road. Not only did he assault the woman while he was driving, but he did so while driving seventy miles per hour on eastbound I-20, an interstate crowded with numerous other vehicles. Additionally, two small toddlers were in the back seat.

He complied with my order to pull over, and I checked out with dispatch providing a mile marker for the stop and advising her that it was a Signal 15 in progress (domestic violence). I walked toward the vehicle and invited the man to step out of the vehicle. I immediately placed him in handcuffs, advised him of his rights, and placed him in the rear of my patrol car after frisking him for contraband and weapons.

I returned to the passenger side to check on the woman, who was in tears and offered evidence of the assault from a large red mark on her left cheek. Movement in the backseat caught my eye as the two toddlers neatly buckled in their car seats started crying. I asked the woman to step outside, so I could ensure she was not suffering any further injuries and asked if she felt that she needed medical attention. She assured me that she was fine and complied with my request to step outside the vehicle. She begged me not to arrest the man whom she identified as her husband. She assured me that he had a right to be mad and I assured her that he had no right to assault her, especially while driving, which endangered her, her children, and all the other motorists on the interstate.

She agreed and began crying. She told me that they were on vacation and on their way back to their home in west Texas, allegedly just west of Abilene. Once again, she begged me not to arrest her husband because they did not have money to bail him out, much less afford any more motel costs while waiting for his release on bail the next morning. I asked for her ID and asked her to return to her car and comfort her children, who were severely frightened by the presence of an officer in their life. She provided her ID, which did indeed show a residence outside of Abilene, Texas.

I returned to the patrol car and retrieved the husband's ID as well, as he sat in silent rage, pondering his future in the Parker County Jail. I verified the identification of both individuals with dispatch, who additionally verified that no warrants existed against either individual. I returned to the suspect's car to visit with the man's wife again. I asked her what the probability was that her husband would conveniently pull off the side of the road after they left Parker County and continue his assault against her and her children. She assured me that she and her children were in no real danger. I was not convinced, but she refused to file charges. Since they were indeed en route to their home in another county, I complied with her request with a final warning.

I returned to my patrol vehicle and allowed the man to step out of the car. As I removed the handcuffs, I told him that I was not going to arrest him even though the laws of the State of Texas allowed me the privilege to intervene on behalf of his battered wife. I assured him that if he was a resident of our county that he would already be in jail. I told him that his saving grace rested with the fact that his wife refused charges against him.

However, he left knowing that I would follow-up with a radio warning to every officer between Parker County and Abilene alerting them that he was heading their way. I promised him that I would provide his and his wife's full identification as well as the license plate number and description of his vehicle to every law enforcement agency, including the Texas Department of Public Safety, between our present location and his destination. I also assured him that I was going to write up the offense in an official report and forward a copy not only to the local law enforcement agency in his area but also to Child Protective Services to ensure that they were aware of his tendency to assault helpless women and children.

The offender did not receive the words of warning well, but he knew better than to protest. I returned his ID and assured him that I would keep all his information in my files so I could welcome him to Parker County again in the future. As he drove away, I notified dispatch of my desire to pass the information forward to all law enforcement agencies along I-20, especially DPS, and to make the agency in his hometown aware of the incident to ensure they took the opportunity to follow up on the safety of the wife and children.

Pulling back into traffic, I negotiated a path into the far-left lane to take advantage of the faster flow of traffic. The shift was approaching the end, and I had numerous reports to write before returning home. I had driven no more than a mile when a vehicle between me and an 18-wheeler suddenly veered into my lane. I swerved away from the vehicle onto the middle shoulder of the highway as I looked ahead for parked vehicles, as well as to the rear, to determine if any drivers behind us were in danger of colliding. The suspect car swerved drastically from the left and right as it proceeded forward around seventy miles per hour.

The driver appeared to react out of control as he swerved back toward the 18-wheeler, forcing that driver to hit the air brakes on the fully-loaded, 40,000-pound trailer to prevent the truck from jackknifing and creating a major, multiple-car accident on westbound I-20. His professionalism showed as the large trailer skidded the 18-wheel vehicle to a stop.

Cars behind us began to brake to avoid collision with each other or the truck. The offending vehicle narrowly missed the 18-wheeler and crossed three lanes of other approaching cars before it careened sideways against a guardrail preventing a drop to a creek bed below. Following immediately behind the out-of-control vehicle, I activated my red and blues and hit the siren. I kept my patrol car between the oncoming traffic and the path of the crashing vehicle, ensuring that the patrol vehicle avoided collision with any other vehicle. Fortunately, the path was clear. Every vehicle on the westbound side came to a screeching halt without colliding with another vehicle. We were all very fortunate.

I pulled up behind the wrecked car assuming I had to deal with another DWI/DUI. The car was resting halfway on top of the guardrail with steam rising from the damaged radiator. Providing the location and license plate number of the stranded vehicle to dispatch, I stepped out of my vehicle, advising that I was out with a major, single-car accident on westbound I-20. I could smell no odor of leaking fuel, but asked dispatch by handheld radio to ask emergency personnel to proceed to the scene regardless and to invite DPS to assist as well. As I approached the vehicle, the driver's door swung open and a man fell out onto the interstate, bleeding from injuries. He attempted to stand up, but I held him down assuring him that he needed to remain still until we could assess his injuries.

I saw no evidence of alcohol and detected no odor from the interior of his car or on his person. He looked up at me with tears in his eyes and said, "I'm sorry, officer. I fell asleep at the wheel. I did not wake up until the car hit the guardrail and my head slammed into the steering wheel." I glanced inside and saw that the airbag had not deployed. The man was lucky to be alive; so were numerous people behind him. I remained with him until DPS, and Life Care arrived at the scene, along with the wrecker service and the fire department, which ensured that the vehicle was not in danger of fuel ignition at the scene or during wrecker transport.

As mentioned in Chapter One, helping those who remain helpless on America's roadsides is an equally important job for all officers. Unfortunately. I have witnessed officers drive by a disabled motorist with no apparent concern for the safety of the occupants, which is, to me, dereliction of duty. Those who assume people are safe on the roadside, especially in respect to women, children, and the elderly, are ignoring what different types of offenders see as easy prey. Just recently on I-10 Louisiana, stranded motorists suffered a wanton crime of attempted murder without provocation or reason.[15]

During a violent thunderstorm, I was patrolling a stretch of I-20 that is typically ignored by county law enforcement because it offers only about two miles of interstate before I-20 fades into Tarrant County. As I followed the curve of the I-20 split off from the I-30 junction on the far east side of Parker County, the torrential rain reduced traffic to a crawl, which was fortunate for two women driving a small, four-door sedan. The car engine suddenly coughed and died with smoke flowing from under the vehicle. The female driver barely managed to maneuver the car from traffic onto the shoulder before it rolled to a stop. Steam and smoke radiated from underneath the car. I trained the spotlight on the underside of the car revealing oil pouring from the engine compartment. It appeared the engine was blown, leaving the women stranded in the torrential thunderstorm, which made them easy targets for offenders, especially during a rainstorm, which served as cover for criminal actions.

I activated the emergency lighting and stepped out of the car to check on the passengers. Bothering with a raincoat seemed futile because of the torrential rain. I laughed at the idea of concern about rain on my back after spending a year in the jungles of Viet Nam.

The women were huddled in fear in the back seat as the storm raged on and a strange man approached, tapping on their door. The Stetson hat sheltered my face from the pouring rain as one of the women lowered the passenger window. I said, "Howdy, Ma'am. It appears that you have blown the engine based on the evidence provided by the vast pool of oil underneath your car. I can offer you a ride to the nearest truck stop where you can contact your loved ones while I arrange for a wrecker if you would like."

Tears fell down the lady's cheek while she shook her head yes, which was confirmed by her teenage daughter. I told them to wait just a minute. I returned to the patrol car and repositioned to align the rear passenger doors. Popping the trunk, I grabbed the raincoat from storage and moved forward to open both car doors as I held the raincoat overhead to enable the women to complete the transfer to the back seat of the patrol vehicle without becoming too drenched in the process.

After they were comfortably seated and secured with the seat belts, I returned to the driver's seat and advised dispatch of the situation. The mother quipped, "Never had a ride in a patrol car before." She looked at me in the rearview and smiled. I assured her that was good news as I confirmed the issue with dispatch, providing the license plate number and location of the vehicle.

The truck stop I had in mind was in Willow Park, and it offered covered parking, which enabled me to continue to help them without forcing them back in the path of the blowing rain. I advised dispatch that I was transporting two females and gave my starting mileage. I provided information concerning the disabled vehicle and asked her to pass the information to the next wrecker rotation and have the vehicle picked up when the storm abated. I assured the mother that she could contact the Parker County Sheriff's Office the next day or even later that evening and ask the dispatcher for information about the wrecker's identification and location to enable her to recover her vehicle. I provided my ending mileage to dispatch and helped the two women out of the rear of the patrol car since the rear area always remained locked from the inside.

Before returning to duty, I made sure they were okay and that they had a loved one en route to pick them up. As I left, I asked the store manager to keep an eye on them but doubted they would have any trouble since Willow Park was a quiet, roadside town. However, being adjacent to the interstate assured easy access, once again, to offenders. I-20 was indeed a typical haunt for local human trafficking offenders.

Thirty days later, I received a call from dispatch advising that the sheriff wanted me to meet him in his office. I was patrolling the southwestern part of the county and advised that it would be about thirty minutes before I could arrive. Dispatch informed the sheriff, and I chose the quickest route back to the office. I could not imagine why the sheriff needed to see me. Maybe it was just me, but one typically searches one's mind for any mistake that may be coming back to haunt the present.

Arriving with only moments to spare, I knocked on Sheriff Whiteman's door and heard his voice command, "Enter." I opened the door, and he motioned for me to take a seat and as I moved toward the chair in front of his desk, Sheriff Whiteman extended his hand for a handshake. As I shook his hand, he said, "I called you in to thank you for outstanding service and to give you this." With his free hand, he lifted a handwritten paper from his desk and handed it to me. As I took a seat, I reviewed the document, which was from the driver of the stranded vehicle I had helped on that rainy day. The letter stated that unknown to me, she and her daughter were returning home from a funeral of a relative in West Texas and were already emotionally distraught from the death of their loved one, her sister. To her and her daughter, I was their guardian angel that day. I shook my head in disbelief and promised Sheriff Whiteman that it was no big deal. He extended his hand again and said, "Apparently it was to these two ladies. Good job, Sergeant." I thanked him and returned to my patrol car to finish my shift.

That moment was a real eye-opener for me. As an officer goes about his or her daily duties, he or she encounters events that are nothing more than routine to that officer, such as helping a stranded motorist. My thoughts never considered what it meant to the victim for the officer to help him or her to rise above difficult circumstances. However, it means much more than we recognize and could even save that person's life.

Therefore, patrol officers should keep in mind, as they traverse the city, county, or state roadways and byways, that there remain only two viable outcomes in situations that we as officers may perceive as mundane, a daily routine. The victim can create a positive or negative perception from the few minutes of our intervention in their lives, which I found remains true even with offenders. That perception by the person with whom you interact on patrol can indeed save that person's life or your own life in the future. It did mine.

Chapter Five

Domestic Violence

Domestic violence remains one of the more prominent, frustrating, and complicated crimes in the criminal justice system. Disputes are complicated by drugs, alcohol, pent-up emotions, mental illness, physical and sexual abuse, and thousands of outside influences. It affects the lives of almost every American because children who are traumatized may evolve into abusers as well. Statistics vary concerning domestic violence but primarily focus on the victims, who are predominately women and children, with men falling into a significantly smaller category, one rarely reported and largely ignored by the criminal justice system.

When one turns to research results in America, noteworthy statistics develop. According to the U.S. Department of Justice, in a study concerning murders committed during domestic violence, "6% were murders of sons or daughters by a parent"[1] which creates a questionable picture of the violence levied against children in domestic violence across America.

A later report from the U.S. Department of Justice (2014) reveals the following:

From 2003–12, domestic violence accounted for 21 percent of all violent crime.

A greater percentage of domestic violence was committed by intimate partners (15 percent) than immediate family members (4 percent) or other relatives (2 percent).

Current or former boyfriends or girlfriends committed most domestic violence.

Females (76 percent) experienced more domestic violence victimizations than males (24 percent)[2]

Further research reveals the statistical correlation of same-gender communities across America to the standard for opposite-gender relationships. A report from American Progress (2011), shows that one out of four domestic violence victims in same-gender relationships is a man,[3] which correlates with another study from the National Domestic Violence Hotline (n.d.) that reveals similar statistics for opposite-gender relationships.[4]

From a law enforcement perspective, statistics ignore violence against children in the home with statistical concentrations on domestic partners. In contrast, children, although they may suffer less reported physical abuse, do indeed suffer extreme emotional abuse. This abuse leads to psychological trauma that may in turn lead to sibling abuse as well as create an individual prone to domestic violence in the future. The Childhood Domestic Violence organization (2014) offers the following statistics that remain worth considering throughout this chapter:

1. 5 million children witness domestic violence each year in the US.

2. 40 million adult Americans grew up with domestic violence.

3. Children from homes with violence are much more likely to experience significant psychological problems short- and long-term.

4. Children who've experienced domestic violence often meet the diagnostic criteria for Post-Traumatic Stress Disorder (PTSD) and the effects on their brain are similar to those experienced by combat veterans.

5. Domestic violence in childhood is directly correlated with difficulties learning, lower IQ scores, deficiencies in visual-motor skills and problems with attention and memory.

6. Living with domestic violence significantly alters a child's DNA, aging them prematurely 7-10 years.

7. Children in homes with violence are physically abused or seriously neglected at a rate 1500 percent higher than the national average.

8. Those who grow up with domestic violence are 6 times more likely to commit suicide and 50 percent more likely to abuse drugs and alcohol.

9. If you grow up with domestic violence, you're 74 percent more likely to commit a violent crime against someone else.

10. Children of domestic violence are 3 times more likely to repeat the cycle in adulthood, as growing up with domestic violence is the most significant predictor of whether or not someone will be engaged in domestic violence later in life.[5]

During my tenure in law enforcement, almost 100 percent of the homes I entered in defense of a victim included one or more children during the violence. Since self-report surveys serve as the source for most of the statistics mentioned above, there is some chance of inaccuracy in these numbers.

Most of the studies I have read describe the presence of alcohol or drug issues in the home during domestic violence. Does that mean that alcohol or drugs cause the domestic violence? Most likely alcohol and drugs enhance the probability of violence in the home, but they serve only as influences or trigger mechanisms that lower one's resistance to the basic urges to commit violence; a propensity toward violence already exists.

Regardless, one must also ask whether such tools are absent in the home, would those family members eventually still turn to violence, but in a more controlled and aware mental state? Would their rage lead to a higher propensity toward a more violent outburst, such as murder rather than a lesser form of assault? If that is true, then emotional abuse may build over the years to the degree that victims may suffer extreme emotional trauma possibly leading to a higher level of Post-Traumatic Stress Disorder (PTSD). More studies need to address the degree to which the absence of these outside contributors empowers the victim and the offender to absorb and release violence at more acceptable levels.

Based on my personal experiences in law enforcement, domestic violence occurs primarily during the evening shift, which is usually the time the entire family gathers together. People who once could not spend a moment away from each other suddenly find themselves jeopardizing the life of the person they would, at one time, have died for.

Another challenge officers face is that quite often, neighbors on either side of the offender's home are relatives who may pose a threat as the officer attempts to place the offender under arrest. This danger is even true with victims who were brutalized by the offender before the officer arrives.

As reported by Jeremy Nikolow, "When responding to a domestic dispute, officers must remain cognizant that anyone on the scene could pose a threat. Domestic disputes are peculiar in that offenders often remain at the scene until police arrive. These situations are inherently problematic for officers due to an elevated propensity for continued violence to erupt, despite the officers' presence."

It is not uncommon for suspects and victims to attempt to attack each other during the investigation, usually when they hear what the other is telling the police. If officers develop probable cause for an arrest, there is undoubtedly a risk of harm when attempting to take the suspect into custody. Even the victims often attack officers when they try to take a loved one into custody.[6]

One case in Parker County involved a man, under the influence of drugs, who beat his wife so severely that he put her in the hospital with multiple contusions and broken bones. She was lucky to be alive. There was little doubt he wanted to kill her. In his drug-induced state, he grabbed a wooden ax handle and chased her through the house, cornering her in a back bedroom. Had it not been for their children calling 911, his wife probably would have died that night. While the officer handcuffed him, the offender commented, "I was just teaching her a lesson. The bitch folded my underwear wrong."

In another instance, an elderly woman caught a neighbor going through the mail in her rural mailbox. Instead of fleeing to evade arrest the man grabbed a pipe wrench from his truck and beat the poor woman severely, leaving her lying on the roadside next to her mail, which he scattered around her on the ground. The investigation proved that the offender was searching for welfare or retirement checks.

Most of the domestic violence cases I worked ended up in an arrest of the adult male in the home (husband/father or common-law lover). After I made the arrest and ensured the injured wife and/or children received proper care from Life Care, I would transport the offender to jail for Assault Bodily Injury: Domestic Violence, which could range from a Class B Misdemeanor to a felony assault or murder charge, depending on the level of harm committed against the victims.

In the absence of poetic justice, the victim typically arrived at the jail with a bail bond person to arrange the immediate release of the very person who had just attempted to kill her or at least severely injure her and her children, which is a paradox that defies explanation, regardless of the psychology behind such relationships.

One such victim commented that she was the entire cause of the domestic violence within their home, where the violence consumed four young children. When asked why she chose to live with a man who assaulted her almost daily, her comment was, "Officer, you do not understand. He treats me like a queen the rest of the time. Therefore,

I look for ways to upset him because I live for those moments when we make up." Her attitude was appalling. Her approach to the entire situation overlooked the trauma and PTSD issues that were mounting in the children she supposedly loved. One can only imagine how consumed, emotionally and physically, America's children become as their parents weave a web of deceit and violence for their own gratuitous satisfaction.

One of the lesser domestic violence calls I encountered remained overshadowed by the actual control the offender had over his family. When I entered the home, the husband and wife were yelling at each other, but nothing more. The home revealed no evidence of violence. Nothing was broken or out of place, except for a little three-year-old girl lying in the corner of the living room, curled up in the fetal position. The father answered the door, instantly changing his aggressive demeanor in hopes of thwarting discovery of violence in the home, at least verbal violence. As I entered the home, the little girl broke from the fetal position and ran to wrap herself around one of my legs, hoping beyond hope that this stranger would bring peace to her troubled world. Her father looked down at her and began apologizing to me while openly scolding his daughter for wrongly calling 911 when all that allegedly occurred was that mommy and daddy were arguing.

I dropped to both knees in front of the sobbing child and took her hands into mine and waited for her to raise her eyes to mine. I looked at her for a moment and told her, "You should always call 911 in any situation where you feel you need help. Your daddy is wrong. Even if he and your mother were just arguing, their argument scared you so much that you tried to escape it all by hiding in the corner. You were definitely right to call 911."

She smiled. I stood up, facing the irritated father, who did not take kindly to my words, which countermanded his control of the child. She wrapped her arms around one leg again and stood looking up at me and then daddy. I locked eyes with her father and told him and his wife that should I ever hear of either of them chastising their children for calling

911 when they were in fear for any reason, I would drive by his home daily until I was satisfied that his family was safe. The father assumed an apologetic posture, assuring me that he would indeed ensure that his family remained safe and that this was just one of those ridiculous arguments over finances in which he lost control of his emotions.

In a similar situation, I received a dispatch to investigate violence between a teenage girl and her father. Dispatch warned that other officers, in the past, had encountered violent resistance from the father even to allow an officer into his home. I approached the home with caution and heard yelling inside. Instead of knocking on the door, I only turned the unlocked knob and walked into the home, announcing my presence as I entered the living room.

The father, standing next to the bar, was apparently caught off-guard. As with the little girl in the situation above, the teenage girl in this scene walked over to stand behind me as her father continued his fit of rage. I noticed a sling-blade knife with about an 8-inch blade was lying open on the bar within the lunging distance of the father. I encouraged him to concentrate his wrath against me as I moved forward slowly as if to increase his wrath. When in reach of the knife, I grabbed it and secured the open blade into the housing, then deftly dropped the knife into my pocket.

Outraged, the man yelled, “What are you doing? You cannot just take another man’s property.” I smiled at him and said, “I am only ensuring that I do not have to shoot you in front of your teenage daughter.” I commanded him to sit down at the kitchen table and to remain silent while I talked with his daughter and assured him that if he moved from the table, I would place him under arrest.

Turning to the daughter, I asked if he had any other weapons in the immediate area and she assured me that was the only one. Sergeant Ken Smith arrived to serve as a backup officer. I asked him to watch the violent father while I took the daughter out of his earshot. As we stepped outside, I asked her to explain what made her father react so violently toward her. She told me that he always became violent when she wanted to attend Wednesday night services at the local Baptist church.

Her father did not attend church and held strong personal feelings concerning what he considered were lies forced upon his daughter by the church. Additionally, he could not stand the other teenagers who came to take her to the church with them. A carload of teenagers arrived as we spoke. I let the teenager go with her friends and returned to issue a further warning to her father and return his knife.

As mentioned earlier, quite often, the catalyst for domestic violence is some form of alcohol or drug, which not only lowers the offender's resistance to emotional reactions but in the case of some drugs fuels that action with an unbridled fury. For example, Phencyclidine, known by many street names such as PCP, Angel Dust, Supergrass, Boat, Tic Tac, Zoom, and Shermans, may cause extraordinary strength in the addict.[7]

In the early 1990s, I received a call from dispatch to investigate a report that a woman was attempting to murder her six-month-old baby girl. Fortunately, my proximity to the scene put me only a few minutes away. I asked dispatch to notify Life Care to stand by but not to make the scene until receiving word from me. I arrived at the offender's sister's home, which was next door. I immediately noticed that a woman was waiting outside with a baby in her arms. From the body language of the woman, I felt sure she was the offender's sister and that she had managed to remove the child from any immediate danger. However, dispatch could not advise if the offender had any form of weapon that would threaten others from a distance.

I verified the physical description of the offender through dispatch. The woman was a known offender who was extremely slender, had shoulder-length blonde hair, and only stood about 5-feet 3-inches high. Additionally, she had a tattoo of a shark on the left side of her neck. Dispatch warned that when on PCP, the offender displayed abnormal strength and violence. The woman standing in front of the sister's home holding the baby was indeed a blonde, but her hair reached to her waist.

Additionally, this woman was slightly plump. Therefore, I assumed she was not the suspect. I checked out at the scene relying on my handheld for communication. The baby appeared to be fine if what I was seeing in the arms of the sister was indeed the endangered child.

The woman with the baby walked toward me as I stepped from my vehicle and identified herself as the offender's sister. She stated, "Janice is lying in her bed, but she is only playing like she is asleep. She is ready to attack you, so, be careful."

My backup officer, Tim Dean, arrived at the scene. Janice's sister told us that the bedroom in which Janice was waiting for us was located on the far end of the single-wide trailer, to the left as we entered the front door. I suggested to Tim that we team up against Janice based on her propensity toward extreme violence when under the influence of PCP. I proposed that if we found her on the bed, playing as if asleep, that he would grab the woman's hand that was on his side of the bed and I would do the same on my side, effectively enabling a rapid pinning technique that would force the woman securely on top of the bed. We could then proceed with a speed-cuff technique. The plan was sound under normal circumstances with both officers disabling the offender by stretching her arms outward, making the arrest rather simple.

We entered the home. All was silent, not even a television or stereo to greet us, which meant that she heard us enter the home. I led the way down the narrow hallway to the open door of the master bedroom. I stopped just shy of the doorway and peered cautiously around the corner.

Janice was not playing like she was asleep. Instead, she was crouching on the bed on her hands and knees as if she were a wild animal. Without moving her body, Janice's head turned mechanically around toward me and cocked sideways. Her eyes were piercing with hatred as she spat out in a growling, menacing tone, "Go away! I am sleeping."

Tim entered the room as I approached Janice from the left side of the bed. The bed offered access on both sides with the headboard pushed up against the exterior wall. I motioned Tim to move toward the other side and slapped my right wrist with the open palm of my left hand, signaling to him to target Janice's right wrist. We approached cautiously, remaining alert for any hidden weapon. Janice wore a pair of jean shorts and a white T-shirt and had no shoes on. Janice's only hidden weapon at that moment was the inner strength we had been warned would be beyond measure.

However, since I stood at 6-feet 3-inches with a weight of around 200 pounds and Tim being similar in size, I assumed that we would have Janice in handcuffs within a few minutes. We anticipated nothing more than a struggle from such a small woman, an easy arrest for a former combat, special ops Marine. Tim had a military background as well.

That was a rookie mistake. I had been on the force no more than a few months and never encountered anyone under the influence of PCP —other drugs and alcohol, but none on PCP. I nodded to Tim, and we both lunged forward, grabbing for each respective wrist.

Speed cuffing is a powerful tool during any arrest because of the action implied by the name. The key to the strategy is to ensure the handcuffs are in the last notch before the action swings open against the slightest force, thereby enabling the officer to force the handcuffs against the offender's wrists rapidly. This action forces the cuffs to instantly encircle the offender's wrist to an immediate lock position from the opposite side, effectively immobilizing the offender.

The act of handcuffing an offender can be one of the more life-threatening events in an officer's career. Quite often a savvy, felony offender will remain calm, waiting to feel the first cuff lock around his or her wrist at which time, the offender will unleash full fury to jerk the handcuffs out of the officer's hands, which empowers that offender to use the cuffs as a deadly weapon against that officer.[8] George Demetriou, a retired, NYPD Detective wrote,[9] "Since 2007, at least five police officers have been killed or seriously wounded while handcuffing – in some cases after getting one handcuff on the violator. The offenders 'rip' or pull the handcuffed arm away suddenly after cooperating with the officer and then draw a concealed firearm and shoot the officer. It should be noted that in every case that this has occurred the offender was being placed into custody for a minor offense."

Unfortunately, Janice was focusing on me and as soon as I lunged forward and grabbed her wrist, she ignored Officer Dean, rolling toward me as she curled around my right forearm. She unleashed a scream that sounded like a wild animal.

With her other hand completely free, she grabbed my right forearm and dug her long fingernails deep into the flesh of my arm. With as much force as I could muster, I tossed the assailing demon to the opposite side of the room where she slammed against the sheetrock wall, crushing the sheetrock, which only softened the blow of her body. She laughed wildly as she slid to the floor and sat, as if she was indeed demonically possessed. I quickly tossed a look to the ceiling and said, "God?" He did not answer. Therefore, I assumed we would have to wrestle the demon alone.

Suddenly Janice leaped to her feet, this time focusing on Tim, which enabled me to jump across the bed and tackle her to the floor, forcing my body weight against hers. Tim assisted with her clawing hands and flailing legs as we gradually managed to secure her arms behind her back and speed cuff her wrists before she could squirm free once again. Lifting her to a standing position we forcibly walked her to the door as she fought incessantly.

As we stepped through the front door, we were forced to loosen our grip to allow her to step through the doorway between us. She lunged backward toward Tim, gnashing her teeth like a rabid animal while striking out at me with her right foot to disable me with a kick to the groin.

Fortunately, the teeth fell short of Tim's throat, and her foot proved only to be a glancing blow to my right thigh. We forced her against the exterior wall and held her as a struggling mass, while I called for the ambulance to make the scene. They moved forward, unloading the gurney and wheeling it into position beside us. We forced Janice onto the gurney and held her down, remaining clear of her gnashing teeth and flailing feet and legs, while one of the EMT medics entered the home, returning with a sheet that he rapidly cut into strips, which he used to tie Janice head to toe to the gurney. She remained a gnashing, gnawing mass as she twisted and squirmed in vain.

They checked the baby despite protests from Janice's sister who assured us the baby was unharmed and then we cleared the scene. Tim returned to his duties on patrol to wait for the next evening shift call. I followed Life Care to Campbell Hospital, the county hospital in Weatherford, which was about a thirty-minute drive. My presence ensured the EMT personnel received immediate assistance in case Janice managed to struggle free. The drive to the hospital proved to be uneventful. The EMT personnel assured me the effects of the drug were wearing off.

Janice remained calm as the EMT removed her, still tied to the gurney, from the rear of the ambulance. As they started wheeling her toward the ER (Emergency Room), I noticed that she had managed to free the strip holding her head, but decided it was not worth worrying about since the effects of the drug were supposedly diminishing.

A male nurse met us outside the entrance to the hospital to begin an immediate assessment of Janice's condition and to receive the report from the EMT personnel. Janice began crying, assuring the nurse that we had mistreated her in every way. Sympathizing with her plight, the nurse moved forward, reaching out to stroke her head as she lured him closer. The gurney allowed her head to be just below the waist of the nurse. He continued to soothe her, asking if the big, bad cops had treated her wrong. Moments later Janice lunged her head toward the male nurse's groin area as hard as she could, almost tilting the gurney over as she unleashed a ferocious effort to latch onto his groin with her teeth, instead, locking only onto his scrubs.

Frantically, he pushed against her head and the gurney as we moved forward to try to assist with Janice, who was now laughing through her clenched teeth. She released her grip with her teeth as we approached, and the gurney launched sideways away from the nurse. He looked at me and yelled, "Get that bitch out of here!"

I laughed and assured him that she was safely in his hands and the hands of the local law enforcement officer on duty in the ER. I thanked the ambulance personnel as I followed alongside the gurney as they wheeled her inside. Blood from the wounds left by Janice's initial attack still trickled down my forearm. The ER doctor surveyed the wounds and assured me that other than the unknown factor of the AIDS that Janice was known to carry, my wounds should heal without issue. Were Janice's hands and nails free from contamination at the moment of the attack? The doctor could not assure me that my future would not bring an attack on my body by the dreaded disease. All he could promise was that he would willingly keep testing me for AIDS for the next ten years, which was the projected span of time for the AIDS to reveal itself.

My thoughts turned to my wife and my children. How could I interact with them with any genuine feeling of security, knowing that I could be a carrier of AIDS? I cleared the scene, returning to duty to finish out the evening shift with additional domestic violence calls to answer, a part of me hearing the old saying, *you can never go home...*, in my mind. Ten years is a long time to worry about whether you would become a deadly menace to your family.

As mentioned earlier, domestic violence calls can offer some of the more challenging and deadly consequences. However, quite often a bit of verbal judo will alter the outcome if the officer merely listens for clues from the offender. I was dispatched to a domestic violence call in the north-central area of our county at a single-wide trailer about five miles east of our Springtown home. The victim's home was just to the north, off Midway Road on an unmarked side road. I had never met the family in the trailer, which suggested to me that they had probably recently moved into the area. Officers rapidly become very acquainted with most domestic violence offenders in the county because of the tendency to repeat the violence sometimes two or three times a week.

I approached the scene cautiously, turning my headlights off and stopping the car on the roadway rather than entering the driveway. Dispatch was unable to provide any information because the call disconnected as soon as the dispatcher heard a scream for help. The dispatcher attempted to return the phone call but to no avail.

As I stepped from the patrol vehicle, a scream echoed from inside the trailer, followed by a sudden loud thud as if someone or something was slammed against the interior wall. I ran forward and attempted to open the front door; it was locked. I heard another scream and yelled, "Sheriff's Office" and kicked the front door open, which is rare for a mobile home since most front doors are hinged to open toward the outside. This home offered a standard door, opening to the inside, which readily facilitated forced entry from a massive kick near the door handle.

The door slammed against the interior wall. I looked across the living room at a man holding a baseball bat and standing over the body of a woman who was crumpled between his legs. She showed no signs of life. Blood dripped from the bat clutched threateningly by the offender as he leered at me, less than ten feet away.

Quickly, I keyed the mike on my radio and asked dispatch to close the channel and have Life Care en route. The man started moving slowly toward me, gripping the bat with both hands and saying, "I am not going back to prison and you sure as hell can't stop me from finishing her off." He took one step forward and then his entire countenance changed as I considered the appropriate level of force, which would have been deadly force since he already expressed an intent to murder the woman lying before him.

The man stopped in his tracks, lowering the bat to a non-threatening position and said, "Wait a minute. You are that cop from Lakeside."

Lakeside was a small law enforcement agency in a beachside community on Lake Worth about thirty miles east of our location, boasting a small population of about 500. The area was known for gang activity and drugs. Violence was common among the inhabitants. I could only imagine what that officer in Lakeside had done to make this violent man suddenly turn pale, but silently thanked him for that memory.

My initial reaction to his comment was to truthfully deny any previous encounter with him and promise that I had never served with Lakeside PD, but something suggested to me that an opportunity to alter the violent ending of our present altercation had just been presented.

I decided to pretend that I indeed was that officer and stepped forward menacingly, saying, "That being the case, you know what is about to happen to you." Suddenly the bat dropped to the floor, and the man turned to the wall behind him and placed his hands behind his back. I walked forward with handcuffs ready for a speed-cuff technique. The handcuffs were the hinged type in contrast to the old-style held together with a small chain.[10] His wrists were in perfect position as I grabbed two fingers from both hands and rapidly forced the cuffs over his wrists and breathed a sigh of relief as the resounding click from both sides assured me the handcuffs secured him. With him leaning against the wall, I searched his clothing and body for other weapons and contraband and discovered a large, sling-blade pocket knife. I secured that weapon as further evidence of his violent nature. With the man secured, I led him to the patrol car and placed him in the back without further incident.

Contacting dispatch, I asked her to return the channel to normal traffic, advising that the suspect was in custody and requested that she send Life Care to the scene immediately to check for signs of life and render aid if required. I returned to the living room and checked the woman for vital signs. She was still breathing but unconscious. Her face was a bloody pulp as was her head with blood flowing from numerous blows. Life Care arrived and I stepped aside.

As the EMT Officers provided immediate care for the woman, I took pictures of the crime scene to ensure the Crimes Against Persons Investigator and the court received pictures of the bloody, aluminum bat lying beside the body of the wounded woman. I trained my camera on the furniture and walls of the living room where further blood splatter confirmed the offender had unleashed numerous blows against the victim. Finding paper towels on the kitchen counter, I retrieved the baseball bat and wrapped it in the paper towels to protect the blood evidence as well as his blood-stained fingerprints on the bat. The final photos included multiple shots of the victim as she lay motionless on the floor. One photo included a close-up shot of the eye-glasses that I assumed belonged to her, broken in half and covered in blood. I collected the glasses as evidence as well. Stepping outside, I took one final photograph of the home, assuring evidence of the location of the crime. With the photo processing over, I asked another deputy arriving at the scene to watch over the suspect so he made no attempt to break the glass out of the rear doors of my car. With the deputy providing such security, I returned to the crime scene to continue final collection of evidence and to ensure no other victims were lying unobserved in the other rooms in the house.

Life Care confirmed that the victim had indeed suffered numerous blows to the head, face, and neck and that she probably suffered from skull fractures as well as severe facial and neck injuries. They recommended Care Flight for immediate transport to a hospital in Tarrant County that could offer emergency services.

I contacted dispatch, requesting the medivac of the victim.[11] Because of the proximity of towering trees and power lines surrounding the home, the EMT personnel would have to transport the victim to a church parking lot about quarter-mile to the north. It was an ancient, historical church known as Midway Baptist Church. However, the congregation abandoned the church because it was too small for today's congregations. The building enjoyed a reputation as a haunted structure that invited cult invasions regularly. Regardless, the small church offered a sufficiently large parking lot to facilitate landing the Care Flight chopper.

I asked the other Deputy to help Life Care with the temporary transfer of the victim to the church parking lot and to facilitate a safe landing of the medivac helicopter. Returning to the patrol car, I checked to ensure the offender remained secure. He was quiet. I secured all the evidence in the trunk, and advised dispatch that I was 10/17 to 10 (en route to the jail) with one white male suspect in custody for Assault Family Violence/ Aggravated Assault and asked her to run a complete criminal history on him. I would be sure to include the criminal history in my report so the judge would take it into consideration when deciding whether to grant bail.

Not every domestic violence call takes place inside the home, and quite often neighbors are equally involved as participants or silent observers as the offense progresses. Therefore, an officer must remain vigilant when approaching a violent scene with neighbors, seemingly innocently, observing the action. Quite often, they are relatives of one or all the people involved and will attack an officer in defense of the offender.

During one such call, Deputy Gary VanY received a call to a neighborhood brawl involving multiple offenders. I contacted dispatch and advised that I would be en route to serve as his backup unit because I was in proximity of the offense as well. Dispatch advised that no weapons were reported to be involved, at the moment. Gary made the scene just a few minutes before I arrived.

I parked my car on a side street and made my way up behind the house to the front yard where the brawl was taking place. As I approached, I observed a group of eight men who were slowly maneuvering to encircle Gary, assuming that he was alone and an easy target. They had ceased their brawl between each other to focus their attention on the intruder. As the circle began to close, I walked up behind a large man who kept touching the small of his back. His shirttail was hanging outside his pants, providing easy access to whatever kept drawing his attention.

Their focus on Gary provided the opportunity for me to move forward undetected. I stopped just to the left and behind the large man, making sure my gun hand and my weapon remained free as I reached out with my right hand and felt for the object in the small of his back. My hand landed against the hilt of a large Bowie knife. Instead of trying to disarm the man, I leaned forward with my hand against the hilt of the weapon and said, "If you move a muscle, I will kill you." The man stiffened as I simultaneously drew my weapon and shoved my hand underneath his shirt to retrieve the Bowie knife, which boasted a massive blade over twelve inches in length.

I ordered the man to drop to his knees and ordered the remainder to do the same. I placed the large man in handcuffs and forced him to lie face down on the ground. I kept my weapon trained in the general direction of each offender as Gary moved forward and disarmed each of the offenders who were in possession of any weapon, which was almost every man at the scene. With the search completed, we had two men in custody for possession of illegal weapons. We allowed the other men to return to their respective homes with a promise that if we had to return, they would be taken to jail as well.

Deputies and other law enforcement officers face dangerous situations almost daily, which requires a commitment of vigilance. Quite often, a deputy must face that danger alone. Officer discretion becomes more of the rule instead of the exception as each officer makes a decision, in a millisecond, whether to employ deadly force during a given situation.

Late one afternoon, shortly after I had left the station and headed to my typical roving patrol of the northeastern, crime-ridden territories of the county, dispatch advised that shots were fired at a home on Arvel Circle, just west of FM730 and north of Azle, Texas. I was the only unit north that evening but had a reserve officer riding with me, which was rare but required by the sheriff to maintain their certification. Dispatch told me that the call came from the neighbors next door.

As I turned off Reno Road and drove toward the small, wood-frame home, I could see an elderly man, about eighty years old, standing on the porch waving a chrome-plated revolver above his head. His grip on the pistol assured me that he was ready to fire the weapon at any moment. I advised dispatch that I was at the scene and asked that she close the channel to emergency traffic only. I asked the reserve officer to stay behind me. He readily agreed as we both stepped out of the car. I wanted the man's concentration on me to ensure he received no perceived threats from anyone but me.

I parked on the street to provide temporary safety behind the vehicle if the elderly man began firing again. As we approached, the man began screaming obscenities relating to threats and issues with his neighbors. He remained oblivious to our presence, intoxicated beyond measure. I walked slowly toward the man until the distance between us was less than ten feet. I decided not to draw my weapon because the man was not an immediate threat to me since he was all but unaware of my presence.

I yelled out to the man, "Sir!" He failed to respond, continuing to wave the weapon wildly in the air. I tried again, a bit louder, "Sir!!" Again, no response. Finally, I yelled as loud as I could muster, "SIR, Sheriff's Office!!!" This time the man stopped waving the weapon in the air and pointed it directly at me. He leaned forward, trying to peer through his intoxicated, bloodshot eyes to discern the man standing before him and said, "Yeah."

I finally had his attention. The weapon did not waver, remaining pointed directly at me. Once again, I stated loudly, "Sir you need to understand that you are about to die!" He stumbled backward a bit and stammered out, "Die? Why?" I said, "Because you are pointing that gun at me." All hostility left the man's eyes, and his demeanor changed immediately. He reacted by pointing the weapon at his head, only to look at the weapon to assure himself that he had indeed been pointing it at me. He looked back at me and held the weapon sideways asking, "What should I do?" I laughed to ease his tension and said, "Sir, that weapon is too beautiful to ask you to drop it. All I want you to do is to lower the weapon to the porch at your feet and step back against the house." He immediately complied.

As soon as he set the weapon on the porch, I picked it up and cleared the cylinder, placing the cartridges in my pocket and placing the empty revolver in my belt. I contacted dispatch on my radio to return the radio to normal traffic and to stand down any responding backup units. I then turned to the reserve deputy who was standing behind me with his weapon drawn, obviously a bit shaken. He assured me that he was okay but had never been in such a situation before. I assured him that none of them were ever the same and that he did the right thing. He holstered his weapon as I invited the elderly man to allow us to enter his home where we could talk about why he was firing his weapon into the air and to discuss if he had threatened or shot any individual.

He readily agreed as he turned and stumbled toward the front door. We entered his home where we sat next to each other on his living room couch. The old man began to tear up as he related his story about how the neighbors, the entire family (husband, wife, and pre-teen boys), constantly berated and bullied him by calling him names and throwing rocks against the north side of his house. He told me that they were attempting to hit his dog by throwing rocks over his fence as well. I asked the reserve officer to step outside to verify if any loose rocks lay on the ground near the wall facing the neighbor's home. Additionally, I asked him to check for contact marks from rocks on the side of the house. He returned with confirmation. I turned to the senior man and told him that I wanted him to go to bed early and sleep off his intoxicated state and assured him that I would drive by occasionally during the night to make sure he remained behind closed doors. Once again, he agreed.

I promised him that I would go next door immediately and deal with his neighbors to ensure that their bullying stopped. I told him that I would store the weapon in a safe place in his house and would return the next day to reveal the location of the weapon. Additionally, I planned to continue our discussion about his decision to take the law into his own hands, as I knew he would remember very little from our conversation. He agreed to go to bed immediately and soon was fast asleep. The reserve officer helped me secure the home and check on the man's dog to ensure the animal had not been harmed. I photographed the outer wall, providing evidence of the harassment from the neighbors.

I advised dispatch that we were moving the investigation to the complainant's house and walked next door. The husband and wife were a bit surprised when I delivered my message since they felt sure their strategy would encourage law enforcement to place the old man behind bars. Instead, I quoted a few laws to them concerning assault by threat, criminal mischief, and animal cruelty to list a few, assuring them that if anyone went to jail, it would probably be them. I told them that I would place a request for each shift to patrol Arvel Circle every day and night to make sure that they left the elderly man and his dog alone. I assured them that I would return for a daily visit during the next thirty days, unannounced, to ensure they left him alone on my shift as well and that if I observed any new marks on the old man's house or received a complaint from him, I would file charges against them for retaliation, which was a felony offense.

The next day, I returned to visit the elderly gentleman as promised and helped him locate his firearm and returned the six cartridges. I helped him clean the weapon as we sat and talked about the issues with the neighbors and how I felt they would finally leave him alone. I left with his promise that he would never mix alcohol and weapons and that he would call 911 before attempting to take on any intruder on his own. I kept my promise to visit, unannounced, the next thirty days and guaranteed that the neighbors decided they would comply with my order to leave the elderly gentleman alone. Before the thirty days slid into history, however, the old man's neighbors disappeared, leaving the house empty. The landlord told me that they left without warning as well as without paying the last month's rent.

Domestic violence varies tremendously from simple arguments to murder. Quite often, the victim or friend of the victim will call 911 to report the assault in progress. The latter can impose weighty issues for the responding officer simply because neither the victim or the offender wants law enforcement intervention.

Such was the case when neighbors called about a father returning home drunk and beating his two teenage boys with a baseball as he chased them around the front yard. The complainant was a concerned neighbor who said the mother had tried to intervene on behalf of her battered children, which temporarily encouraged the patriarch to unleash his assault against her. Dispatch assigned the call to me with Corporal Danny McKnight responding as the backup officer. We both arrived at the scene simultaneously and saw no one outside. As we approached the front door, we could hear screams from inside the home, accompanying by muffled voices pleading for mercy. We walked up to the door and Danny stood on one side of the door opposite my position. Even Hollywood movies recognize the dangers of standing directly in front of a closed door, providing an easy target for an offender firing blindly through the door. I reached forward and delivered a loud knock on the door and returned to my waiting position, clear of the doorway. The door opened rapidly as a man yelled, "What do you want?" Then, in the same breath, "Oh hell! It's the cops!!!" He immediately attempted to slam the door as I swung around from my position and delivered a hard kick to the door.

The force pushed him back onto the living room floor as Corporal McKnight and I found ourselves wedged in the opening, each screaming out, "He's mine!" We shared a brief laugh at our awkward approach and regathered as I relented, allowing Danny to enter the home first where he launched himself on top of the struggling drunk who was reaching for the bat. Following immediately behind Danny, I saw a woman running across the living room wielding a pair of over-sized scissors, aiming toward Danny's back. I intercepted her effort of aggravated assault, wrenching the scissors from her hands just as she dove forward. Tossing the scissors to the end of the adjoining hallway, I forced the woman to the floor where I stabilized her with a pair of handcuffs behind her back. I checked over towards Danny just in time to see him doing the same with the drunken father. He was unaware of the woman's attempt to stab him. I left the woman lying on the floor, face down, struggling under my foot as I turned my gaze to the opposite side of the room. Two teenage boys lay unconscious on the floor with blood oozing from wounds from various locations. Danny keyed up his mike, requesting Life Care be allowed to make the scene.

Any patrol officer may provide numerous examples of domestic violence. Some officers working the evening shift, which is the prime time for domestic violence, may make every attempt to be busy on a different call when dispatch issues a domestic violence call.[12] However, even though some agencies may allow such options, deputy sheriffs are typically pulled off a previous, non-threatening call like a burglary or theft investigation or even an evening meal to serve as primary or backup officer for a domestic violence call. I agree with the written or unwritten policy imposing immediate response from officers to a domestic violence call regardless of the threat against that officer. Quite often, if an officer does not make the scene in time, the offender can murder or seriously harm his or her spouse, or even worse, his or her children.

For example, we only had two officers on duty one evening. I covered the north while the other officer covered the south. We agreed to not stray more than five miles or so north or south of Interstate 20, running east to west and roughly dividing the county. In theory, that is an excellent strategy. However, calls for service rather than theory dictate where an officer must go, and during the evening shift, that might be in some of the more remote locations, leaving that officer virtually alone.

I was patrolling on the west side of Weatherford (the county seat of Parker County) when dispatch advised that a known offender in Millsap, Texas, was attempting to murder his girlfriend. Dispatch advised that he was wielding a large hunting knife against the victim and that he had already inflicted severe injuries. She was fleeing from his attack while she talked with dispatch on her wireless phone. Fortunately, I had just turned on Ranger Highway when I received the call, which would put me on the scene within a few minutes.

I told dispatch to tell the victim to attempt to escape outside if possible, but otherwise, find a room where she could lock herself in to attempt to delay the offender's attack. Dispatch advised that Life Care was en route and that they would be waiting near the scene.

I arrived at the remote, rural home just a few minutes later to hear crashing noises from the back side of the house. Suddenly the front door swung open, and a man wielding a large knife ran almost into my arms. I wrestled the knife from his grasp, forcing him to the ground as I managed to handcuff him and hold him to the ground until he stopped resisting. I contacted dispatch advising that I had the suspect in custody, but that I had not been able to enter the home to verify the location or the safety of the victim.

Dispatch told me that the woman had locked herself in the bathroom as I had mentioned, and that the offender began stabbing the knife through the door as well as attempting to kick the door down during the process. Dispatch assured me that she encouraged the victim to flee through the bathroom window, which she did, but had to break the window. The victim remained in contact through the wireless phone connection. I told dispatch to have the victim stand by while Life Care moved forward to render aid.

I pulled the offender to his feet after I completed a search of his clothing and person for other weapons and contraband and then secured him in the back seat of the vehicle. Dispatch advised that the victim was hiding in the woods behind the home but would move forward when I assured her it was safe. I encouraged her to do so, immediately. Life Care was already entering the long driveway to the country home nestled in an alcove cut out of the surrounding trees with an open front overlooking a quiet prairie.

Somewhere, a coyote let the world know of his presence. The wounded woman stumbled around the corner of the home, falling to the ground. Running over to catch her, I encouraged her to just lie still while I checked her wounds. Blood was flowing from her arms and her torso. Life Care moved forward and immediately began to care for her wounds while I requested Care Flight for an emergency extraction. As I stood watching Life Care perform the same, lifesaving duties they complete numerous times almost every evening, I wondered who else was a victim at that moment in time.

The chopper arrived and dropped into the open prairie in front of the home. Another deputy arrived to help as we assisted Life Care with the transfer of the wounded woman to the gurney and then to the waiting helicopter. They were unsure if the girl would live because of blood loss.

The other deputy and I returned to the home and began processing the crime scene, first taking photographs of all evidence, taking care not to contaminate or destroy any evidence, which would empower a defense attorney to ask for a dismissal. Fortunately, no other calls came in, providing time to process the crime scene before returning to duty. I completed the report later that evening, unable to finish until the early hours of the morning, making sure that it was complete in every detail, including the witness statement from our dispatcher. Once all the evidence was logged correctly and turned over to the property clerk, I headed home, effectively serving a double shift.

Sadly, this is where an officer can become wholly dismayed with the criminal justice system. The case did not come up for trial until about three months later. The suspect was released on bail but did indeed appear for the trial as ordered with his latest girlfriend wrapped around his arm. The trial appeared to move along smoothly as the offender watched the jurors' emotional body language responses to the presentation of evidence by the District Attorney. Soon, as the State's Witness, I was called to the stand, but just as I settled in for the questioning following being sworn in by the Bailiff, the judge slammed his gavel down and yelled out, “Case dismissed!” Only minutes had passed from the beginning presentation given by both attorneys.

Without explanation the judge stood up and left the courtroom. The startled Bailiff yelled out, “All rise!” He did not even take the time to dismiss me from the witness stand. The District Attorney stood leaning against the rail on the witness box for a moment and then looked over at me and said, “Let’s grab a cup of coffee.”

I stepped from the witness stand, more than bewildered. I looked over at the victim, who sat sobbing uncontrollably, as her parents made every attempt to offer consoling remarks. I considered attempting to offer my apologies as well but considered the better of it and followed the District Attorney to the small, courthouse square café across the road where he assured me that the issue was a personal argument between him and the judge.

We sat nursing our coffee for a moment. I looked up at him and said, “Tell that to the victim. That man almost killed that woman and dared to walk into the courtroom with another victim wrapped around his arm.” It is one thing to tell an investigator that such things happen, but the investigator is the one who must face the surviving victim or victim’s survivors and attempt to explain why courts allow offenders to blatantly walk away with no consequences for their actions.

Rarely will an officer (city, county, or state) happen upon the scene of a domestic violence act in progress. However, when it occurs, that officer must be ready to accept immediate control over the scene and quite often too quickly to warn dispatch that he or she is about to step out of the car, which is one of the more dangerous moments in an officer’s line of duty.

I was driving in a far remote southern part of the county toward an area known as Horseshoe Bend, which was one of those developments created by a shady individual offering weekend retreats and retirement homes along the quietly flowing Brazos River. Unfortunately, the alleged development became a few beautiful homes surrounded by numerous single-wide mobile homes populated mostly by transient drug dealers, addicts, and sex offenders along with a host of other well-known offenders who found that the remote location was safe from discovery and prosecution because most of their victims were hiding from the law as well.

A massive, horseshoe-shaped, wooden structure serving as the only entrance to the resort, spanned across the roadway entering Horseshoe Bend. The Brazos River etched a lazy trail along the far back side of the area, which also served as the county border between Parker and Hood county, offering fleeing offenders any easy swim across the shallow depths to the equally remote border of Hood County.

The sunset rays darted between the trees as my cruiser rounded the last curve leading to the giant horseshoe, which was about 100 yards further down the road. A small wooden sales hut that had long since been abandoned by the development company offered a small, gravel parking area for would be customers. I noticed two vehicles parked in front of the building. However, what caught my attention was the actions of two women, one in her fifties and another in her early thirties at best, who were grasping the arms of a young girl, about six-years-old, suspending the girl between them and yanking back and forth on the child as if they were two dogs fighting over a piece of meat. I sped up, slamming on the brakes in front of the women who were so intent on their mutual abuse of the child that they did not notice my presence until the car slid to a stop in front of them.

They each remained unyielding, clinging desperately to their intended prey as I leaped from the patrol car and yelled out, "Drop her! NOW!" The women complied. As soon as the little girl's feet touched the ground, she ran over to me, bursting into tears as she jumped into my arms. I opened the patrol car's rear door and sat her in the back seat with her facing out through the open doorway. I kneeled before her and asked her if the women harmed her. She stopped crying for a moment and pointed to the two women saying, "They were fighting over me."

The little girl started sobbing, begging me to help her. I asked her to remain still for a moment as I popped open the trunk, grabbing one of the many stuffed animals I kept stored there for just such occasions. I gave her the teddy bear, which she clutched dearly and returned a smile through tear-stained cheeks. I then asked her if she had been harmed by the two women as I visually checked for injuries. The women started to walk toward me, but I ordered them to stay where they were. A man stepped from one of the cars and started walking toward me. I ordered him to stop as well. He hesitated, then complied. I returned my attention to the little girl as I advised dispatch on my handheld that I was out on a domestic violence in progress at the entrance to Horseshoe Bend but assured her all was well.

I asked the girl to tell me who the people were and why they were treating her that way. She told me that the younger one was her mother and that the older woman was her grandmother and the man was her grandmother's new husband. I hunted through the console for one of the many candies I kept there for consoling children as well and handed her a lollipop. I told her that I would like for her to stay where she was while I talked with her mom and grandparents. She assured me she would remain where she was, but once again told me that the man was not her grandfather, just grandmother's husband. She obviously fostered no love for the man, which made me wonder if she was a victim of some level of abuse from him as well. I told her I understood. He appeared to be part of the problem.

I walked toward the three adults who were already involved in a heated argument. I stopped in front of them, and the man stepped forward saying, "Officer, you need to let us handle this and back out of this situation. I am a security guard, and I know my limitations and powers in this situation." I looked at him for a moment and said, simply, "Sir, you need to step aside while I talk with these two women." He began again, "You have no authority..." I interrupted him as I reached behind my back for my handcuffs and said, "You are interfering with a lawful investigation.

If you truly are a security guard, you are about to jeopardize your career with charges for obstructing justice, so, what is your decision?"

The man turned and walked back to his car. I placed the handcuffs back into the protective case. I pointed to the girl's mom and invited her to join me out of hearing distance from the grandmother, whom she identified as her mom and confirmed that the man was a new live-in boyfriend, not a relative in any manner. I asked her why she would jeopardize the health of her child by yanking her, suspended, between her and the girl's grandmother. She told me that her mother was upset because she thought that she was smoking too much marijuana at the risk of the health of her child.

I smiled and politely asked mom if she had any marijuana on her person or in her vehicle. Fear crossed her face as she considered my question but verbally agreed to allow the search of her car. She handed me her purse and her car keys and encouraged me to do so. I told mom to stay put for a moment and returned to the little girl and asked her whom she would like to ride home with, mom, grandmother, or me. She assured me that she would like to stay where she was in my car, which worked for me because it provided an opportunity for me to see the conditions under which the child had to live. I agreed to take her home but told her that I was going to look in mom's car first and then talk to her grandmother. Before I turned away, I asked her, "Does your mom smoke marijuana or do any other type of drug?" The girl's eyes shot to the ground and then she looked up at me, her eyes locked on mine. "Are you going to take my mom to jail?" I smiled at her and said, "That depends on your mom." She accepted that and assured me that mom did smoke occasionally, but not all the time and that her grandmother did not like her to smoke at all. I asked her to stay put a bit longer while I searched her mom's car and purse for any paraphernalia and signs of drugs.

The search revealed no contraband, and no odor of marijuana attacked my senses when I opened her purse or car doors. Returning to the child's mom and I asked her to step aside while I talked with her mother.

Grandma was almost hostile as I listened to her side of the story. She assured me that her only concern was the safety of her granddaughter to which I answered, "You could have fooled me. From what I could see, the two of you were trying to yank her apart." Grandma agreed her actions were out of line, then broke into tears. "What am I supposed to do?" She asked. I assured her that the solution was simple. If her complaint was valid, she should have contacted the sheriff's office or Parker County Child Protective Services (CPS) and filed a complaint against her daughter. I assured her that the subsequent investigation would have proven or disproved her daughter's abuse of marijuana or other drugs as well as provided further evidence that the grandmother's daughter was endangering the health and security of her child. I assured the grandmother that a second investigation would reveal whether it was safe to turn temporary custody of her granddaughter over to her, depending on a background check and verification of the new man she had just allowed into her life. I assured her that if the investigation held in her favor, she would be awarded temporary custody of her granddaughter through legal procedures, not through her efforts to kidnap her.

I told her that I was going to drive her granddaughter home and complete a search of her daughter's home. Additionally, if I saw anything that I felt would jeopardize the girl's immediate health that I would contact Child Protective Services immediately. Otherwise, I planned to file a written report with CPS regardless, to ensure the security and the safety of her granddaughter, even if it meant placing her granddaughter in foster care.

I assured the grandmother that if her daughter indeed did have a drug habit that the best thing she could do would be to turn her daughter in when she knew she was in possession of drugs; only then could the criminal justice system move in and provide help. I told her that after I filed a report with Child Protective Services (CPS), she should look for a visit from a CPS Officer shortly. I left her with the reassurance that if I saw such actions endangering her granddaughter again, she would assuredly spend her own time behind bars, along with her new boyfriend.

Returning to mom, I told her I was going to follow her to her home, based on her daughter's request. I assured her that with her permission I would search her home to determine if any drugs or other dangers were present that might threaten her daughter's safety, and if I discovered any drugs or paraphernalia, I would contact CPS immediately and request an emergency extraction.

The girl's mother was a bit crestfallen over her daughter's choice to ride with me instead of her, but I imagined the little girl needed just a few more moments of security before returning to the woman who had participated in a tug-of-war with her. The event was not a pretty memory for any child or grandchild. Mom agreed to allow me to search the house, which told me that she had her drugs so well hidden that she felt assured that my search would reveal nothing. Mom's house proved to be the typical single-wide trailer but was surprisingly well-kept inside with no evidence of empty beer cans or drug paraphernalia in plain view. The home offered a neatly mowed yard, and the kitchen offered no evidence of mom's concentration on drugs instead of her daily chores to ensure the safety and welfare of her child.

I left the little girl with another lollipop and told her she could keep the teddy bear. Since I uncovered no evidence of drugs or other dangers, I released the little girl back into the custody of her mom along with the reassurance that she could expect a visit from CPS soon. Leaving the entire situation behind and providing a stern warning to all adults involved in the child's life, I returned to the office to file the report that would no doubt impact all their lives in the immediate future.

Indeed, domestic violence plagues America's homes and reaches across all boundaries, leaving scars passing from one generation to the next. Maybe, sometime in the future, we will discover the key to domestic violence and rid our nation and our world of a plight that destroys homes and creates physical and emotional scars lasting a lifetime.

Family Code and Penal Code laws have evolved considerably, even since the 1990s. However, during my tenure in law enforcement, very few women's and family shelters existed to offer an alternative source of care, custody, and control of her and her abused children. The few facilities that did exist did so solely because of private contributions, which always seemed to sway with the political climate, whatever priority society felt important at that moment in time.

During the late 1980s and early 1990s in our area, as patrol officers, we could not arrest an offender in a domestic violence situation unless probable cause existed to lead a normal, prudent person to believe that an act of family violence had indeed occurred. This requirement meant that we had to witness the assault or receive a statement from the victim or other witnesses (child, spouse, or neighbor) before we could affect an arrest. If no injury was visible on the victim and that person could not express true pain and harm to his or her body, then the probable cause could not develop, regardless of the situation.

If probable cause did not exist, the only option remaining was to dissolve the aggression by forcing one of the parties to leave the scene for a minimum of twenty-four hours. Quite often, that proved to be a challenge as well, since the aggressor and the victim were typically high on drugs or intoxicated, which eliminates the option of allowing either party to drive or walk away from the scene. However, another alternative was to invite a neighbor to assume care, custody, and control of the children or to contact Child Protective Services (CPS) to assist with some form of intervention. Fortunately, a caring neighbor or a family member living nearby could sometimes offer an immediate solution that enabled the two feuding parties to be separated.

Another challenge patrol officers faced in previous decades is that regardless of the harm to the victim, she or he still had the right to withdraw charges filed in the heat of the moment. Quite often, the victim arrived at the jail with a bail bonds agent to release the offender before the officer even booked the offender into the jail. The report then reflected that the victim filed a notice of withdrawing charges against the offender. The case became unfounded even though the patrol officer knew he or she would return to that same couple's lives later that week.

The State of Texas political element finally resolved the issue with a new law requiring patrol to arrest one or both people involved in domestic violence. This law assured the officer that he or she would leave the scene secured because the aggressor would be going to jail. However, the other problem of the victim dropping the charges remains an issue. The State of Texas created an answer to this dilemma by passing a new law that allowed the patrol officer to act on behalf of the State of Texas and the victim and file charges against the offender. Additionally, the patrol officer could seek an immediate remedy by requesting a Temporary Exparte Emergency Protective Order, which is a civil order from a judge ordering the victim and the offender to separate for a period of up to one year and remains criminally enforceable. Once the order is in effect, the officer files a copy with the primary dispatch office of that jurisdiction. Any patrol officer discovering the offender, in plain view, violating the protective order may arrest the offender and take him or her before the judge.

The victim is bound by the court order as well. However, typically, the victim is not arrested at the time of the violation (typically because children are involved and would require immediate care, custody, and control, which may or may not be available). Therefore, an officer files the case report with the court naming the victim as in violation of the order, and the court deals with the victim during regularly scheduled activity.

Most domestic violence offenders are more cowardly than their victim chooses to believe, leaving the victim in fear of even attempting to leave the offender. However, the offender typically chooses to flee before law enforcement can make the scene. One situation empowered by the new Emergency Protective Order ruling involved a four-year-old girl who found herself caught in the middle of a violent altercation during which she tried to stop daddy from beating on mom.

Daddy reacted with a swift kick to the child and then picked her up and threw her down the single flight of stairs in their two-story home. Fortunately, the carpeted stairs offered sufficient padding to cushion the child's fall, and the child suffered no debilitating injuries. However, when I arrived at the scene, her visible wounds were oozing blood as was her mom. The violence that had transpired before my arrival was obvious.

I contacted dispatch and asked that the EMT be allowed to move forward and care for the wounded to ensure neither victim required hospitalization. I photographed the wounds and left a victim's statement with the mom after Life Care personnel arrived. Mom told me that daddy had friends who lived right over the county border and she provided the address of the friend's home. I left the crime scene, leaving orders with the EMT to notify dispatch immediately if the father or any other hostile associate showed up in my absence, which was just as predictable as fleeing the scene. Quite often the offender would conveniently hide in a wooded area or some other obstacle until the officers left the scene. He or she would then return to the scene to finish the assault and intimidation of the victim or victims.

This man was easy to find. As I turned down the street, he was facing the other direction, leaning up against his friend's car on the roadside. I stopped my vehicle right in the middle of the road, jumped out of the car and assisted the man across the hood of my patrol vehicle. I searched him for weapons and contraband. Finding none, I forced him into handcuffs. I searched through his wallet until I found his Texas Driver's License, which contributed information to my report.

Unfortunately, since all I had was the word of a child and mom alleging that daddy threw her down the stairs, I had to allow the suspect to remain free, after the ensuing investigation. However, he would see his time in court, facing charges of Aggravated Assault of a Child less than five years old. Thanks to the new law, I filed a copy of the report with the local Justice of Peace in that precinct and received an Exparte Emergency Protective Order that would empower the offender's arrest at any time or place he approached his spouse, his child, or the victims' home, school, or workplace. I was thankful to see the State of Texas improving laws allowing officers and courts more leeway in filing domestic violence cases.

Photo 1. Chief Deputy Charles "Chip" Shumaker, Parker County Sheriff's Office 1990

Photo provided by Chip Shumaker (retired)

Photo 2. Parker County Sheriff's Office (PCSO) SWAT practice, early 1990s

Photo provided by Sheriff Ben Whiteman (retired)

Photo 3. Sheriff Ben Whiteman and Chief Deputy Charles "Chip" Shumaker in the mid-1990s

Photo provided by Sheriff Ben Whiteman (retired)

Photo 4. Sheriff Ben Whiteman during a media interview, mid-1990s

Photo provided by Sheriff Ben Whiteman (retired)

Photo 5. Deadly traffic stop photo in chapter two

Photo by author

Photo 6. Previous home of the Johnson Brothers (significantly improved since 1990s)

Photo by author

Photo 7. My son Brad saying goodbye as I am heading out on patrol

Photo by author

Photo 8. One-car roll-over involving PCSO reserve deputies responding to a call. Story related in Chapter 2.

Photo provided by Sheriff Ben Whiteman (retired).

Photo 9. Entrance to Horseshoe Bend today. The original, massive horseshoe covering the entrance to the area has long since been replaced.

Photo by author

Photo 10. Main entrance to Western Lake Estates today. Like Horseshoe Bend, the original entrance of the 1990s has long since deteriorated and been replaced.

Photo by author

Photo 11. Alleged glowing tombstone that has presently been altered to stop the glow during the night.

Photo by author

Photo 12. Alleged glowing tombstone to reveal the distance from the entrance to the tombstone

Photo by author

Photo 13. Alleged glowing tombstone from the side that previously offered the "glow" that was visible from the front gate of the cemetery entrance

Photo by author

Photo 14. Historical Marker designating the previous location of the Veal Station Settlement, which served as the first stagecoach stop west of Ft. Worth

Photo by author

Photo 15. Turn off from I-20 during the pursuit of the burglary suspect while on patrol in response to a burglary in progress call from dispatch

Photo by author

Photo 16. Goodson as a Criminal Investigator for the Parker County Sheriff's Office

Photo by author

Photo 17. Goodson served as guest speaker at a Memorial Day service at the Greenwood Cemetery in Ft. Worth, Texas, in 1997, on behalf of PCSO and *CAP MOT* publication release.

Photo by author

Photo 18. Award ceremony for officer of the year with PCSO

Photo by author

Photo 19. KKK rally, which Sheriff Whiteman had asked Goodson to take command and provide riot control

Photo by author

Photo 20. Ceremony on behalf of Officer of the Year involving officers from all agencies in Parker County

Photo by author

Chapter Six

Community Policing

Another best practice of controlling domestic violence and other crimes in a community stems from a program called "Community Policing," which has roots back in the late 1960s and early 1970s. Some researchers give credit to recognized needs in the Civil Rights Movement while others believe that the Civil Rights Movement was just a catalyst to those who already possessed the innate desire to organize community efforts.[1] Gayle Fisher-Stewart (2007) of the United States Department of Justice, confirms that the community policing movement began in the 1960s and 1970s, although many agencies were still adjusting to the concept in the following decades.[2] Community policing provides law enforcement entities the opportunity to share thoughts and concerns with community members, but serves primarily as a way for law enforcement to respond to expressed community needs. Texas communities expanded the idea a bit further with the pro-active involvement of community members.

Texas communities appear to have led the way in expanding community policing in a program called Citizens on Patrol (C.O.P.), which authorizes unarmed citizens to report crimes and suspicious activity in progress to law enforcement and provides them with uniforms, vehicles, and radio communications. This proactive form of community policing allows

C.O.P. members to serve as witnesses in court, which helps to increase the reliability of the case filing based on the witness statements for C.O.P. validation. China has sent law enforcement leaders to Texas to copy prime strategies employed in C.O.P. programs.[3]

In Parker County, community policing began during the early 1990s under the guidance of Sheriff Ben Whiteman, who in cooperation with the Weatherford Police Chief, Jerry Blaisdale, started working toward a viable concept to increase crime control and better response to high crime neighborhoods, especially those overwhelmed with drugs and domestic violence.

Unfortunately, Sheriff Whiteman's directive lacked proper funding from the County Commissioners, federal government, or any other reliable source. Therefore, the actual success of community policing projects fell on the shoulders of the lead sergeants of the patrol division. Sheriff Whiteman asked me to serve as the lead officer of the community policing program, placing the organization and evolution of the plan solely in my hands, without funding or directives. Most of the other patrol sergeants ignored the concept, promising to work toward the goal as soon as they encountered a citizen to take on the responsibility, which left the entire approach up to the patrol officers on my shift.

Based on the directive provided by the federal government, we proceeded with a written policy incorporating the powers and limitations of community policing programs along with the dictated policy proposing cooperative efforts from patrol leadership. I initiated community policing in the northeastern sector in an area known as Quail Run as well as in three communities in the southern sector, one being in Western Lake Estates and the other two being Horseshoe Bend and Lake Country Estates. Each of these locations required the most calls for service south of Interstate 20, typically for domestic violence between families or neighbors or that involved drug and alcohol abuse, burglary, theft, or criminal mischief.

Quite often, professional burglars or thieves turn to theft of expensive construction equipment as well, especially during increases in new home or commercial construction. Thefts from construction sites, farms, and rural homesites pose a significant challenge for community policing in a rural area. However, homeowners who do unite in a remote area can positively impact such criminal enterprises. Sheriff Whiteman established a cooperative effort with the Texas Department of Public Safety Theft Division to help gain control of heavy equipment thefts in Parker County.

However, community policing efforts can contribute to this cause as well. Community policing members in a new community enjoying growth in the eastern part of Parker County called Sheriff Whiteman one day advising that a thief had stolen a D-10 Caterpillar from a job site, pulling the Caterpillar on a trailer with a white Ford diesel crew-cab. He ordered dispatch to issue an all-points bulletin based on this information. The witness reported the offender going west on FM 1886, which connects with FM 730. The offender had only three options when he turned onto FM 730. If he headed north, he had to drive through downtown Azle. If he drove south to Weatherford, he stood a strong chance of encountering Texas DPS, Weatherford PD, or Parker County officers. Therefore, his best bet was to take the back-country roads crossing Parker County to the west. The fastest route across the northern part of the county is Veal Station Road, which is only about five miles north of FM 1886. I assumed the offender would choose that route because it took him to FM 51 where he could turn south and hook up with Carter Road nearly a mile away, enabling him to continue west to Palo Pinto County.

Equipped only with my drug seizure Ford pickup, I headed north on FM 51 with a plan to set up a blockade with the small truck at one of the narrow bridge crossings on Veal Station. Two ideal bridges on Veal Station were about one mile east of FM 51. Minutes later, I turned onto Veal Station and drove to the first narrow bridge. Allowing one citizen in a small car to continue her route to FM 51, I parked the small green pickup diagonally on the narrow bridge. Unfortunately, the more substantial pickup pulling a massive D-10 could easily plow through the small truck. However, I felt the slugs in my 12-gauge shotgun would probably provide the extra compensation required to stop the offender.

Dwight (DD) Stevens, the head of Parker County Burglary Investigations, radioed that he was closing the gap behind the offender and agreed that the offender would probably choose Veal Station as an escape route. I stood waiting in front of my diminutive blockage. A white Ford diesel truck crested the hill about a quarter of a mile in the distance, but I could not see a trailer. A few seconds later the pickup rolled to a stop in front of me. The driver was a local farmer I knew well. I explained that he needed to take a different route and apologized for the inconvenience. However, he waved it off as something that was good for him as well, since his farm also offered prime targets for such criminals. He completed a 180-degree turn and headed back east.

As his truck passed over the crest of the same hill, a second white Ford truck passed him, headed toward me. This one was pulling a trailer laden with a D-10 Caterpillar. Rechecking my weapon to ensure the first shell was a slug, I stood ready for the worst. Seconds later the truck came barreling at me as it crested the small rise in the roadway before the bridge. Fortunately, the offender felt discretion was the best option as he rapidly brought the big rig to a halt. I greeted him with my shotgun, encouraging him to exit the vehicle and assume a spread-eagle position against the body of his truck. Knowing Investigator Stevens was en route, I decided to keep the suspect against the truck under threat from the shotgun instead of risking a one-handed cuffing technique. A few tense moments later, DD's car skidded to a stop beside us. This professional thief failed to research law enforcement activity in Parker County. Had he chosen to commit the theft during the midnight shift his effort would probably have succeeded since only a handful of city, county, and state officers cover the territory during those hours. However, construction crews leave the keys in their equipment when they break for lunch, which makes the theft of heavy equipment much easier since one is not required to hotwire the heavy rig. Community policing saved the construction company thousands of dollars that day.

One of the primary challenges to developing an active, civic-minded, community policing organization rests with finding a motivated person who is drug-free and not besieged by family violence in such high-crime areas. We were never able to find anyone qualified and brave enough to face the wrath of the drug lords governing the northern territory. Without further empowerment from funding through the County Commissioners or private sources, the best my officers could do was to commit to a block-long area in a remote location and risk foot-patrol. Most officers resisted the idea.

Western Lake Estates offered one individual who was recognized and respected by most members of that community. I had met Larry Haney and his wife Ann during an early evening shift patrol of Western Lake Estates in 1991. His twelve-year-old daughter was riding a bicycle in the roadway and waved at me as I approached. I rarely had time to visit with the good citizens in Western Lake Estates because of the frequent domestic calls dominating my time. However, most calls did not start until after 4:00 pm, after mom and dad returned home from work and the kids were dropped off by the school bus.

I rolled slowly to a stop, and Larry's daughter stopped her bicycle beside the driver's door. She was bold and friendly in her approach, which is rare for the youth in a drug-ridden neighborhood. I lowered the driver's window as she smiled and said, "Hi, I'm Suzie." We carried on a brief conversation during which I quizzed her about her home and school life hoping to uncover information concerning the strength or lack of within the family unit. She told me her last name was Haney and pointed to a single-wide trailer, quickly adding that they owned seven acres near the entrance of Western Lake Estates and would be moving over there as soon as her father could afford a double-wide mobile home. Their present home was pleasing to the eye, showing a well-manicured lawn and clean deck, which is rare in a mobile home community. Most mobile-home yards, driveways, and porches are cluttered with trash, mostly dismantled junk cars, and even old toilets or bathtubs turned into flower pots. The Haney home offered a pleasing shift away from the norm.

Suzie and I talked about her aspirations to become a school teacher in Weatherford, and about her life with her family. She assured me that her father and mom were the best people in Western Lake Estates but quickly added that she did have a drug addict sister that her father had forced to move out. I had indeed met her sister on a few occasions when serving a warrant for her or her boyfriend.

I asked her if she would introduce me to her parents and she readily agreed as she turned and pedaled as hard and fast as she could to warn her parents. I allowed her time to jump from her bike and run up the steps of the porch to her home just as I pulled to a stop alongside the roadway adjacent to their home. She stuck her head in the door and then returned to continue talking with me.

"They'll be out in a minute," she said. We chatted more about her desire to become a teacher, and I assured her that if I could help, I surely would. I knew the principal and several teachers at the Weatherford High School and thought I could probably let them know about this young lady's desire to follow in their footsteps. Based on Suzie's openness and obvious love and caring for her parents, I felt I may have located a man who could help establish a community policing program in Western Lake Estates.

After a few moments a middle-aged man and woman stepped outside. They both extended their hands, offering firm handshakes with sincere appreciation for the presence of a law enforcement officer in Western Lake Estates. Suzie introduced her father as Larry Haney, who in turn presented his wife, Ann. I instantly felt a common bond with both parents as well as with Suzie. We chatted for a moment, then Ann asked if I had time to share a glass of iced tea. I checked the sun, which was slowly starting its descent toward the tree line to the west. I knew I would be swamped within the next hour, but I did have a brief window before that. I checked out on a Signal 51 (investigation) with dispatch and provided the address of the Haney home as I followed my newfound friends into their house. Larry perked up immediately, confirming that he wanted to discuss the idea. He said he was willing to do anything to fight crime in Western Lake Estates. Ann agreed with Larry, especially since their older daughter suffered from drug addiction.

We all found a seat in the living room as Ann and Suzie handed out cool glasses of tea. Ann continually apologized for what she perceived as a dirty house as I reassured her that the house appeared fine to me and offered that lived-in feeling one grows to appreciate in the country life. We began discussing the crime they felt to be prevalent in their area as well as possible solutions. Additionally, we discussed other people they felt would want to join the effort. I was beginning to think we had a chance to develop community policing in Western Lake Estates.

Western Lake Estates is located in a quiet valley surrounding a small but beautiful clear-water lake, hence the name of the community. The community is about ten miles south of Weatherford just off Tin Top Road, which led residents further south to the Brazos River and then down into Hood County to Lake Granbury and a popular small town with the same name.

I had enough information to convince me that Larry and Ann may be good candidates to serve as community policing leaders. I shared my thoughts and concerns with Larry, Ann, and Suzie. All three were very excited about the idea and assured me that they were not interested in directly taking on any of the drug addicts or dealers in the area. Additionally, they were indeed willing to head up a group of good citizens who could provide other officers and me with information to combat the drug abuse and drug dealers in their community. I assured them that I only needed them and the other good people in the area to serve as my eyes and ears. Additionally, I invited Larry to ride along occasionally with me during a patrol, to provide insight concerning known troublemakers or locations of drug dealers. He welcomed the idea.

Soon, Western Lake Estates became a viable addition to much-needed crime control efforts in the southern area of the county and gave us considerable information relating to days and locations of drug deliveries throughout the area, including down to Granbury. Western Lake Estates became my model community policing program, my reference point as proof to other officers that one could gain cooperation from good citizens in a community, even one engulfed in drugs.

Years after I transferred from patrol to the Criminal Investigation Division (CID), I received a phone call from a notorious drug dealer who had long reigned over Western Lake Estates. He struck fear in residents by allegedly toting a double-barreled shotgun while riding a mule down the roads of Western Lake Estates, daring anyone to defy him. Thanks to Larry and those who followed him, we brought such actions to an end.

The drug dealer's phone call no longer threatened aggression against our patrol officers but served as a cry of help from a loving father. His activities as a drug dealer had taken a toll on his family. His daughter had risen to the top in the local drug trafficking and, unfortunately, fell to the clutches of the very drugs she delivered to other addicts. The earnest plea for help came as a surprise since he and I had butted heads so often in the past. "Sergeant Goodson, I need your help, please," he pleaded. "My daughter is following the same path I chose in the past." I told him that I could not believe he wanted my help after all the battles we fought, but he assured me that he had put that life behind him since his last parole and that he desperately wanted to ensure his child did not fall prey to the same lifestyle.

Unfortunately, his plea came too late. His daughter was well into her teens and had dropped out of school to pursue the brief lucrative career offered by the drug life she wanted. I assured him that I would gladly meet with him and his daughter anytime...anywhere, but I never heard from him again. I checked his home in Western Lake Estates, but it was abandoned, leaving no trace of his whereabouts behind, which is typical of those dealing in illicit drugs.

Horseshoe Bend became the second successful venture in community policing under the leadership of Mike Amandellero and his wife, Nancy. Mike was a retired U.S. Marine Gunny Sergeant, who had served his country well, and he and his wife Nancy continued to serve in a reduced, but essential facet as leaders of the community policing effort in Horseshoe Bend.

Unfortunately, their efforts were a bit more challenged than Larry's success in Western Lake Estates. However, both men and the members who chose to join the community policing projects in their area served as excellent sources of intel for wanted felons. Horseshoe Bend was several miles south of Weatherford, even further south than Western Lake Estates. We desperately needed help in that community because of the relative ease with which drug dealers, rapists, burglars, and other criminals could operate without fear of discovery, even by Mike and Nancy. Mike stayed busy with his service as head of the Horseshoe Bend Volunteer Fire Department, which found itself continually battling fires set by rebellious teenagers or careless outsiders who enjoyed their vacation homes with uncontrolled fires, leaving the remains for Mike and his volunteers to deal with.

Mike entrusted the leadership of the community policing program to other members of the community he thought were good people. However, one evening I received a call from dispatch to meet the Horseshoe Bend Fire Chief at the Horseshoe Bend Country Club. I was in a northern sector of the county. Therefore, it was almost an hour before I pulled into the parking lot where Mike was patiently waiting.

Even though Mike had retired as a Gunny Sergeant from the Marine Corps, he seemed to have left that moniker behind in exchange for a meek and mild manner, which I knew was a cover for a very strong-willed person. Mike walked over to me as I stepped from my car. Gunny Mike told me that the men he left in charge of the community policing were driving around the neighborhood in a pickup truck with many of them in the bed of the truck and all were carrying firearms ranging from pistols to rifles and shotguns. He said they had been waving the weapons in the air and threatening all the citizens to remain inside their homes or suffer the consequences. I could hear echoes from firearms in the distance as we shared concerns. He apologized for entrusting the wrong men to do the job, but I waved it aside, assuring him that some people just cannot be trusted with power over others, hence the reason why dictators rise to power.

I asked him if he wanted to show me where they were. Gunny Sergeant Amandellero stood tall and said, "Hell yeah. Let's go get 'em." Mike entered the passenger side of the patrol car, and I made sure he was armed. I made sure he understood that no firearms would be used except against the threat of deadly force and only by my command and he agreed. We drove toward the roadway from which echoed the continuous gunfire until we reached a "T" intersection. I stopped briefly to listen. Suddenly, the sound of firearms came toward us from the left. I wheeled the car in the direction of the threatening gunfire. Moments later, the pickup could be seen driving ahead of us, heading south, while the men inside the cab and the back of the truck fired their weapons indiscriminately. An occasional beer bottle hit the side of the road as well.

I notified dispatch that an altercation was about to occur, giving her our location and a description and license number of the suspect vehicle. The men were so intoxicated that they remained oblivious to our presence until I flipped on the red and blues and hit the siren. The driver of the truck slammed on the brakes, sending one of his men over the edge of the bed of the truck onto the pavement below. The others fell in a bundle against the rear window of the pickup as the driver tried to exit the vehicle and run for cover. The passenger remained in the truck and made no move to exit or create any issues. I jumped out of the car and chased down the drunken driver, wrestling his weapon from him. When I returned with the handcuffed driver, Mike had already disarmed all the other men and had them on their knees in front of my vehicle. The man who fell out of the truck had been fortunate. He only suffered a few cuts from landing in a briar patch.

I read each of them their rights and placed them under arrest for disorderly conduct and the driver for driving while under the influence. Additionally, I confiscated all their firearms under the protest of the driver, who was the self-proclaimed leader of the alleged community policing group. He promised he would have my badge. I waited for another unit to show up to assist with transport before we all cleared the scene.

Thanks to Mike, we managed to regroup under the banner of community policing in that area, but most of the citizens refused to participate or cooperate, which left Mike with another torch to carry on his own. He and Nancy served that community faithfully for years, fighting fires and drug dealers, hoping to secure the Horseshoe Bend they had grown to love. Indeed, it could have been a beautiful area if only solid citizens had committed their lives to the betterment of the community. As it was, Mike and Nancy faced angry, demanding vacationers who remained easy prey to the drug dealers and other offenders who indeed controlled their community, leaving the residents of Horseshoe Bend intimidated by the lack of respect from outsiders and the drug dealers catering to their whims.

My last dispatch to Horseshoe Bend was as an investigator based on a tip from Mike. A Horseshoe Bend drug dealer had given his six-month-old baby a lethal dose of cocaine and then slammed the baby against the bedroom wall to make it stop crying. He was successful in his quest. The baby's lifeless body dropped to the floor. The drug dealer managed to gain a release on bond but failed to appear in court. The judge issued a warrant for his arrest and patrol had made numerous attempts to locate him, but to no avail.

Mike called one day to tell me that the escaped offender was presently enjoying a drink in the bar of the Horseshoe Bend Country Club and that he would engage him in a conversation until I arrived if I was free. He knew my answer. I assured him that I was already heading his direction.

He told me that the reason the drug dealer managed to evade patrol successfully was that friends who lived near the entrance of Horseshoe Bend called him as soon as they saw a patrol car enter the area, giving him time to evade arrest, even if he had to make his way across the Brazos River. I assured Mike that would not be an issue. As a member of CID, I drove a drug seizure vehicle, a little Ford Ranger pickup, which meant that his friends would not recognize me as I drove past the entrance. I entered the parking lot of the Country Club and parked out of sight of the bar entrance. Entering quietly, I noticed Mike and the offender sitting at the bar. Mike responded appropriately to my approach by ordering the offender another round. I walked up behind the man, who was sitting with his back to the door. I stood for a moment wondering whether to immediately force the man to the floor or trust him to not raise a ruckus inside the bar.

I chose to give him an option. He still was not aware of my presence, and Mike was holding his own in the conversation. I leaned forward and whispered in his ear, "We can do this the hard way, or you can simply put your hands behind your back." The man froze in mid-sentence as he glanced behind him to identify the source of the threat. I smiled. He stood up and asked if we could take it outside because he did indeed not want to ruin his reputation with the bar. I laughed at the idea of a baby murderer remaining concerned about his reputation. However, I agreed. Mike remained in the bar to settle the tab. I knew he would be right behind me. As we stepped into the sunlight outside, the offender looked at me for a moment as his eyes began to adjust to the sunlight, then glanced to the left and right. He was about to make his move.

I glared at him, putting my hand on the butt of my pistol and said, "Go ahead. See if you can outrun my .45 slugs." He glanced at my grip on my Colt .45, and then turned and put his hands behind his back. I completed a speed-cuff technique and shoved him against the wall of the Country Club as I searched him for any contraband or weapons. The Marine part of me wished that the man would choose to try to escape, a felon who had murdered a six-month-old baby. I had shot men during the Viet Nam War for a lot less.

Mike came outside, walking by us as if nothing had happened, ignoring the handcuffed man. Mike's performance reached beyond the call of duty, and I was not about to let the offender know that Mike had endangered himself by making the call and keeping the offender busy until I arrived. I returned the offender to the county jail where he remained without bail until his day in court where he was promised a life sentence without parole for Capital Murder of an Infant, much too lenient for what he did to the baby. To my horror, his case was later dismissed because of a technicality.

Mike is no longer with us. He and Larry never knew each other, but I like to think the two of them are still watching over families in Western Lake Estates and Horseshoe Bend. They both left behind loving families and a community that remains grateful for their devotion above the call of duty.

Lake Country Acres was another remote community nestled against the northern shores of the Brazos River as it made its way through the southern sector of Parker County and remains the southernmost community in the county. The drive to that remote location is long and arduous, even longer than the trip to Horseshoe Bend. However, the area demanded our attention because of the criminal element controlling it.

To make matters worse, the first home at the entrance to Lake Country Acres belonged to a drug-dealing mom and her two felonious sons. Both sons served time in prison for felony drug and murder charges. They were known as the Johnson brothers. The plot of land owned by their mom provided enough space for a three-bedroom frame home and a single-wide trailer. One of the sons lived in the house with mom, while the other lived in the single-wide, which sat perpendicular to the home, facing to the south.

During my early years on patrol, I was dispatched to investigate a complaint from a Lake Country Acres resident who chose to remain anonymous alleging that one of the sons was roaming the streets wielding a pistol and threatening other residents. On the night I received the dispatch, Sergeant Ken Smith contacted me by radio asking me to wait for his arrival before making the scene. About twenty minutes passed as he doused his headlights and pulled next to my already blacked-out patrol car. I had never entered Lake Country Acres before, so I welcomed the backup. Ken told me that he just wanted to remind me about the two felony brothers, one of whom was a Viet Nam veteran. He told me that they were all dangerous, even their mom. Sergeant Smith said that my headlights would shine right on the Johnson brothers' houses as I passed through the entrance to the community. I assured him that I had heard about them from other officers but was not aware that one of them was a combat veteran of the Viet Nam War. Ken told me to watch my back and that he would accompany me if I felt that I needed a backup. I could sense that Ken was testing my mettle. I was not going to disappoint him with my first call as a rookie officer. I told him I would give him a shout if I walked into a hornet's nest but felt that one or two combat veterans would not pose too much of a threat. He laughed and drove away, heading back north.

I drove the last two miles to the entrance of Lake Country Acres, turning my lights off before I closed in on the location of the Viet Nam veteran. I despised the idea of a fellow Viet Nam Veteran being a felony offender, but scoffed at my false sense of security, thinking that all veterans were honorable individuals. I toyed with approaching the Johnson brothers' home but decided to visit the trailer instead, which should enable meeting only one of the Johnson brothers at a time. I stopped the patrol car about fifty yards shy of the houses and checked out with dispatch, advising her that I would be confronting the individual in the trailer home instead of the homestead.

I crept toward the entrance of the home, which had a small, wooden deck leading to the front door. I tested the first step and found it to be sound, providing no significant noise to give away my approach. I made it to the front door and tapped on the door with a loud knock. "Come on in," sounded from within the interior, seemingly on the right side of the living room. I announced myself, "Sheriff's Office. You need to step outside, please." A laugh echoed back at me, followed by a man urging me to go ahead and enter the home. I glanced toward the mother's house, but it remained dark, offering no visible signs of activity or threats. I opened the door with my hand on my weapon as I entered. A scruffy-looking man sat in a lounge chair with a television offering some form of entertainment to its viewer. The man appeared to be alone. He noticed my hand on my weapon and assured me that no such action was needed.

I told him that I had been dispatched to investigate a man threatening neighbors with a weapon earlier that day. He told me that it must have been his brother, if it was anyone in his family, because he was prone to irritating the neighbors; he himself did not have time for it. I had already checked with dispatch to see if any active warrants were out for the Johnson brothers before I arrived, and she confirmed that none existed. I told Mr. Johnson that others informed me that he was a crazy Viet Nam veteran and that he has just met another and that I was probably equally unpredictable.

He laughed and stood up, extending his hand. We shook hands as he quizzed me about my branch of service and where I had served in Viet Nam. I shared a brief history of my start as a machine gunner with Alpha Guns with Alpha 1/7 on Hill 10 and then how I made the transition to the CAP Marine program after completing three months in-country. Ironically, we shared a bit of kinship based on our mutual service on behalf of our country during that horrific war. He showed me a few pictures, and I observed a couple of medals hanging alone on the wall above his television. I told him that it was a shame that we were on opposite sides of the law. Otherwise, we might have been able to share memories over a few beers someday.

He laughed again, saying that he and his brother would never be a threat to me, but they assuredly had no love for any other officer with Parker County. I left him to enjoy his remaining beers and advised dispatch that one home was secure and that I had indeed contacted one of the Johnson brothers. I told the dispatcher that I would file a written report providing cause for further investigation. Before I left, I promised Mr. Johnson that I would return the next day around 4:00 and that I wanted to meet his brother and mother.

I kept my promise, meeting with all three the next day and issued the same warning I had given the brother in the trailer the night before. I assured them that I would be committed to routine patrol and expected them to refrain from any further acts of harassment or face more time in jail or prison.

I did return to Lake Country Acres at least two or three times every week until I transferred to CID many years later and always stopped by for a visit with the dreaded Johnson boys.[4] They ceased their threatening behavior, and the brother living in the house with mom returned to prison after a parole violation. Unfortunately, other inmates killed him while he served his time, leaving a grieving mother. The Johnson brother I met suffered through his parole with no other known violations.

During my numerous visits to the community, many of the residents near the entrance began to report that the remaining Johnson brother had seemingly turned over a new leaf with offers to help them with repairs around the house as well as just sharing a glass of tea with them. I was not surprised. His mom assured me that she was afraid she would lose the only son she had left if he did not change his ways. Presumably, the man had seen the light and chosen the better route. I checked with his parole officer who assured me that the man was free and clear, had completed all parole requirements and lacked further reports of committing other crimes.

Months later, during my patrol of Lake Country Acres, the remaining Johnson son was mowing the yard. I pulled over in front of his house, and his mom waved from the front door. Mr. Johnson shut down the riding mower and walked over to me, extending his hand with a hardy handshake. He asked me if I was on routine patrol or if I was hunting for a specific offender because he knew all of them. I laughed and told him that my actual intent was to knock on a few doors and see if I could find someone to help me start a community policing program in Lake Country Acres. He stopped for a minute as if searching his mind for a suggestion. Most of the good citizens in the area had already refused my requests because they did not want to endanger their family since Parker County Deputy response was sometimes an hour's drive away. The good citizens were not angry, only frustrated at the situation that came with their desire to live in such a remote location. They were right. Parker County could only offer protection when an officer was present, and since we were always understaffed, we were fortunate to have an officer available when they called 911.

Additionally, only one county road led to the entrance of Lake Country Acres, which meant that any officer in other parts of the county would have to make his or her way to that county road before making the long drive to Lake Country Acres. They knew they were alone and none of them fostered the expertise or the will to stand against the drug dealers in their area. Instead, they remained behind locked doors when the dealers were on the move.

High cyclone fences with locked gates surrounded most of the homes. Numerous dogs guarded the houses. Citizens did file cases, but none of the residents chose to witness in court against any of the offenders. Therefore, our only hope rested with the drug task force to infiltrate the ranks of the offenders and bring them to justice. Unfortunately, the task force covered a tri-county area, which meant that they concentrated only on the primary drug dealers, not the petty marijuana and crack-cocaine dealers found in the remote locations such as Lake Country Acres.

Mr. Johnson shoved the toe of his boot in the ground underneath his feet, like a boy about to ask a girl out for their first date. I was taken aback by his words. "What about me?" He asked. I said, "You? You mean as head of the community policing program?"

He smiled meekly, lowering his shoulders and said, "Man, I need to do something to make up for all the wrong I have done in this world. I need to let these people know I am the one they can turn to in their hour of need." He stopped for a minute. His eyes continued dropping to the ground. He then looked straight at me as he squared his shoulders and said, "Just give me a chance to prove myself, will ya?"

I studied his eyes for a moment and then mom came outside, joining the conversation after overhearing his request for me to trust him. She pleaded with me to trust him, promising she would help all that she could. He looked at me and said, "Man, we fought together against a common enemy in 'Nam. Doesn't that mean something." I thought for a moment and wondered if the people in the community would accept a known felon as their crime watch leader. I turned back to him and said, "I tell you what. If you can gather enough residents who are willing to trust you together, I will come back, and we will hold a meeting and let your neighbors decide." He smiled and shook my hand assuring me that I would not be sorry.

About two days later I received a call from dispatch advising that I needed to meet a complainant in Lake Country Acres. I arrived about an hour later to see Mr. Johnson standing outside with his mom, talking with a handful of other neighbors. I stepped from the car as Mr. Johnson began walking my way, with one hand waving back to the small group of people. He said, "I have a few neighbors right here who have agreed to consider the idea and about a dozen more waiting for us in the clubhouse if you are still game."

I said, "Lead the way," and everyone got into their cars and drove to the clubhouse where I discovered another dozen or so people awaiting my arrival. After everyone took a seat, I asked for a show of hands from all those who knew why I was there. They all raised their hands and one blurted out, "Because he [pointing at Mr. Johnson] assures us that he can help us clean up the neighborhood and get rid of the drug dealers and drug addicts." Mr. Johnson had not taken a seat but instead stood beside me.

I asked him and his mom to wait outside while I discussed the idea with the other residents. I wanted to make sure that none of them were there under duress and that Mr. Johnson and his mother had not threatened them in any way. Each community member assured me that he had approached them with his hat in his hand and offered to stand up against the criminal element plaguing their community. I made sure that they understood that meant only to serve as the eyes and ears on behalf of the Parker County Sheriff's Office.

They all promised me that they indeed did understand the duties of a community policing organization and were well prepared to accept the leadership of Mr. Johnson with the full knowledge that he was an ex-con. They felt confident that he had proven to them over the past few months that he was sincerely interested in helping improve family life in Lake Country Acres. They told me that Mr. Johnson showed no fear of the drug offenders in the area, which was far more than the rest of them could offer. A few stepped forward saying that every person deserved a second chance and besides, Mr. Johnson knew all the criminals in the area and knew that they feared him. I called Mr. Johnson and his mom back into the clubhouse and asked for a show of hands, again, and once again, all hands went up in favor of the new crime watch commander. I inwardly hoped that I was not committing a grave error by empowering this man. His mom excused herself and returned with platters of cakes and cookies and urged others to return to her car to bring in the coolers with tea and Kool-Aid. The new commander began shaking hands as he almost burst into tears with the solid vote in his favor. He then made his way over to me, extended his hand for a hearty handshake one more time and said, "Thanks. I know you doubt me, but as one Viet Nam veteran to another, I give you my word...I will protect these people with my life."

I returned his firm grip, patted him on the shoulder and said, "I accept your promise, Mr. Johnson and to think I was prepared to shoot you that first night I entered your home." He laughed, "Yeah, I thought so too."

I dropped by to visit with the members of the community watch group a few times a month afterward but soon realized that the only calls we were receiving from Mr. Johnson were to advise us of the location and time of a drug drop along with the identity of the offenders and the vehicles they drove.

Within a few months, calls for dispatch to Lake Country Acres began to dissipate to almost nothing. The once drug-plagued community offered clean, manicured yards and neighbors going for walks along the roadside or heading for a moment of fishing in the nearby bend of the Brazos River, knowing that a drug-crazed individual would not harass them or cause them any harm. Mr. Johnson stood by his promise, showing that one person can indeed make a difference. Most of all, he proved that a felon could be rehabilitated.

Other than the areas mentioned above, a few individual blocks of a half-dozen homes in the northern sector agreed to establish nothing more than an agreement to watch each other's houses but refused to develop any truly organized effort toward a community policing program. However, three of the worst communities in Parker County did indeed gain control of the criminal elements threatening their community through the commitment of a handful of residents who took the time to make a difference.

Chapter Seven

Cult Crimes

One of my more challenging and unique assignments stemmed from an impromptu meeting with Sheriff Whiteman in the early 1990s. Dale Pilcher served as my Patrol Corporal at that time. He was a rather unique individual with a love of anything military, which he expressed through his war-era Willys Army Jeep that he restored to mostly original condition along with the standard-issue trailer to complete the package.[1] The finished product was indeed beautiful, and he drove it regularly.

I grew fond of Corporal Pilcher, not because he had the robust, hell-bent for leather mentality that some expect in officers, but more because he always remained focused on the spirit of the law, insisting that we should explore the unique criminal element that seemingly falls through the cracks. During a conversation one day he shared his concern that certain sectors of Parker County were occupied by what appeared to be clandestine Satanic cult operations. One was a ranch in the Aledo area that boasted the upside-down cross as the brand for their livestock and boldly displayed the brand on a billboard at the entrance to their ranch, which consisted of several-thousands of acres.[2]

Even though the 1960s and 1970s offered popular cult movies relating to human torture and sacrifices, I never accepted the reality of such cultic activity, dismissing it as just Hollywood hype, far from the truth, or as strange, small sects of people caught up in an alternative search for validation in life. However, Dale insisted that demonic cults were indeed at work in Parker County and that we were wrong to ignore the signs, some of which were explained as attacks by wild animals on livestock. Additionally, one must question the fact that some of these attacks left no signs of blood at the crime scene, leaving only a carcass. Generally, the chosen sacrificial animal was a pregnant nanny or cow about to give birth to a new life.

As mentioned in the book *The Satanism Scare*, some people remain unaware that some cultic practices can indeed violate criminal laws, especially laws relating to criminal trespassing, animal abuse, and desecration of a graveyard. The authors of *The Satanism Scare* propose that Satanism is nothing more than an alternative religion and that laws restricting such worship are based on illogical social influence from other religious entities and social powers. The basis for this theory appears to rest on the belief that laws declaring an act to be criminal are solely based on the ruling class's beliefs and cultural practices in societies juxtaposed to Satanism as a viable religion. The authors, therefore, purport that such laws are merely further intrusion of the ruling class on the average citizen in societies.[3]

Some theorists suggest that organizations searching for specific livestock body parts for medical research are responsible for cattle mutilations. One rancher in the U.S. reported a helicopter flying in a total blacked-out mode (no running lights) dropping to the ground on his ranch one evening for unknown reasons. The next morning the rancher told investigators that he found mutilated cattle in the area where he witnessed the helicopter land.[4]

A third theory arises from conspiracy theorists and UFO (Unidentified Flying Objects) theorists. Such researchers provide findings they believe substantiate reports of bright lights in the areas where cattle mutilations were discovered. Sightings of strange flying objects and unexplained lights in the nighttime skies abound across the United States as well as around the world.

To date, no viable evidence verifies any theories relating to cattle mutilations. However, peer-reviewed research remains severely lacking in this area, suggesting that livestock mutilations remain an under-investigated phenomenon.[5]

I worked numerous livestock mutilation cases throughout my career, but since no human tracks were ever be found at the scene, many assume the offense was committed by a predatory animal. However, no known predator prints were left at the scene and wounds defied the typical ripping marks predators leave. Additionally, the unborn offspring (lamb or calf) always appeared to have been removed from the womb in a precise pattern with a sharp knife, possibly a scalpel. The slaughtered animal was always missing genitals, heart, udder, and occasionally the horns as well. The death of the animal appeared to have been caused by a solitary hole in the jugular, which does not suggest a natural predator. Predators rip and tear at their victim's throat and body, leaving gaping wounds and spilt blood, with the primary focus on the edible portions of the body.

More disconcerting evidence rests with the scalpel-like cutting of the skin, as if someone was intent on a surgical process. No animal is prone to such precise, controlled wounding of their prey. Therefore, although lacking definitive evidence, investigations point toward human intervention. With the absence of evidence, these cases remain unsolved, although they are prevalent. In 2013, a rancher in Missouri reported that her cattle suffered from similar mutilations to those in Parker County. The rancher accused extraterrestrial beings.[6] However, all such reports remain based on theory alone. One Parker County rancher whose 1,000-plus-acre ranch lies in a valley area roughly ten miles south of Weatherford, assured me that he loses close to 100 animals a year to an unknown offender, be it animal or man.

The information Dale and I shared with each other began to clearly point toward the actions of humans. Therefore, either the ranchers were involved in some form of cultic activity designed to strike fear in neighboring livestock operations, or unknown suspects were deeply involved in torturing and murdering the animals as well as trespassing on private property. One report I received from another location on the east side of Parker County supports this theory. The preliminary investigation revealed a newborn calf had been skinned and then the hide turned inside-out and forced back onto the dead calf. Two young boys found the calf in an open prairie lying on a pile of stones. The stones were apparently stacked to provide some semblance of a table. No evidence provided any clues as to the owner of the calf or the offenders who committed the crime. The boys' parents told me that a man from Dallas owned the property and subsequent investigation led to the discovery that the registered owner of the land was a corporation and that no livestock were kept on the property. No further evidence developed.

Sheriff Whiteman shared Dale's concerns, which led to his request for me to join him in his office during the beginning hours of evening shift in the early 1990s. He shared the fact that the animal cruelty reports from deputies had caught his eye and that he had asked his secretary to create a chart of locations, dates, and times of such killings throughout the past five years. He showed me the results. I was not surprised to see proof that thousands of livestock were disappearing annually from ranches, farms, and private homes (as pets) throughout Parker County. Sheriff Whiteman assured me that he had chosen Corporal Pilcher and me to serve as Cult Crimes Investigators for the county because of the attention to detail in our reports concerning these crimes. Sheriff Whiteman supported Dale's theory that cult organizations were working Parker County with relative impunity.

As I mentioned, the animal murders did concern me, but not to the degree that I could pull myself away from domestic violence calls or other crimes that permeated every evening of the week, seemingly nonstop. Regardless, Sheriff Whiteman chose to send me to several federal and state cult training programs to ensure that I would be certified as a cult investigator as well as fully aware of the numerous forms of cults in the state and the crimes predominately associated with each group.

I remained skeptical of my new assignment and was warned by my patrol sergeant at that time to refuse it because of the probability of becoming labeled as a Devil Hunter by the other patrol officers, not only in the Parker County Sheriff's Office, but also with every agency in the county. I considered his warning but felt compelled to accept the assignment from Sheriff Whiteman.

Other information Dale shared with me led him to realize that these cult organizations were fronts for organized criminal activity. This included not only weapons and drug trafficking, but also human trafficking. Dale had begun working closely with a local FBI contact a few years before we joined forces. Through his efforts with the agent, he managed to formulate plausible theories that he believed gave answers to many mysterious missing person's cases, especially where wayward youths were concerned.

According to Dale, cults acted much like the Nazis did during the early days before WWII, when they developed compulsory recruitment of German youth to create an underground army of servants devoted to the Fuhrer, Adolf Hitler. Many people suspect that these dark underground organizations were funded by people in powerful places and that such criminal acts haunt our communities today.[7]

This is one of the reasons why Dale, even though we worked closely together, would keep some information secret, even from me. His strategy ensured that if something went wrong, he alone would be the likely victim of their retaliation. Based on this theory, Dale chose to never reveal his identity to informants, nor did he invade their anonymity. He only knew them by nicknames he issued to them. However, with no cases filed, fear of retribution remains unfounded.

The federally sponsored cult training program, which took place in the Ft. Worth Police Academy Training Center, presented one of the more heinous crimes relating to a case that developed in East Texas. Objective research does not confirm this case or the cult group, with the exception of a deluge of information confirming the reality of a group known as the Werewolf Order, an alleged sect of Satanic organizations. Regardless, according to the studies and photos provided during our Sect/Cult Investigations class in the 1990s, a cult group known to the instructors as the Werewolf Order operated in East Texas and the cult consumed city, county, and state judges, dentists, pharmaceutical distribution centers, members of the clergy, teachers, and even some law enforcement officers. According to the training report, the Werewolf group was a cult organization that based their beliefs and practices around the legends of the werewolf or Lycanthropy.

In her writings, Charlotte Otten (1986) confirms the existence of numerous offenders across the United States who suffered psychological fixation on their perceived lives in Lycanthropy. Ms Otten describes a U.S. Navy veteran and a farmer from the eastern United States who believed that they were werewolves and resorted to living in the Appalachians. Therefore, one must admit that, to some degree, Lycanthropy remains an issue in our country.[8]

The Sect/Cult Investigations training in Ft. Worth alleged that dentists created the fangs worn by each member of the cult that served as the tool or weapon of choice in sacrifices.[9] State and federal officers became aware of the group when a young girl about six years old became involved in a situation where her parents divorced, strangely leaving her in the custody of the father, which is rare in the State of Texas. The courts awarded the mother and father shared-custody of the child six months out of the year.

After each visit with her mom, the child returned home with small wounds on the inside of her thighs, which grew worse with each subsequent visit. The girl always told her father that she hurt herself playing in the area around her mother's country home. According to the instructors, this was exactly what the cult group and her mother had taught her to say. Allegedly, the sect required that outsiders should remain unaware of the girl's visits. Mom sufficiently groomed the girl's response so that she believed that the pain she endured was the cult requirement for all new members, assuring the child that she had endured the same membership process. The daughter was proud to be a member of a special organization alongside her mom and was willing to hide the truth that offenders were leaving bite marks on her body.

However, her father decided that his daughter was purposefully being harmed and shared his concerns with Child Protective Services (CPS), from his own jurisdiction. CPS officers determined that the man's daughter was suffering from some form of assault and the best they could ascertain was that the girl was being subjected to bites from some animal based on the depth and shape of the bite marks suggesting fangs rather than human teeth.

The subsequent investigation led to the involvement of state investigators based on the probability that local government entities may have been involved, since the mother was employed by a government entity. The final investigation revealed the true cult organization. The state called in the federal authorities and within a short time, numerous sect members were discovered, and charges brought forth to close down county-wide operations and to bring cult members to justice. Unfortunately, even with the involvement of the federal investigators, little was completed to extend the investigation past the county level.

The investigation uncovered the fact that the mom was grooming her child for sacrifice by the Werewolf Order. Therefore, that one child was saved from future harm. Regardless, one may wonder how many other children suffered, horribly, at the hands of this cult before its demise.

I have since searched for media verification of this crime, but none appears to exist, short of a missing girl, who remains missing today.[10] However, based on the attempts by news media and business leaders in our own county to cover up the offenses Dale and I ended up filing,

I believe that communities nationwide refuse to accept the reality of cult activity.

In the mid-1990s, a person in Azle, Texas, posted an ad in the local newspaper claiming that his cultic group planned to kidnap a local, blonde-haired, blue-eyed boy in the immediate area. The *Azle News* could produce no records of the person placing the ad and assured law enforcement that the clerk accepting the payment and forwarding the ad to the newsroom assumed the ad to be a practical joke. Local newscasters also quickly dismissed the scare as nothing more than a practical joke. However, being involved in cult investigations for Parker County and having a son who met the physical attributes required for the alleged kidnapping victim, led me to be on alert for any possible clue to the ad becoming a reality. No one kidnapped a child during the year that ad made history in Parker County, at least not to our knowledge. However, Azle is equally divided between Tarrant and Parker Counties. Missing juveniles and smaller children can easily slip under the wire in larger counties. Evidently, during that time, a scare existed concerning such threats, which is confirmed by an Internet blog discussion.[11]

I must admit, I never question training provided by the federal government to assist local investigators with investigating possible criminal cult activities within their jurisdiction. Repeat case studies and advanced cult investigations training provided by federal and state entities soon empowered me with investigative credentials that I dared not hang on my walls or even show to anyone, especially family members because I did not want my family to be aware that such dangers lurked in the dark shadows of night, even in Parker County, Texas. Dale never had the opportunity to attend formal training since he resigned from the Sheriff's Office shortly before the decision was made to send me to specialized, advanced investigation courses. However, Dale benefitted from direct association with a local FBI agent whose assignment was cult investigations in the southern states.

Cultic activity seemed to prevail in four major areas of the county: Springtown, Azle, Aledo, and the county line joining Palo Pinto and Parker Counties along Highway 80/180 in an area adjacent to Mineral Wells, Texas, which officers from Mineral Wells PD claimed served as the home of the Church of Satan in North Texas. However, Dale and I could never confirm this claim and research does not confirm the existence of the organization in Mineral Wells.

However, Mineral Wells PD encountered numerous cult investigation requirements as well, some of which alleged that sacrifices were being conducted by Satanic cults in the abandoned underground bunkers located on the old Fort Wolters base. Some of the antiquated military buildings had been either purchased or leased by various businesses and organizations, which helped provide a limited level of security on the Viet Nam-era base. Unfortunately, the underground bunkers were located on the far side of the base where only the curious chose to venture. Fort Wolters served as a military base from 1921 to 1973. According to the base's website, the last service on the base involved helicopter training not only for U.S. soldiers, but also for select Vietnamese who were chosen to become pilots on behalf of the Vietnamese efforts during the Viet Nam War. Mineral Wells PD did find locations inside some of the bunkers that offered evidence of human presence, but nothing that would lead one to believe that human or animal sacrifices occurred.

Around 1993 in Mineral Wells, Timothy Ray Bridges walked into a convenience store with a machete and hacked away at a store clerk. Normally, investigative practices will demonstrate that such actions are motivated by the offender's hatred for the victim. Alternative scenarios involve the victim reminding the offender of someone he or she hated in the past, but lacked the ability to retaliate against, leaving him or her forced to tolerate the abuse throughout his or her young life. During a conversation with one of the detectives working the case, he revealed to me that the offender confessed to the murder, claiming he was compelled to commit the heinous crime because Satan told him to, specifically, to slash and kill the victim with a machete.[12]

Springtown proved to be a major attraction to cult groups—witch covens, ghost hunters, and curious travelers—because of the renowned glowing tombstone one could find in the Veal Station Graveyard about four miles south of Springtown near the junction of Old Springtown and Veal Station Roads. The cemetery dates back to the early days of old Fort Worth, which served as a U.S. Army outpost as well as the location of the Veal Station Stage Coach Station and settlement, which was the first stage stop north of the county seat, Weatherford, Texas. The settlement began in 1850 with the primary business man in the community known as William Veal, hence the name.[13] Veal Station Road meanders west from FM 730 to a junction with FM 51. However, visitors to Veal Station Graveyard, especially during Halloween and blood or full moon nights, ventured in from locations from all parts of the United States. The blood moon is legendary among religious zealots based on the alleged relationship with the end times, with the moon turning blood red during those final days. This Biblical prophecy was made famous in a book authored by John Hagee, *Four Blood Moons: Something Is about to Change,* published in 2013.[14]

During my years on patrol, I encountered many strange individuals who chose to violate the sanctity of the Veal Station Graveyard, some with devious intentions and others with morbid curiosity. I decided, as time allowed, to make it my quest to squelch the legend of the glowing tombstone, which allegedly was haunted by the spirt of an evil presence from the past.

When I first arrived in Springtown in the late 1980s, living only about a mile northeast of the graveyard, I soon became enthralled with the tales of the ghosts in the graveyard, said to be caused by a tombstone that glowed in the dark. I decided to see for myself and drove to the old burial grounds. As my research continued, I was rapidly disappointed when the legend was immediately displaced with reality.

As I approached the graveyard, I fully expected to see an eerie radiating glow from only one tombstone. My country gentleman neighbor who was serving as my local guide, assured me it was there. He walked forward toward the main gain, side-stepped a few times, and then abruptly came to a halt. "There!" he exclaimed, pointing a shaking finger at a tombstone on the far, backside of the graveyard. The glow from the massive rock did indeed create a glow that separated it from all other tombstones. Locking the tombstone's position in my mind, I retreated to my previous position, which still offered a clear view of the same tombstone but offered only the same reflected light as the other stones surrounding the same area.

I laughed and called my friend over to my position and pointed the beam of my flashlight at the alleged glowing tombstone and asked, "Is that not the same one?" He readily agreed. I turned the light off and the tombstone still offered no radiant glow. I walked back over to his infamous spot and the glow returned, but only to that tombstone. I assured my neighbor that the tombstone did not glow, but only reflected light in a given position because those who installed the tombstone placed it in a unique angle to the full moon. I provided proof to him by making him return to the alternate location, once again, to see if the glow remained. He was puzzled for a moment and then assured me that it even glowed on moonless nights. "How do you explain that?" He asked. I pointed toward a floodlight radiating from the Hinkle Dairy barn, one of the few, privately owned dairy farms remaining active in the Springtown area. I assured him that the floodlight was probably the culprit.

We returned on a moonless night and confirmed my theory. My neighbor was a bit dismayed with the fact that I had debunked a legend that had captivated his youth. I was happy because this knowledge empowered me to pass this knowledge to everyone who chose to venture to the legendary graveyard for a glimpse of the glowing tombstone.

One of the more worrisome encounters I had at the Veal Station Graveyard came on a night following Halloween in the mid-1990s. The massive cedar trees surrounding the graveyard offered ample cover that even darkened the presence of my all-white patrol vehicle as I backed into the shadows on the west side of the graveyard to wait for sect members who frequented the place to commit their devious acts, including turning over the tombstones, a felony offense in the State of Texas (Desecration of a Grave).[15] As I sat in the dark shortly after midnight, a dark, four-door sedan drove toward me from the west, which led those leaving FM 51 to the junction of Veal Station and Old Springtown Roads. I waited. The driver turned off the headlights of the sedan as the vehicle slowly coasted from Veal Station Road into the shallow parking area of the graveyard.

During this time, the graveyard only offered a short, decorative iron fence enclosure that provided no hope of protection for the graves, making them easy prey by those with bad intentions. The fact that the driver killed the headlights while the car was still traveling on Veal Station Road aroused my suspicions.

I keyed up the mike advising dispatch that I would be out with a suspicious vehicle at the Veal Station Graveyard, lacking the usual license plate number because of the darkness of the night and the absence of artificial light. I had made sure that the dome light in my vehicle would not illuminate as I opened the door and walked slowly toward the suspicious vehicle. Two men and a woman stepped from the vehicle and walked to the rear, as the driver hit the button to release the trunk. The trunk light provided dim lighting radiating into the darkness, which momentarily blinded the three people, leaving them unaware of my approach. I altered my path to remain out of the radiant light and walked along the short fence at the front of the graveyard. I hoped to see the contents of the trunk before they noticed my presence. The woman and both men leaned into the trunk as I made my final approach.

My strategy worked. They were so intent on the contents of the trunk that my presence surprised them. The two men, dressed in black robes, stepped back in full defensive posture and the woman, dressed in a robe of red, stood tall, next to the open trunk. Calmly, she approached and said, "Good evening, officer. What can I do for you?" I assured her that she almost stole the same question out of my mouth. "Maybe you would like to tell me why three adults dressed in strange robes would be visiting Veal Station Graveyard in the dark of night, when the sign above the gate fully assures you that the graveyard closes daily at dusk to all visitors?" She glanced at the sign, which revealed to me that she was very aware of the presence and intention of the sign. She stated, "But, we have not entered the graveyard at this point, just parked alongside." She smiled at her moment of victory.

I smiled back, assuring her that I intended to keep her and her clan from desecrating the graveyard. Indeed, I could have remained in my patrol car until they entered the graveyard, but I chose to run them off instead, after I identified each person, checked each one for warrants and criminal history, and inspected the open trunk, which revealed piles of bleached white bones. She reached for the top of the trunk and I commented, "Don't even think about it, Ma'am. All that is in plain view now, thanks to you and your friends. Therefore, anything I find in the trunk may be legally seized and used in a trial against you and your men, should such discovery lead to evidence of a crime." She dropped her hand to her side, waving me forward.

I ignored her offer and asked all three for legal identification. Both the men stood silently and produced their Texas driver's licenses. The woman assured me that hers was in her purse inside the car. I asked the two men to stand back-to-back in the full light of the beam radiating from the trunk and followed the woman to the passenger side and shined my flashlight on her searching hands as she sought out her purse lying on the passenger seat. I glanced back at the men, who still stood silently, in full compliance. The woman retrieved her driver's license from her purse and I asked her to join her friends in the light of the trunk.

As she moved toward her friends, I contacted dispatch on my handheld, asking for verification of each ID as well as verification of the ownership and title of the vehicle. The vehicle returned to the driver. The license of each showed addresses in Ft. Worth, Texas, and offered no available warrants or criminal history. Therefore, if I was going to generate an arrest out of the confrontation, I would have to go through the contents in the trunk that were in plain view.

As they sat on the ground in view from the light of the trunk, I did not bend over to search the contents, but instead stepped to the side, which enabled me to reach inside the trunk while keeping the suspects in sight. My search of the trunk revealed only animal bones and skulls, which does not violate any laws of the land in the State of Texas. No human bones were in plain view. I decided to engage the suspects in a conversation by tempting them with the legend of the glowing tombstone. The woman confirmed that she was a practicing witch and worked as a theater manager in White Settlement, a small community on the west side of Ft. Worth. She assured me that the men were card-carrying warlocks, but they did not practice any evil destruction of humans. However, she did not volunteer information relating to animal sacrifices. I decided it was practical for me to retain a copy of their information to measure against future livestock mutilation and sacrificial cases in Parker County.

She assured me that they came to the glowing tombstone to gain power from the supernatural source of energy generated by that one tombstone. I laughed, which obviously upset her considerably. She quipped, "What's so funny? We take our practice very seriously." I envisioned her and her male friends attempting to turn me into a goat or uttering some other legendary curse. I motioned for her and her friends to follow me and walked until the glow from the tombstone disappeared and stopped. They looked toward the stone and wanted to know what I had done to stop the stone from glowing, as if I was a warlock as well. I laughed again and asked if they ever heard of the reflective properties of polished granite. They seemed a bit bewildered, so I invited them to join me on a quick jaunt into the graveyard.

I chose a path that kept the glow from the tombstone shining toward us. Once we were within a few feet of the tombstone, I stepped to the left and the glow all but disappeared. The witch was dismayed. I turned on my flashlight and allowed the beam to embrace the entire tombstone, revealing the polished finish of the granite. I turned the beam on all the neighboring tombstones to reveal that none of them offered the same brilliant finish as that solitary stone. I managed to shatter their dreams as the illusion disappeared before them and we returned to their vehicle. I asked them to promise me that they would scratch the Veal Station Graveyard from their list and never cross our county lines for their evil purposes again. The witch agreed that since the tombstone was a hoax, she indeed could not expect any true increase in powers from such a venture in the future. I released them, and they immediately headed north on the Old Springtown Road in search of Highway 199 that would lead them back to the security of the illusions offered by the glimmering lights of downtown Ft. Worth. I never saw them or their vehicle in the area again.

Tiu Snider published an article in 2014 debunking the legendary glowing tombstone of the Veal Station Cemetery in Springtown. I laughed when I read her article but chose not to tell her that she was only about twenty years late with her significant discovery.[16] I have no doubt that many tombstone artisans laugh every time they hear about similar legends arising from other polished granites.

Sect/Cult activity is not reserved to adults. Children fall prey as well. Children left alone either from their parent's lack of desire to force them to attend school or more practically, by working parents who simply can not be home are labeled "latchkey kids." Sadly, latchkey kids fall prey to their own devices and curiosities, which can lead them to being recruited by local cult groups or enticed by Hollywood productions or cultic articles to create their own venture into the world of the occult. Regardless of the source of temptation, children across our nation find themselves tempted to join the ranks of others in their quest for the unknown, a possible source of power over others.

One of the more chilling cases I worked as a Cult Investigator stemmed from a call from dispatch to meet a school principal at the Aledo High

School. I changed my plans and headed for the high school, which is located right off FM 1187 on the north side of Aledo. When I arrived at the principal's office, I observed a young man sitting in one of the chairs in a row against the wall. The principal stood up as I entered, extending his hand to welcome me to his school and to thank me for responding so rapidly.

The principal introduced me to the young man, who was about fifteen years old, and instructed him to tell me what he knew. The boy looked around as if someone may be listening. He was visibly shaken by the information he was about to reveal. According to him, one of his friends had been recruited by a Satanic cult operating in Mineral Wells, which was surprising because of the vast distance between the two towns. However, the principal reminded me that the boys and girls involved in any of the numerous sporting events, especially the farm and ranching programs, were constantly visiting remote sites to participate in events hosted by the school.

The boy's words brought a chill to my spine as he told me that his friend's initiation by the adult Satanic cult required that the boy must kill his parents, and he was supposed to complete the sacrifice that evening, leaving little time to confirm the boy's story through normal channels of investigation. I asked the boy to reduce his thoughts to paper as a witness statement as I asked the principal if the suspect boy was at the school. He assured me he was and the teacher was ready to send him to the office. To ensure that the suspect boy was not aware of the presence of his friend in the office, I asked the principal to delay his request until the boy completed his written statement. We still had plenty of time before the class change bell rang.

When the boy completed the written statement he asked with tears in his eyes, "You are not going to hurt him, are you?" I assured him that I had no intention of hurting his friend. The boy could offer no information about whether or not adult members in the cult were planning to participate in the act. I had a feeling they were. We allowed time for the boy to return to class before calling the suspect boy into the office. I had no doubt the boy would attempt to flee when he saw me waiting in the principal's office, so I stepped outside for a moment, and asked the principal to feign a visit with someone else to allow the boy to wait inside his office alone.

A few minutes later, I was standing before the boy and advising him of his rights to remain silent but assuring him that he was being taken into custody for suspicion of planning a murder. The boy laughed at the idea but became solemn as soon as I produced the handcuffs. He studied the idea of attempting to overpower me since I was blocking the only exit from the office, but I did not give him time to think and completed a speed-cuff technique, forcing his hands behind him.

As I left the school office, I asked the school to notify both parents and ask them to meet me at the Parker County Sheriff's Office immediately. Both parents were employed by separate companies in Ft. Worth, which was about a thirty to forty minute drive, providing sufficient time to process the boy and turn him over to Juvenile Probation.

The parents did indeed arrive just as I returned from the Juvenile Probation Department. Both parents were appalled that their son would be considered such a risk and adamantly denied that he fostered any association with a satanic cult. They demanded his immediate release. I asked them if they would allow me to examine the boy's room before we released him into his parents' custody, informing them that the only other option was to proceed with a probable cause warrant affidavit to search their entire home by force, based on a witness statement, on file, if they refused to cooperate. They finally conceded and signed a release allowing the search of the boy's room, which is allowed by Texas laws. Mom looked up at me with tears in her eyes and said, "You will need a pry bar or some other tool to get into this room though. We respect our son's privacy and he keeps a padlock on his bedroom door. We never enter his room and I leave his clean clothes in a basket by his door."

She then turned her eyes toward her husband as fear visibly changed her demeanor. She looked at him for a moment and said, "Do you think…" She never completed the question as she slumped into her husband's arms. I gave her a moment to recuperate before I insisted that time was not on our side because of the state law requiring that their boy be released to a juvenile court or a parent/guardian within six hours of being taken into custody.

The parents returned to their car and led the way out of the parking lot as I followed in my cruiser. Within a few minutes they turned into the driveway of a very affluent home in a gated community in Willow Park. I had retrieved a set of bolt cutters from the Parker County Sheriff's Office and carried the cutters with me as we entered the home. Both parents led the way down the hall to a sculpted door, complete with large padlock, leading to their son's bedroom.

I photographed the boy's bedroom entrance door to provide proof to the courts that the door was indeed padlocked. Photograph in hand, I forced removal of the padlock.

The shackle of the padlock snapped with a loud groan as it dropped to the carpeted floor. I removed the remains to save as evidence, as the parents stepped back, waiting to assure me that their words were true. They were positive that the bedroom would reveal no evidence of occult practices in any form. I pushed the door open and was greeted by nothing but darkness.

The large bedroom window and doorway to the pool outside had been completely painted black and covered with black drapes. I asked the parents to flip the light switch on, which they did. The interior of the bedroom came alive as a red light in the ceiling light fixture radiated an eerie presence across a room painted entirely black, including the tile floor. Red and black candles covered every flat surface in the room and an actual goat skull complete with horns sat on a shelf above the headboard of the boy's bed. A white pentagram covered the entire floor in front of the foot of the bed. The shelves and desk in the room held numerous cultic figurines and strange devices ranging from steel claws to knives with twisted and curved blades, all laid out on back felt.

It appeared that the room had indeed been set up for a sacrifice. Mom fell back into dad's arms once again as the reality of the scene overwhelmed her. I asked the parents to step out of the room to allow me the opportunity to photograph all the evidence. He complied as he helped his wife return to the living room. When I'd finished photographing the evidence, I asked to borrow their phone and immediately contacted dispatch to advise her that I had discovered a crime scene and that I would be contacting Juvenile Probation immediately. I asked her to activate the crime scene unit. A few minutes later, I completed my conversation with the Juvenile Probation Officer in charge of the custody of the juvenile. He assured me that the boy would be taken immediately before the juvenile court judge. I left the parents with strict orders to not alter the crime scene and placed crime scene tape across the bedroom door.

The probation officer contacted me about an hour later to advise that the juvenile court judge had ordered the boy to be transported to a mental health facility in Ft. Worth. He asked if I could serve as transport officer because the boy had attempted to become violent during the hearing before the judge. I agreed and headed for the courthouse. I checked with dispatch to determine the status of the team of investigators at the home to complete a collection of the evidence for the final hearing. The parents agreed without hesitation and I turned them over to the Juvenile Probation Officer who shared the process they and their son were about to endure.

Did we prevent a murder, a human sacrifice in the name of Satan? We could never be sure. The boy refused to talk to anyone and remained in the mental hospital based on court order until he properly responded to therapy treatments. The hearing never took place, to my knowledge. I returned to my normal patrol duties and never received a notice to appear for a hearing and never heard anything further concerning the case.

Cult investigations dwindled after that as winter took over, which discourages murdering helpless livestock, I suppose. Even when spring and summer passed by, cult reports never seemed to return to the normal function of our patrol efforts until about a year later. Dispatch contacted me and asked me to meet Corporal Pilcher at the Sheriff's Office. Dale was sitting beside a red-headed, white female who appeared to be in her early twenties. She had long, flowing, red hair and wore an equally long white silk evening dress. Sheriff Whiteman introduced me to the young woman.

Sheriff Whiteman told me that the woman had arrived in Texas from California as a passenger in one of two black Ford vans with black-tinted windows. He said that the woman told him that the vans contained holographic presentations of the pentagram as well as a human skull hidden within the black paint on the sides of each van. Sheriff Whiteman allowed the woman to take up the story from that moment.

She assured me that she had ventured to Texas as her Satanic cult did every year with two vans loaded with eleven young females who would be sacrificed in a remote area on private land in Parker County. She confessed that she had participated in several sacrifices in the past, but discovered, by chance, that this trip was to be her own offering of marriage to Satan, which meant that she would be one of those sacrificed. She told me that they stopped for fuel and refreshments at a convenience store on the west side of Weatherford, which afforded her the opportunity to escape and eventually be found by a Baptist pastor who brought her to the Parker County Sheriff's Office.

The woman began sobbing, which I doubted was real since she had just confessed to murdering people in Parker County in the past. Sheriff Whiteman assured me that, to his knowledge and based on his secretary's research, no dead case files existed addressing multiple murders in Parker County. The woman insisted that the bodies were buried on the site of the sacrifice as well as on other private property in Parker and surrounding counties. She assured us that the young women were typically homeless or juvenile runaways and that they chose Parker County because the citizenry in our area refused to believe that cult activity truly existed. I remained skeptical of her story as well, along with Sheriff Whiteman and the Baptist pastor.

Sheriff Whiteman pulled me and Dale off patrol duty and assigned us to take the young woman into temporary custody so she could guide us across the southern part of the county to the site of the alleged sacrifice, which was supposed to occur at midnight that evening. Dale and I kept black utilities in our patrol vehicles to wear when we needed to remain undetected in our surveillance of alleged sacrificial operations. To date, we had never realized a need for such attire. We left the woman in the custody of corrections personnel in the jail for her own protection as we planned our approach for the evening.

The woman had told us that the cult drove to a location south on FM 51 to the last road turning to the east, right before the farm road crossed the county border into Hood County. She claimed the ranch was about two miles down that road and on the north side of the road. To confirm the location, we referenced a large map, which unfortunately did not provide locations and names of the ranches in Parker County. Therefore, we could not correlate map information with phone contact information to notify ranchers to be on the lookout for the two vans.

However, the female cult member could offer no ranch name anyway. This meant that a bulletin release to the public, if the threat was real, would inform the offenders that we were aware of their presence and intention in Parker County and the leaders would be compelled to go into hiding as well as possibly escalate the sacrifice of the other women.

The young woman assured us that we should approach with caution because the California cult was like a gang and owned supreme firepower and the latest technology designed to warn them of our presence, even if we were able to locate the intended sacrificial location. The only thing that added true credibility to her story, other than the confirmation of the visual sighting of the vans by one of our detectives, was her knowledge of the organization of Satanic cult practices, based on the training that

I received from the state and federal sources. She assured us that they would set up a three-ring perimeter, with the outer perimeter being nothing more than electronic sensors to warn of anyone or anything approaching their position. The second ring supposedly would consist of armed guards complete with fully automatic weapons, with similar coverage for the inner circle where the sacrifices were to occur.

With assurance that the sacrifice would occur precisely at midnight, we decided to make our approach around 10:00 pm and would limit the scouting strictly to the two of us, along with the female cult member to serve as our guide through the perimeters, should such defenses truly be encountered.

The Parker County Sheriff's Office had a SWAT team and I served briefly as a member of the team. However, without some level of confidence or intel providing sufficient cause to believe that a crime was truly about to be committed, we could not justify activating the SWAT team. Additionally, Dale and I decided that if such sensors and perimeter guards existed, the two of us along with the Satanist bride would have a better chance of negotiating a path through the defenses without discovery.

As we prepared to depart for the location, the Satanist bride expressed fear that we could be discovered and that she would fall prey to the sacrifice anyway. Consequently, we opted to place her in a hotel on the west side of Weatherford and request that Weatherford PD complete an occasional welfare check to ensure she was okay. We left word with the hotel manager to contact 911 immediately if either of the black vans entered his parking lot. As soon as the woman decided to cancel her willingness to participate, something assured me that the entire situation was a hoax. However, it was an elaborate hoax since the exact markings on similar blacked-out vans were witnessed by a PCSO investigator as they were driving down Highway 80/180. We had to proceed based on the slightest suspicion that eleven women were about to be murdered.

To minimize alarm to the citizenry in the area, which was limited anyway because of the broad stretch of ranchland between each ranch, we chose to drive our personal vehicles to the location, which imposed radio communication through handhelds only. With the witness safely in the hotel, we approached the area we determined to be the most likely prospect for the sacrifice, which was a guess based on the woman's pointing finger. We pulled off the road under the shadow of a large oak tree and slipped into the cover of the undergrowth.

Our search turned out to be in vain. We either chose the wrong location or my suspicion was correct: the Bride of Satan was enjoying an elaborate hoax. Just to be sure we did not miss something, we contacted dispatch and asked her to call the woman's room at the hotel. Dispatch advised that no one answered the phone. We asked her to dispatch a Weatherford unit to verify that the woman was still safe and sound based on the theory that she may have fallen asleep or was taking a shower. We drove immediately to the hotel to see a Weatherford officer chatting with the hotel manager. When the manager was unable to arouse the woman with a knock on the door or by phone call, he unlocked the door to allow the officer to complete a welfare check. The room was empty, with no signs of forced entry or foul play. The woman's luggage was gone, leaving nothing behind to provide a clue as to her disappearance. The Weatherford officer had already asked his dispatch to notify all other shift personnel of the woman's disappearance, providing personal identification information from the woman's registration as well. We exhausted the search a few hours later and assumed the woman had followed through with her fear and simply fled the county, or worse, that she fell prey to the cultic group.

My thoughts returned to my previous suspicion, wondering if the Parker County Sheriff's Office had been the victim of some elaborate hoax based on an initiation requirement for a new recruit. Regardless, we left the bulletin active for thirty days, and it expired without providing further information. We shared the limited information we had about the vans with the Texas Department of Public Safety and all law enforcement agencies located on major highways leading back to California, hoping that the vans would be stopped during a return trip. However, no jurisdiction ever reported encountering the vehicles. The personal information provided by the woman turned out to be false. However, I have to wonder, even today, if skeletal remains are scattered across Parker County and other areas, never to be recovered and provided a proper burial.

Although we rarely hear about cultic crimes in the news today, the infamous MS-13 gang made news in 2017 concerning possible sacrifices of young women and girls from California to Texas with charges being filed against two perpetrators for kidnapping and murder in Houston, in March 2017.[17] With such stories still surfacing, one must ponder the true dangers, especially considering our nation's countless runaways and missing children.

During the few years that we devoted to cult investigations, we were never able to uncover any concrete evidence of the true existence of cultic activities in Parker and surrounding counties with the exception of the animal mutilation cases, which remained a perplexing challenge. I encouraged ranchers to install game cameras, but they refused to incur such an expense and what they deemed a waste of time, simply writing off the losses as a part of their business in livestock. However, cultic reports diminished considerably, which led to the disbanding of our small, cult investigation unit, leaving us to return to more normal duties fighting more prominent, repeat crimes such as domestic violence, but still, one must ponder.

Chapter Eight

Explosives

Often, a duty befalls a law enforcement officer because no one else possesses the talent, training, expertise, or experience to deal with the unique issue. One such challenge in Parker County arose from the former military base, Fort Wolters.

While I was in combat in Viet Nam, my parents sent a letter describing how the base was a training ground for the few lucky Vietnamese who were chosen by the U.S. Department of Defense to attend helicopter flight school so they could serve as Huey gunship pilots. The letter mentioned how one of the would-be pilots turned a helicopter upside down on a highway somewhere west of Mineral Wells. I laughed when I read that portion of the letter but shared concerns about the quality of pilots returning to Vietnam, which may prove costly to our military in need of a medivac or gunship to help during a dire situation.[1]

By the time I joined the Parker County Sheriff's Office, the federal government had closed Fort Wolters. Unfortunately, unexploded ordnance (UXO) remains one of the legacies left behind by the once active military base. UXO were dropped from military aircraft as they flew over Parker County or by military ground forces traveling to and from military maneuvers elsewhere in Texas. Why military personnel chose to dump explosives remains a mystery, but, one may surmise that someone chose not to go through the process of inventorying the left-over ordnance.

During the Viet Nam War, CAP command sent me to basic explosives ordnance school in Okinawa. I returned with the new MOS 2100. The MOS came in handy for me as a CAP Marine Squad Leader of CAP124 later in my service. After a few dangerous encounters, combat experiences raised the level of the playing field, requiring me to deal with any explosive threat within our area. This knowledge helped our unit deal with improvised explosive devices (IEDs), which were a constant danger as were UXO. This training and experience provided the Parker County Sheriff's Office a relatively well-trained bomb threat/post-blast investigator, even as a rookie officer.

During the late 1980s and early 1990s, Parker County experienced spurts of growth that led to gated communities and large acreage being surveyed and sold in small parcels of land. My first call to investigate a UXO came from an individual who had purchased a small parcel of land surveyed out of a large ranch on the west side of the county, adjacent to Fort Wolters. The man had decided to clear all the scrub brush near his home to bring some semblance of landscaping to his new home in the country. During the effort, his spade uncovered what he determined was a grenade.

Dispatch advised me of the call and assured me that the complainant had not moved or touched the threat and would meet me at the junction of Highway 80/180, commonly known as the Mineral Wells Highway, and the dirt road that led to his new home. As I neared the junction I observed a young man about thirty years old waving wildly. We briefly shook hands as he remained eager to return to his land where his wife and children were awaiting my arrival to remove the threat.

His home was a picturesque, newly constructed home nestled among a grove of live oak trees. He told me he had decided to clear the undergrowth to enable the installation of a white picket fence that would satisfy his wife's dream of a country home surrounded by the classic, white picket fence. His wife and children were standing on the front porch. He showed me the area where the alleged grenade lay in wait and I asked him to return to his home and take his family inside the house, preferably to a room on the opposite side to ensure their safety should the device detonate.

I checked out of the car with dispatch and grabbed my flashlight to show the way to the spot, as the sun was setting. My mind slipped back to the moments in Viet Nam when I approached similar devices. However, during combat in Viet Nam, unless a farm or village lay in the kill zone of the device, I typically planted C-4 (Military Grade Plastic Explosive) on the device and detonated it. The use of plastic explosive was not an option in law enforcement.[2]

My thoughts returned to the present as I cautiously approached the location of the alleged explosive, occasionally pausing to ensure no other explosives lay in the path. The flashlight beam glanced off a familiar object, the partially exposed relic affectionately known as the pineapple during WWII. The man was correct. I took out my pocket knife and gingerly cleaned dirt and debris to reveal the entire weapon.

With the grenade exposed, I gently stabbed the surrounding area with the knife blade to ensure that no brothers or sisters were hiding in the soil below. One must assume that whoever dropped the grenade may have left an entire crate. I was not fond of the idea of celebrating a victory by removing one threat while leaving behind a whole box to harm the family I had promised to protect. The gentle probing revealed nothing more.

By the light of the flashlight, I studied the grenade a bit closer before completely freeing it from its home in the undergrowth. Satisfied that the handle and cotter pin holding the handle in place were still intact, I carefully picked up the explosive device, allowing it to roll to the palm of my hand. As I studied the grenade, I noticed that the color was a faded blue and the bottom of the device had an indentation, suggesting that it was only a practice grenade, an inert device used by troops during field training maneuvers.

I cleared part of the debris with the point of the blade of my knife and then completed the removal of the debris, revealing the hole to assure the property clerk that the grenade offered no threat to anyone. I tossed the inert device onto the passenger seat and told dispatch the device was harmless. I drove to the gentleman's home and assured him and his wife that the device offered no real threat. However, I promised them that did not mean that any future discoveries would be harmless as well. Leaving them with encouragement to contact the sheriff's office if any further issues arose, I returned to the office, completed my report, and placed the grenade in the property locker to be handled by the property clerk in the morning, which was a rookie mistake.

Although I was a seasoned combat veteran, I did not consider the emotional reaction of an average civilian when opening a property locker to discover a grenade, albeit a harmless one. I received a notice to report to the Chief's office as soon as I arrived on duty the following day. When I knocked on his door he smiled and waved me to a waiting chair. "Barry, you managed to scare about twenty years off our property clerk's life this morning," he said. I thought for a minute, and then reality hit me. I stammered out an explanation that the report confirmed the grenade was nothing more than an inert, practice grenade. Chief Shumaker readily agreed that the report was well written, but assured me that typically, the property clerk did not read the report copy left with the property deposited in the locker, because she must ensure the copy of the report remains with the property in question to ensure chain-of-custody. He laughed and said, "I would have loved to have been present when she opened that locker, though."

As I left Chief Shumaker's office, I headed directly to the property clerk's office to apologize for the frightening experience. Although she accepted the apology, she remained obviously upset with the encounter. As time progressed, the incident evolved into a comical memory. However, she told me that she always checked my reports before opening any further property submissions bearing the name of Deputy Goodson.

Throughout my career, I received numerous calls to investigate UXOs. Most of the explosives were inert but still caused alarm, which one would expect from any citizen. As mentioned earlier in the chapter, typically a military practice grenade or similar inert devices are painted a pale blue. However, should one assume by color alone? Couldn't someone intend to harm another by adding explosive material to a device, making it a danger to others? The answer is, yes, unequivocally, yes.

During my service as a CAP Marine as well as in law enforcement, it became very apparent that almost anything could be retrofitted to change a harmless object into a deadly, explosive device. For example, one can paint two specific chemicals on separate pages in a book and insert a photocopy of a $100 bill between those two chemicals. The book may be left lying in plain view or stuffed in a bookshelf where it remains harmless, awaiting a victim. When the victim pulls the alleged $100 bill out of the book, the two materials meet, causing an explosive chemical reaction, which could maim or kill.

Military explosives, such as the one described above, were the most common calls received by the Parker County Sheriff's Office, as farmers, ranchers, and new residents haphazardly discovered a mortar round or grenade lying exposed by recent rains. The more dangerous calls stemmed from 81mm mortar rounds, most of which ranchers found on their ranch in the far eastern section of Parker County. All such shells were high-explosive, military-grade projectiles requiring handling with care because the rounds were previously fired from a mortar, which meant the projectile was armed and dangerous. I recovered each round and arranged to meet the Tarrant County EOD at their ordinance disposal center located on the northwestern side of Tarrant County.[3]

One challenging call came from a rancher on the west side of Parker County who had witnessed one of his cattle chewing on what looked like a grenade in a dry creek bed adjacent to a remote country road, which although it did not experience frequent traffic, did offer a potential victim if the cattle stepped on the round or crushed the grenade when attempting to see if it was a tasty morsel.

Sergeant Kevin Salters, another deputy with the Parker County Sheriff's Office and fellow military veteran, volunteered to assist with the call. He shared my concern that the grenade could cause considerable harm, not only to the rancher's cattle but also to any nearby citizen. The killing radius of a grenade varies but can force dangerous projectiles and debris up to about fifteen meters from ground zero.

We met the rancher at the entrance to his property and told dispatch we were investigating a threat involving explosives but did not close the channel since no danger was imminent. Kevin and I noticed one cow nibbling at a small, round object and quickly identified it as an active, WWII-relic grenade. Encouraging the cow to drop the grenade, we wrapped the weapon from top to bottom and then around the center with duct tape to ensure the handle and the firing mechanism could not release during transport, and I asked dispatch to contact our friends in Tarrant County once again. I thanked Sergeant Walters for his assistance and started my journey to the western side of Tarrant County to release another explosive to the Tarrant County EOD.

Although this incident turned out peacefully, it was still frightening. In the words of an email from Kevin in December 2019, "Received call of hand grenade in creek bed near Whitt. Located said grenade in creek bed near road. Contacted dispatch and Goodson responded to my location. Goodson agreed that it was a old pineapple grenade which appeared to be live. We taped the spoon to grenade and Goodson drove off holding it to take to bomb squad in Ft Worth. Scared crap out of me due to the rust."

Typically, we also received bomb threats in the 1990s stemming from schools and county courts. The first question asked by leadership at the location where there was a bomb threat was usually what to look for. The answer is simple. One should not look for an improvised explosive device at all. There are no exceptions to this rule, not only because the explosive could appear as an everyday item, but also because there are too many methods of detonation that endanger unwary, untrained personnel.

One morning, I received a call from dispatch to contact the office by phone. Jay Brown served as Sheriff at that time. He told me that the 43rd District Court Clerk had received a bomb threat by phone claiming that a bomb was set to detonate at 11:30 that morning. I checked my watch... just past 10:30. Since I had been patrolling the northeastern sector of the county, I knew I barely had enough time to make it back to Weatherford to help. I assured Sheriff Brown that I would head toward the courthouse immediately.

I activated my red and blues as well as the siren and headed south. Fortunately, the traffic had subsided at that point, because most people were already at work or school, leaving the country highways relatively clear. While en route to the scene, I advised dispatch to shut down all radio traffic within a mile of the courthouse in any direction, which included, unfortunately, the Weatherford City Police Dispatch Center. However, the County Dispatch Center fell just outside the one-mile area, which empowered our dispatchers to receive city calls until we eliminated the threat.

I arrived at the scene shortly after 11:00 am, leaving only minutes to ensure that the courthouse and all surrounding businesses evacuated adequately. The Weatherford Police Chief, Jerry Blaisdale, and his personnel assisted with diverting traffic away from the courthouse square. Sheriff Brown and the District Judge were standing on the south side of the courthouse, about 100 yards from the building. I joined them. Sheriff Brown told me that he and Chief Blaisdale decided to ask the fire department to enter the courthouse hoping they could discover the location of the bomb. The decision endangered the firemen as well as any citizenry standing within the kill zone of the unknown IED. If the explosive was military-grade, 100 yards remained grossly inadequate to protect innocent bystanders.

Quite often, improvised explosive devices rely on FM signals for detonation, which was why I requested dispatch to shut down radio traffic within a mile of the courthouse. Unfortunately, I assumed our leaders already knew about the inherent dangers of the use of police or other radio traffic in the proximity of explosives. I made a mental note to encourage Sheriff Brown to allow me to develop an explosives awareness class for all our local emergency personnel.

I shared my knowledge with Sheriff Brown and the District Judge and asked to be allowed to enter the building to usher all the fire personnel back outside to a safety zone, which was even limited since we were unsure how large the bomb, if it did exist, was. They agreed, and I trotted off in search of those who were unknowingly risking their lives. Fortunately, most of the men were meeting in the foyer of the courthouse and they knew the location of all remaining personnel. I warned them not to use their radios or cell phones and to even ignore incoming calls to hardline telephones, which could also serve as detonation for the bomb.

After ensuring all fire personnel had cleared the building, I returned to tell Sheriff Brown and the District Judge the building was empty. Sheriff Brown checked the time, 11:25 am. It was far too late to ask him to move the crowd back to a safer distance. The people would probably panic, causing undue harm. I could only hope that, if the bomb did exist, that it would be a pipe bomb that would not extend a blast radius more than a few feet from ground center. My gut feeling was that the call was a hoax. However, bomb threat training will tell you that if a bomber gives a specific time, the threat is probably serious because the intention is to strike fear more than to kill innocent people.

However, one must consider the other side of the equation as well, which makes it difficult to decide in such cases. A terrorist may very well use a bomb threat to bring his or her prey outside where they are easy targets. For example, the Parker County Courthouse, in the middle of a square, is surrounded by typical retail and office buildings, separated from the courthouse only by small parking lots. Additionally, each building has an old-style flat roof with a brick, stone, or concrete curb creating a false front above the flat roof. This design provides a perfect hiding place for a sniper or someone wielding a remote-control device to detonate devices placed outside the exits of the courthouse or even in the parking lots. The caller issuing the bomb threat encourages victims to flee to the promise of security away from a dangerous situation only to step into a well-placed trap.

Another reason I felt the threat might be just a distraction was that major felony cases were being tried in the 43rd District Court that day. Some of the offenders were out on bail, meaning that one of those offenders could have decided that he or she wanted another day of freedom. Therefore, the best way to ensure an approved absence without legal penalties added to sentencing rested with the risk of being caught calling in a bomb threat. Should such an offender choose that option, he or she would want to tie the threat to a specific time to ensure that the threat covered the time the court required that person's presence, hence the reason to assign the threat with a detonation time of 11:30 am.

I rechecked my watch. It was precisely 11:30 am. The District Judge was talking with the District Attorney and waved me over. "Well, Sergeant Goodson," he said, "It is now a couple of minutes past the scheduled detonation time. I assume that means the call was a hoax?" I glanced at the courthouse and considered my response. I knew the judge wanted me to accept responsibility for the decision and the bomb, which could indeed have failed to detonate, or the bomber was waiting for us to invite all the courthouse personnel and civilians to return to the courthouse before he or she activated a remote detonation device. I decided to drop the decision back into his lap: "That's a tough call, Your Honor. Do you want to go by your watch or his?" He looked at me for a minute, then turned to his secretary and said, "Hell, tell everyone to take the rest of the day off." He looked back at me for confirmation. I assured him that I felt it was a wise decision and shared my concerns that the bomber could indeed be in the crowd, watching and waiting until the judge ordered all personnel to return to work. He agreed and officially declared the courthouse closed for the remainder of the day.

The judge asked what he was supposed to do about locating the bomb. I told him that I would check all the public access areas in and around the courthouse, but all areas that were only accessible by his personnel would have to fall back on them because I would have no idea what belonged in each office. I informed him that anything could be made to house an IED. I suggested that I meet with all the courthouse supervisors before the day began the next morning to explain my reliance on them to ask their personnel to survey their office area and to let me know if anything looked out of place. I assured them that a bomb could be as small as a ballpoint pen. I anticipated the next day to be a busy one as I responded to each concern voiced by the courthouse personnel. He was not happy with the time constraint but agreed that it offered the only plausible solution.

The next day, about mid-morning, I had not received one single call from the courthouse. I had spent the rest of the afternoon of the day of the threat going through all public areas inside and outside of the courthouse, discovering nothing foreign to daily operations. Later that afternoon, I received a phone call from the District Judge asking me to meet him in his office.

I went immediately to his office and joined the Judge where he sat with the District Attorney. They were concerned that their lives and the lives of their personnel may be in danger, especially with the recent major drug dealing cases filed with the District Court. I agreed and suggested that they should consider increasing the level of security during the trials. Additionally, I offered to complete a risk assessment that would anticipate any attacks from within or outside the courthouse. They both agreed, and I left immediately with a promise to complete the report by lunch the next day.

To complete the risk assessment, I accessed the criminal history files of the suspects scheduled for trials that week. Additionally, I researched any known criminal associations each may have in the general area and developed a profile based on the probability of any attempt to free their drug lords during the trials or transport of the offenders to the courthouse from the county jail. My report included a survey of the existing courthouse to red flag potential situations that would empower anyone to harm the judge, the district attorney, or any courthouse personnel and civilians or to allow access to the building by suspects without passing through security.

The basement of the building had fixed-glass windows to allow sunlight into the bathrooms ground-level alcoves. However, the primary concern I uncovered was the fact that the judge's inner chambers were located on the ground floor, with a beautiful plate-glass window affording an excellent view of the gardens to the west. Additionally, the judge and all courthouse personnel parked their personal vehicles in an open parking lot leaving them vulnerable to placement of an IED with a motion or heat sensor on the undersides of the vehicles.

However, as I mentioned, my primary concern rested with the judge's chambers. The large window was easily accessible at grade level. Additionally, beautifully sculptured hedgerows lined the exterior of the courthouse providing perfect hiding places for suspects to place a briefcase bomb .

Courthouse security did not include any surveillance cameras other than those aimed toward the four entrances from the interior. Even those cameras offered nothing more than video recording during working hours, with no manned surveillance of the courthouse at any hour of the day or night. The videos served only as a record of those who entered and left the courthouse and security erased the recordings once or twice a week.

I shared my report with the judge with a suggestion that he consider moving his office to the second floor. However, that did not facilitate daily operations within the 43rd District Court, which was adjacent to the judge's chambers, which meant that a bomb could be placed adjacent to the courtroom as well. However, I did not feel that an attack against the courtroom was practical since the goal of an accused's associates would remain primarily to facilitate escape or to impose punishment on the judge for any negative ruling.

Combat veterans pose an extreme challenge to law enforcement searches as well. Aside from the apparent use of explosives, one of the simpler traps is a hollow tube (metal, wood, or plastic) with a nail inserted in the bottom. The offender drops a shotgun shell or live rifle or pistol round into the hollow tube with the primer resting against the point of the nail. The bullet end of the cartridge or shotgun round projects above the end of the hollow tube. The deadly trap is inserted in a hole in the floor with the bullet or end of the shotgun round hidden by the carpet, under a rug, below a wooden or metal step, or under the grass in the yard. As law enforcement advances to serve the warrant, the pressure of an officer's foot will detonate the primer causing the cartridge or shotgun shell to fire, sending the projectile or buckshot through the officer's foot and in some cases into the officer's body.

Explosives serve as other methods employed by offenders, especially those with prior combat experience. Those who possess such knowledge can create an improvised explosive device (IED) from household products available from any grocery or pharmacy. Smokeless black powder is available through cannon and antique gun supply sources as are cannon fuses. From such products, IEDs can be created and placed in just about any location.

Unexploded ordnance (UXO), bomb threats, and risk analysis of volatile situations remain a challenge to every law enforcement agency. Only through proper training and cooperative efforts between all law enforcement agencies and private security agencies, including state and federal law enforcement entities as well as our military EOD[4] can we move forward in a united effort to defeat such challenges.

Chapter Nine

Juvenile Investigations

Every law enforcement agency encounters issues with juvenile offenders, who range from status offenders to juvenile delinquents. Before we begin this chapter, we need to address the differences and commonalities between these two groups.

A status offender is a juvenile who has committed an act that is not against the law for an adult but that is still dangerous to the juvenile. It relates to the parens patriae concept originating in the common law practices of England, along with the concept that it takes a village to raise a child. The parens patriae is a two-edged sword, if you will, in that it provides the government with the responsibility for care, custody, and control of any child who is in need of supervision, which may be lacking in the home. Therefore, when a child becomes rebellious and runs away from home or becomes truant from school, then local, county, or state law enforcement agencies are required to assume control over that juvenile even though he or she has not violated any laws that would be punishable if that juvenile was an adult.[1]

State laws empower law enforcement to take custody of juvenile status offenders or even children under the legal age of juveniles to ensure their protection and care. Typically, children under the age of juveniles (ten to sixteen years) are released to Child Protective Services (CPS) for care, custody, and control based on CPS interaction with the family.

Criminal mischief remains one of the lesser Class C offenses with the Texas Penal Code, when the property damage is less than $100. However, some juvenile criminal mischief cases can include severe property damage, equaling $2500 or more, resulting in felony charges.

One of our more prevalent criminal mischief crimes in a county results from the numerous rural roads with little or no traffic in the evenings or late night. Each rural roadway offers metal mailboxes for sacrifice, a temptation that remains alluring to juveniles on late-night joy-rides with their friends. The mailboxes sit at the pavement's edge to provide easy access for the owner and the postal delivery services, but unfortunately this also encourages drunken or otherwise mischievous teenagers to bash them with a baseball bat while their partner drives. Occasionally a homeowner photographs the vehicle, which provides sufficient evidence to file a case against the offenders.

Usually, mailbox bashing remains an unsolved crime of little dollar value but a frustrating, repetitive crime against property owners; many voice a desire to shoot the offenders or plant dangerous traps that may disable the offender's vehicle but might injure the occupants as well. Once during my career, a homeowner did provide a photograph identifying the vehicle license plate and a picture of the driver. Verification of the license plate showed a Fort Worth Police Officer living in Parker County to be the registered owner. The investigation identified the driver as his son. I managed to identify the other offenders after interviewing the Fort Worth Police Department officer's son. The boys bashed approximately fifty mailboxes that night, which elevated the dollar value of the damage to well over $200. I filed the case as a criminal episode, which increased the crime from Class C offense to a Class B, with the accumulated value of the damaged property.[2] The Precinct One Justice of the Peace accepted the case since it was a juvenile offense. The judge confirmed the charges and turned the boys over to juvenile probation.

One boy's father was not happy with his son's participation in the crime but argued with the judge concerning the filing of the case as a criminal episode as ludicrous since the offense related only to mailboxes. She ignored his plea upon consideration of the emotional trauma imposed upon and expressed by the victims serving as witnesses during the hearing. The judge remanded the juveniles into the custody of Parker County Juvenile Probation, which resulted in community service for six months along with court costs, fines, and probation fees. Ironically, most of the offenders were top scholars at Springtown High School.

The Internet can encourage crimes from the relatively mild mailbox bashing to serious crimes of preying on children. The obscurity of the Internet provides a perfect mechanism to hide the reality that the child is unaware that she or he is chatting with an adult offender as that offender relies on the media source to paint a false presentation of the offender as a child of the same age of the intended victim. Through various forms of enticement, the offender gains psychological control over the victim, convincing the child to flee the troubled home life to seek alleged comfort and security in a new environment promised by the offender.

As juvenile investigator, I treated every juvenile runaway as a missing child until proven otherwise. My priority focused on the root cause of the child's reason for wanting to flee the sanctity and security of their home for an unknown life, possibly becoming easy prey to those waiting in the shadows.

Runaways are indeed troubled youth who are in need of proper supervision, which is lacking, for varying reasons, within the home. The child compares his or her perception of freedom with the perceived freedoms from the alleged oppression or rules of his or her peers.[3] Therefore, juvenile justification for running away stems from that juvenile's perception of a life free of delegated chores that burden their life or freedom from a truly oppressive life at the hands of an abusive parent or older sibling. Juveniles who are simply left to their own devices are enticed to run away because of offerings of an exciting life that caters to their personal whims. Pedophiles and other sexual predators such as human traffickers rely on numerous ploys to entice a child from their home.

During a patrol on a cold winter night with the temperature just above freezing, I was heading north on FM 920, a farm-to-market road leading to Graford, Texas, far to the northwest. We rarely experienced any criminal activity in the western side of the county, but occasionally a farmer, rancher, or someone on vacation would break down while traveling late at night and have to face the elements as well as possibly fall prey to a wandering offender searching for a window of opportunity.

As I proceeded north, I felt prompted to check Cartwright Park, which borders the northwestern side of Weatherford city limits. The park is an excellent place for family picnics or just quiet time beside the still waters of the small lake known as Sunshine Lake.[4] I was not sure what moved me to check an area that was entirely out of my jurisdiction, but the compulsion was strong, reminding me of the impending doom feeling that sometimes warned me of an ambush in the jungles of Viet Nam. Succumbing to the urge, I turned into the entrance to Cartwright Park.

As I drove the wandering road leading westward around the leafless oak trees scattered in the park, I lowered my windows to ensure that I could hear any noise. About halfway through the park, as I rounded a curve, my headlights reflected off something glittering in the undergrowth next to one of the concrete picnic tables close to the water's edge. I turned into the nearby parking area while searching with the spotlight. The light illuminated the area under a bush and revealed a nightgown that served as the only protection against the night for a twelve-to-thirteen-year-old girl lying on the ground beside a birds-eye hedge. Only the fallen leaves offered her some protection from the freezing temperatures.

Immediately, I advised dispatch that I was out with a small child at Cartwright Park and to standby. I did not wait for a reply. Seconds later,

I was reaching under the bush to retrieve the freezing child, already overcome by the first stages of hypothermia. I identified myself as a deputy with the Parker County Sheriff's Office, but she barely noticed as a large butcher knife slid from her hands onto the ground as I scooped her into my arms and rushed her to the patrol car. As I set her into the passenger seat, I reached past her and flipped the heater switch on high. She was all but unconscious as her frail body curled up, defensively, in the fetal position on the seat. Popping the trunk open, I retrieved a blanket and stuffed teddy bear and ran back to the little girl, wrapping her up in the blanket, along with the teddy bear.

Shoving the car into reverse, I simultaneously notified dispatch to advise Campbell Hospital to prepare for a twelve-year-old girl who was in the first stages of hypothermia, maybe more. I told her to have a CPS officer meet me there as well. It was after midnight, with little chance that I would encounter another car on the road; regardless, I turned on the siren and overheads. I wanted nothing in my way as I sped through town down Santa Fe Drive to the hospital.

As I wheeled to a stop, the hospital ER staff ran out to meet me with a gurney loaded with more blankets. They had the girl out of the car and onto the gurney heading for the emergency room before I could even get out of the car. I realized that I had forgotten to give my starting mileage to dispatch and contacted her before I stepped out of the vehicle. She advised that she logged my time, which would conclusively show that I did not deviate from my path to the hospital. I told her I would be at the hospital for a while, at least until CPS arrived. I had to know that the girl was going to live before I left the scene. My heart ached to know what led that child to flee in the dark of night, clad only in her nightgown, clinging to a butcher knife and a ray of hope that someone would find her before she drifted off... forever. I wanted her offender's name and location and I wanted it immediately. No man or woman deserved to live free after putting a child through such a traumatic and dangerous experience.

The hospital staff was working fervently to save the girl's life, so I returned to the waiting room, like a father waiting for his own child. My daughter was just a couple of years younger than the child lying on a bed in ICU surrounded by people dedicated to bringing her from the brink of death. About an hour later, one of the emergency room nurses, Tami Carter, came around the corner and headed directly toward me. I stood up, holding the girl's teddy bear in my hands. It had dropped away as the nurses and doctors scooped the child out of the patrol car. I wanted to make sure Tami returned it to the girl... it belonged to her now.

Tami smiled and assured me that the girl was going to make it. She was still unconscious, but all her vitals were returning to normal, meaning that the girl's organs were regaining the needed heat to ensure her survival. I breathed a sigh of relief. Tami asked me to share how I found the girl and listened with disbelief as I explained my sudden, and inexplicable, compulsion to patrol Cartwright Park.

The Child Protective Services (CPS) Officer, Cindy, walked into the emergency room lobby a few minutes later and I apologized for having to get her out of bed. She brushed it off and asked how the girl was doing. I shared my story with Cindy while we waited for further good news. Tami returned about thirty minutes later with news that the girl was finally awake, but still not fully recovered. A call from dispatch forced my return to patrol, but I left Cindy and Tami with the request to find out who was harming the girl and why she felt she had to flee home that night.

I returned to the hospital following the end of my shift to check on the girl, now identified as Julie. Tami advised that Julie had been moved out of ICU to a room upstairs. I was allowed a brief visit with the girl. I assured her that I was pleased to see her alive and awake. She smiled and thanked me for the teddy bear. I asked her to share why she found herself in need to do what she did the night before. Julie stared into space for a minute and quietly said that she did not want to talk about it. I gave her my card and even wrote my home phone number on the back and begged her to call before she decided to make such a dangerous move in the future. I warned her that evil people were looking for opportunities with little girls like her and running away was only putting herself in harm's way. I never heard from her but picked her up one evening about a mile from her home and, once again, released her to CPS custody. None of us ever saw the girl again. I checked her home numerous times, but it was empty.

Ten years later a young woman about twenty-two years old with a baby in her arms and a toddler clinging to her skirt walked into my office. I was serving as a Juvenile Investigator at the time. She knocked on the office door and peeked in, "Do you have a moment?"

"Do you remember me?" she asked, and then in the same breath, washed the question away, "How could you, I was only twelve then."

She had my interest. She launched into the story to reveal that she was Julie. She told me that she was more than grateful that I rescued her and I attempted to explain to her that it was strictly the luck of the draw. She assured me that it was much more than luck. Regardless, I told her I was glad to see that she was safe and secure as an adult. Her eyes dropped to the floor.

She looked up like she was about to confess her sins. She bit her lip, looked away, and then looked me right in the eyes. "Do you remember telling me that I should call you instead of running away and that evil people were waiting for the opportunity to snatch me up?" I nodded, afraid of what was coming next. "They did," she said.

Her head dropped to her hands momentarily. She regained her composure and shared the fact that after the second time I recovered her she was walking the streets in the evening, on Ranger Highway, where she lived, not a mile from her home, when a car stopped next to her and two men grabbed her and threw her into the back of the vehicle. She told me that she awoke a day or two later, overwhelmed by drugs and tied to a bed. She informed me that she spent the next ten years as a prostitute in Dallas and had her first child when she was sixteen.

Once again, my blood boiled. I leaned over the desk and begged Julie to give me the names and addresses of her offenders and I would ensure they received their just reward. I sensed that the offenders might even be ignorant enough to be waiting in the car outside. She assured me they were not. I calmed down a bit, as she told me how thankful she was that I wanted to stand up for her again, but that it was impossible unless I could guarantee her safety and the safety of her children, 100 percent. She looked at me with pleading in her eyes. I could not lie to her. I sighed, stood up from my desk, and walked over to the window overlooking the parking lot on the north side of the sheriff's office. I turned back to her and said, "I can promise you that I can put you in a safe house and no one will tell anyone, even me, where you are. However, once the trial is over, I cannot offer any further protection than that." I waved my hand through the air, "Hell, I can't even guarantee my wife and children safety 100 percent of the time."

Julie smiled, stood up, and extended her hand. "Then I have no option other than to return to my life in Dallas, as futile as it is." I shook her hand and pled with her to let me work through the issue with her. I could file charges against them for kidnapping and a multitude of other crimes. She told me that her present offenders were not the original ones who had kidnapped her ten years before. She could not even remember their names or provide a physical description of them. That being the case, all the present crimes against her were taking place in Dallas County, far out of my jurisdiction. I sighed again and assured her that I would work with Dallas in every way, but we both knew my thoughts were futile gestures. I did not want to see her leave again but could do nothing to help her.

Today that would not be true. In 2014, I, along with retired FBI Special Agent, Greg Bristol, retired NCIS Special Agent, Joe Martinez, and Human Trafficking Investigative Attorney, Ben Greer, formed the Human Trafficking Investigations & Training Institute (HTITI). Julie's situation served as my motivator to continue the fight against this heinous crime even in the final years of my career. I only wish I knew where she was today. My partners and I could not only set her free but also could help her gain financial support that would help her finish out her life in peace. I can only hope that she finally found a way to break free on her own. Thank you for keeping me motivated, Julie.

Human trafficking offenders rely heavily on the Internet today. I received notice from dispatch one morning concerning a juvenile runaway. I proceeded immediately to the residence of the runaway to interview the parents and to obtain physical evidence (photos, physical descriptions, videos) and other information that would help secure the recovery of the girl. Mom promised me that her daughter, thirteen years old, left on her own volition by climbing out her bedroom window sometime during the night. I asked her mother if her daughter shared her problems with anyone. Mom's reply sent chills down my spine as she recounted how, over the past several months, her daughter spent considerable time chatting with other children on the Internet. I checked the bedroom window from the outside and discovered the screen lying on the ground as if tossed aside. Small footprint impressions, barely visible in the sandy soil, led toward the roadway where tire prints assured me that someone in a car met the girl that morning.

I asked mom for a list of her daughter's friends. With the list in hand, I met with the principal of Springtown Middle School to ask for permission to speak to each girl on the list individually, and he readily complied. According to the interviews, the girl had met another alleged thireen-year-old online and had gradually developed a strong bond with the other supposed girl because of the common issues they both faced in their home life without a father. One of the girls assured me that the runaway had told her that her Internet friend had convinced her to run away during the night with a promise to send her mother to pick her up around two o'clock in the morning. She even told the girl that her mother would be driving a green, four-door Ford.

I returned to the juvenile's home and told the mother that I felt her child was a victim of enticement and that a female offender abducted her child. I asked her if she had ever seen her daughter talking with anyone in a green, four-door Ford. Mom shared that she worked twelve-hour shifts, leaving her daughter home alone most of the time. The girl's father and mother were divorced, and there were no siblings who could provide further information.

With recent photos in hand, I returned to the office where I composed a public notice flyer showing the girl's picture along with her physical description. Unfortunately, mom refused to accept the probability that her daughter was anything more than a runaway and since no evidence existed that could provide probable cause of an abduction, I could not broadcast the missing girl through the Amber Alert System, nor could I encourage assistance from other law enforcement agencies.

One of the girl's friends told me that the victim said that the Internet friend lived in the Hurst/Euless/Bedford city limits, an area between Dallas and Ft. Worth. I contacted the police departments in that area and asked them to be on the lookout for the girl. They accepted the flyer but refused to place much emphasis other than providing the information to patrol during each briefing that day. The Chief of Police of each agency encouraged me to do whatever I felt necessary in their jurisdiction to help locate the runaway. With 300 copies of the flyer, I began a door-to-door, knock and talk, an effort within all the apartment complexes until I exhausted the supply of leaflets. I returned the next day with more flyers and continued my strategy with different apartments.

Around noon on the second day, Hurst PD called advising that they thought they had the victim in custody at their precinct office. I was still in the area and drove to the police station immediately where I discovered the girl in the care of a female officer in the front lobby. The officer told me that a gray van, unknown make or model, had driven to the curbside of the agency property, dumped the girl on the lawn, then sped away before anyone could identify the offenders or the vehicle.

The girl was barely able to stand because she was under the influence of an unknown drug. I contacted dispatch and advised that I had the victim in my possession and needed the mother to meet me at the hospital, which was my next destination. An hour later, the mother met me at the Campbell Hospital, where the doctors in ER immediately began trying to discover the source of the drug. The hospital determined that the offenders put Rohypnol into a drink they gave to the girl.

The female officer with Hurst PD assured me that she would contact me if any evidence turned up concerning the identification of the gray van or the driver. Once the child recovered, she shared what she could remember about her experience, which was horrifying. Additionally, I received information alleging the existence of a small hotel in the area that had been reported to be involved in prostitution. However, Hurst PD could not verify which hotel was involved. No further information came forward, and I closed the investigation since the child's mother still refused to file charges.

During our parting interview, the child assured me that all she remembered was entering the car and chatting briefly with the alleged mother of her Internet friend, whom she identified as a white female, about thirty-five years old. She recalled asking the woman where her daughter was, and the woman assured her that her daughter had wanted to accompany her but that she had fallen asleep before mom left to pick her up. The girl reported that she remembered nothing after the initial conversation because the woman had given her a coke to drink while they headed to her newfound friend's home.

Not all child enticements are specifically related to sex slavery. One juvenile runaway out of an Azle School District area of Parker County developed from temptation through the Wiccan Cult movement on the east side of Ft. Worth. According to Wendy Lozano and Tanice Foltz, Wiccan cults began their development in the late 1960s and remain present today because of the rise in the feminist movement. Wendy and Tanice reveal that the Wiccan Cult relies on the feminist focus on the increase of the powers of leadership in the United States. The cause relates to European roots of the Wicca religion alleging that a Goddess leads the cult. Therefore, one can only imagine the enticing nature of a Wiccan cult to a troubled, female teenager. Such was the cause in this case.[5]

Both her parents were professionals, and she was an only child. Her parents lived in an affluent, gated-community in the Azle area and like many professionals, their careers required they work long hours. Unfortunately, such concentration on professional gains creates the inevitable situation of the latchkey child. Unless provided sufficient adult supervision, these children fall easy prey to enticements catering to their desire to be free from daily chores, which fall on their shoulders so that they feel like they alone contribute to the livelihood of the family.

Mary was in this situation and found herself chatting on the Internet and the phone, daily, with a Wiccan Cult leader in Ft. Worth. Mary was a thirteen-year-old, white female, fed up with having to take care of not only her homework, but also the daily chores of cleaning the house, doing the laundry, and worse, cooking meals for her parents. She felt exploited and believed that she was far from appreciated, staying enslaved to her parents' will.

The cult leader was a white female, and claimed she offered the answer to all teenage girls in the Dallas/Fort Worth area. To emphasize her control and power, she surrounded herself with young black males between the ages of seventeen and twenty-five who catered to her every whim, which included helping her entice teenage girls from surrounding counties. As the girls managed to slip away in the dark of night or not return home from school, they would meet the men in a designated area, away from prying eyes.

Early in the spring of 1994, Mary fell prey to the cult leader's attractive offer to join her cult group in Ft. Worth, which she purported as the ultimate religious experience of female enlightenment. A few hours after slipping out in the dark of night, Mary accepted a ride by two of the Wiccan Cult followers, who delivered the child to the cult leader in their location on the far east side of Ft. Worth in a well-known, high-crime, drug-ridden area. The home was a small frame home located on Vaughn Blvd. just off and west of FM 1187, southeast of downtown Ft. Worth.

Mary's parents reported her as a runaway as soon as they discovered the note she left behind advising her parents that she would no longer be their slave. Fortunately, the mother knew the password to her child's computer, which provided the exact address of the Wiccan Cult. I contacted the Ft. Worth Police Department and asked them to assist with the investigation of a runaway child in their jurisdiction. Once again, the fact that she was listed as a runaway deterred Ft. Worth PD's ability to assist since runaways are status offenders, falling far short of being classified as true missing children.

According to the spokesperson for Ft. Worth PD, the policy did not encourage officers to investigate runaways unless circumstances created more concern. I requested a backup unit from FWPD to meet me at the address. However, they would not commit to the effort even though they advised me that the area in question was a well-known drug area, infested with heinous offenders and no one there welcomed the presence of law enforcement. They encouraged me to take whatever precautions I deemed necessary, but that I was entirely on my own. If the situation became violent, my only hope for help fell on the shoulders of Parker County dispatchers since I had no radio contact with Ft. Worth PD. I hoped to encounter a patrol officer when I turned off FM 1187, but the area was void of any police presence.

This venture of recovering the missing child turned into a highly volatile situation probably because of my required uniform. As investigators, we were required to wear dark blue or black jeans or slacks, cowboy boots, white shirts, and the proverbial Silver Belly cowboy hat, which projected the true epitome of the country cop one might perceive from the Old West days.

Politically, it served as an excellent step because it genuinely separated Parker County Sheriff's Deputies/Investigators from the city police in Parker and Tarrant Counties. Unfortunately, the attire was not conducive to pursuing and wrestling with offenders. My only saving grace was the insight to take my boots to a bootmaker and replace the leather soles with a durable, rubber, tread-like sole that would provide sufficient grip on any surface.

After my failed attempt to gain assistance from FWPD, I proceeded from FM 1187 to the location of the Wiccan Cult on Vaughn Boulevard. Around mid-morning, I pulled my drug-seizure, Ford pickup truck to a stop along the curbside of the Wiccan location, which completed the Wild West ensemble. I remained in the pickup, momentarily observing the neighboring homes, looking for any signs of potential threats. The area offered no visible signs of human presence. I checked my weapon, once again, to ensure a round was in the chamber and that the pistol was still cocked, unlocked, and ready to fire. I had no idea what would happen when I approached the front door, or what awaited me inside. I advised dispatch of my present location, including the address and the exit road I used to locate Vaughn Blvd. I did not ask her to shut down the channel since anything that transpired would have to be requested from Ft. Worth PD. I was on my own, and I knew it.

Satisfied that I was as prepared as possible, I stepped out of the truck, donned my cowboy hat, and walked straight to the front door as I caught glimpses of people peering out of the windows of surrounding homes, wondering why a deputy sheriff was walking toward their neighbor's house. I was surprised not to see someone with a video recorder; no doubt those inside were recording my every step. I imagined the suspect's phone was ringing off the wall. Some of the neighbors even stepped outside to get a better look and then thought better of it and ran back inside. I was not sure if they feared me or the fact that flying bullets may soon fill the air, a sight, I had no doubt, to which they were very accustomed.

I knocked on the front door then sidestepped to my ideal position, relying on the internal building studs to protect me from the bullets I felt would probably immediately follow my knock. Moments passed as my mind raced to bring forth the correct scenario that would demand my immediate reaction. I checked all the windows on the front of the house. I listened intently for any noise that would reveal someone exiting the back door to flank my advance. The blinds on the front windows remained closed, showing no sign of curious eyes.

Suddenly, the door opened about halfway and a young, black male about seventeen years old yelled, “Oh hell, it’s the cops,” as he vainly attempted to slam the door shut. I responded by kicking the door with full force, which sent the young man flying across the room. Quickly, I stepped inside the house, positioning myself with my back to the outside wall adjacent to the front door to ensure no one would be able to take me from behind. My eyes searched the entire area that spread out in plain view, which included a short hallway leading to rooms to the left, a doorway opening into the kitchen area, and the entire living room, which offered the immediate view of eight black males ranging from seventeen to twenty-five years-old.

They all jumped up and started toward me. Loudly, I counted off, “One, two, three, four, five, six, seven, eight...” and said, “Eight, exactly how many bullets I have in my pistol,” as I drew my Series 80, Colt .45, pointing it at the nearest offender. All eight stopped dead in their tracks, with exception to the younger black male who initially answered the door and appeared to be mentally challenged as he began jumping back and forth in a fit of rage. I moved the barrel of my weapon to aim at him and ordered the man beside him to gain control, or the boy would be the first to die. I assured all of them that my semi-automatic weapon would take out each one before they could advance against me.

One of the men said, “What do you want, copper?” I looked at him and then glanced back at the others and said, “I am from another county and here only to pick up a runaway teenage girl. I have no intention of dealing with any of you unless you have harmed the girl. I encourage each of you to return to your seats and bring forth the girl I am here to retrieve.” All the men complied, with exception to the one man attempting to restrain the raving teenager.

A female voice radiated from one of the bedrooms off to the left as I remained in the attack mode. I did not doubt the power of my pistol or the bullets I chose to carry as a law enforcement officer. I loaded my magazines with the infamous Eagle Talons, which offer a serrated hollow-point designed to flatten and open up in a semblance of a serrated claw, ripping flesh and bone away as it enters the body. Someone asked me once why I carried such an imposing round. My answer was simple. I only wanted to have to fire one shot in my defense or the defense of others, and I wanted that round to discourage any further assault against me or any other intended victim. The Eagle Talon served that purpose well.

I yelled for the girl to come into the living area, which she did, followed by another black male. She recognized me as she put her hand to her mouth and shouted, "Guys, do not mess with this man. He is well known in Parker County for not tolerating any crap from anyone." Her words forced me to chuckle briefly, because I never thought of myself as striking fear in the average citizen. However, I chose to use her words to discourage any deadly plans any of the offenders may be conjuring in their minds. However, the girl's words had an overwhelming effect as even the wild teenager calmed down and sat down in the nearest chair. All the men became apologetic, each offering personal excuses. Once again, I assured them that all I wanted was the return of the teenage girl.

At this point the front doorknob began to turn. I sidestepped to the opposite side of the door to keep my back to the wall, waiting for the person to enter. A white female about thirty-five years old entered the room and stopped as soon as she saw me. She started to attempt to flee, but I encouraged her to reconsider the idea. She came in, and one of the young men gave her his seat. I provided the entire group the Miranda Warning and then asked the woman why she was hiding a teenage runaway in her home. She assured me that she had no idea the girl was a runaway and that she was not being held against her will, which, of course, was a lie. She said that they met on the roadside and after she saw the girl was troubled, she took her into her home as a guest to offer food and shelter. She assured me that it was merely the Wiccan way to help those in need. I identified all the people present and placed the girl in handcuffs to ensure she would not attempt to run away as soon as we walked outside. I reminded the men and their female leader that I had no intention of arresting any of them unless they tried to intervene, which included following me outside or attempting to flank me as I left the house and placed the girl in my truck. The girl, once again, urged them not to try to challenge me. She remained completely submissive.

Positioning the girl ahead of me while holding her by the arm to ensure she did not stumble or run at the last minute, I backed out of the house. With my pistol still aimed at the people in the living room, I led us outside. I escorted the girl to the truck, my head on a swivel to ensure no one pointed a weapon at me from any window and that no one was attempting to follow us to the truck. All remained quiet. I placed her in the front seat ensuring her seatbelt was fastened appropriately. I took off my hat and settled into the driver's side, where I immediately keyed up the mike on my radio and advised dispatch that I was clearing the scene without incidence and that I had the white female juvenile suspect in custody. I asked her to notify the parents and juvenile probation immediately and provided my starting mileage.

As I drove the forty-five-minute drive back to the PCSO, I quizzed the girl to determine why she chose to run away and derived from the conversation that she was indeed the classic, latchkey child suffering from lack of appropriate, parental supervision. Upon arrival at the sheriff's office, I immediately transferred custody of the child to the Parker County Juvenile Probation Officer who had answered the call from dispatch. I then returned to my office to complete my report on the entire incident, including pertinent information concerning each of the identified individuals, and filed the case as one of enticement of a child based on the data from her parents concerning the Internet chats their child had with the Wiccan Cult leader. Her parents called later and told me that they preferred to drop all charges. I added the case file to the dead file storage, joining others by parents not caring to bring charges against the people who had endangered their child.

One should note that when dealing with juvenile status offenders or any juvenile offender, an officer is required, in the State of Texas, to transport that juvenile directly to the certified juvenile processing center for that jurisdiction. The disposition of the child, regardless of the crime, must occur within six hours of the moment the officer takes the child into custody. Therefore, even though I did identify each of the individuals in the suspect's home, I did not bother dispatch with a request to verify the identity of those individuals, nor did I ask dispatch to check for any warrants against them. To do so would have forced a need to involve Ft. Worth PD. My focus remained on the girl's safety, nothing more.

The state mandates require that one deals strictly with the care, custody, and control of the juvenile status offender or juvenile delinquent offender and leave the adult offenders for a later encounter. If I had been in Parker County, I would have involved an assisting unit from the local police department or from another county unit to ensure sufficient criminal checks were completed on each adult in the household, while I secured the safety of the juvenile. However, since I was alone, in a neighboring county, I had no jurisdiction for arrest of the adults at that time and since Ft. Worth PD chose not to provide a back-up officer, I had no choice other than to take immediate custody of the child and leave the premises. I did not bother Ft. Worth PD upon my departure.

Juvenile Investigation is an area of law enforcement that some officers prefer to avoid because such calls for service typically address only minor crimes such as criminal mischief, family or domestic violence of a minor nature, theft, and other similar misdemeanor or status offender issues. However, dealing with juveniles requires full compliance with federal and state juvenile laws and mandates, which can indeed occupy a considerable amount of time that the officer could direct toward major criminal operations.

However, when one is dealing with juvenile offenders, it is reassuring to realize that bringing resolution to the present situation may prevent that juvenile from becoming a future adult offender. This effort helps create a better community. Realistically, an officer would probably never notice a percentage decrease in adult crime, because of the incessant calls for service he or she endures daily. However, one of the benefits of serving with a juvenile offender division is the opportunity to witness the fruits of your efforts, as most of the juvenile offenders do indeed respond favorably to juvenile probation's corrective and rehabilitative efforts.

One ever-present danger to the community, as well as to our officers, is the sudden eruption of violence from juveniles, especially in school shootings. Much of this violence seems to be a result of bullying inside the schools or at school-related activities, as well as from the rise of cyberbullying offenses, across the country.

Throughout my career, I worked numerous cases of bullying, from simple threats of assault to actual assaults causing bodily injury. However, most bullying involved intimidation more than anything else, which most people thought kept them from becoming targeted by law enforcement, which was partly correct. Some officers remained unaware or did not care to research the laws relating to assault, which empowered an officer to file charges against a bully even before states enacted proper laws. The laws enabling an officer to take action are the laws of Assault by Threat and Assault by Contact, both of which are Class C misdemeanors.[6]

One such event included a bully in the Springtown Middle School. The boy would choose one boy or girl to threaten every morning, either on the school bus or on the school grounds before the bell rang to begin classes. Then the boy would stop the victim in the hall, in plain view of his peers, and attempt to further intimidate the victim with threats. The negative reinforcement he enjoyed created a seemingly irreversible impact on his victims.

As Juvenile Investigator, I became aware of the situation and suggested that the principal allow me to chat with some of the victims. He readily complied, and I spent the day interviewing every known victim until I found one boy who was willing to contact his parents and request that they file charges against the bully. His parents talked with me, briefly, and confirmed their son's concerns. Once I explained my reasoning as well as the consequences the bully and his parents would face, they decided to file charges against the offender. A Class C Misdemeanor usually includes a fine of $500 as well as other fees, and the bully and his or her parents are put into the probation system.

Upon completion of the interviews and receipt of a written statement from the boy, I asked the principal to bring the offender to his office. As soon as the boy entered the office, I introduced myself and gave him a citation for the offense of Assault by Threat, Texas Penal Code: 22.01 Section 2, which states, "A person commits an offense if the person intentionally or knowingly threatens another with an imminent bodily injury."

Usually, by the time offenders complete their term of probation, and their parents pay the fine, they see the error of their ways and turn from a life of crime. Unfortunately, this bully's parents did not support the actions of the principal or the courts and the bully refused to respond to juvenile probation's rehabilitative efforts, which is sad, because he continued his bullying tactics, which led him to a life of crime into adulthood. He ended up serving time in a Texas prison.

Following my retirement from law enforcement, I found myself recruited to create and teach a criminal justice program for the Springtown High School, which proved to be an excellent opportunity to make students aware of the relationship they could and should develop with the local law enforcement officers. The students learned that the laws of the land do indeed empower them against those who commit criminal offenses, and they don't have to deal with the offender on their own.

A female student approached me one morning, before our Criminal Investigations class. The girl shared the fact that she was being assaulted, daily, by one of the football players on the school bus during transport to the school. She told me that she filed a complaint with the bus driver and the school principal, but to no avail. The student remained forced to endure the assault, daily, without hope. I told her that I could indeed remedy the situation if she would allow me to do so. Additionally, I asked her to let me share the offense with the class to show how the law can be used to stop an offender, especially a bully. She readily agreed.

I shared the situation with the class and asked the students to express their thoughts concerning what actions could be taken to defeat the bullying offense. This moment gave me the opportunity to prove to the students that a person can use the law to bring justice to any given situation in contrast to resorting to personal violence. I contacted the Springtown Police Department on my cell phone and asked them to send an officer to my classroom.

The officer arrived and took a written statement from the victim, who, at the age of seventeen, did not have to rely on her parents' decision to file charges. The officer followed up with the case, and the football player soon found himself standing before a judge to explain why he felt compelled to bully the female student. This offense, although it is a simple assault in the eyes of the law, remains a Class B offense because of the accompaniment of bodily injury expressed by the girl and confirmed by her family physician. The Class B offense carries a penalty of up to six months in the County Jail as well as a fine up to $500, not including court costs and probation fees, assuming the boy would receive the probated sentence.

The officer and juvenile probation followed up, upon my request, with presentations to the students in my class to update them on the actions taken to stop the bullying. The primary consequence of the court requirements forced the school to withdraw the boy from any organized athletic program. This boy responded favorably to rehabilitation efforts.

During the late 1990s, I received a call from dispatch to contact the principal of the Millsap High School located in the far western side of Parker County, a community and school district that was almost void of major crime. This event occurred in the shadow of the Columbine School Shooting in Colorado and shortly after an alleged bomb threat from a student with the Springtown High School.[7]

When I returned the principal's call, I could sense the fear in her voice as she related a story concerning one of the students who had reported that a friend of his, in response to unchecked bullying, brought a firearm to school that day for the expressed purpose of shooting any student or staff choosing to bully him.

Johnny's parents had moved to the rural community of Millsap, Texas, from Houston. The move forced him to leave a 5A school where he was a star halfback and equally excellent student to a rural, county school less than half the size of his previous school. Johnny had benefited from professional training and guidance under a seasoned coach who had once played pro football as well. The town of Millsap should have opened their doors with a hearty welcome to this young man who probably could have put the local high school on the map because of his talents and expertise as a halfback. However, the Millsap coach, teachers, and principal chose a more sinister option that might have led to events like Columbine.[8]

So why did such a promising student encounter issues with this small, country school? Sadly, the sixteen-year-old boy did not fit the physical appearance demanded by the rural community, which only accepted the demeanor and dress of a cowboy. Most of the students wore cowboy hats, western jeans, and boots. Most students, as well as the coaches and some of the teachers, enjoyed a habit of constantly chewing tobacco, a common trait of the western cowboy in Texas, but a juvenile status offense. Additionally, all the boys kept a military-style haircut. The item on their person to reveal any self-expression was the belt buckle some wore to acknowledge the fact that they were considered a bull-rider or winner of some other coveted rodeo event award.

The boy from Houston was a direct affront to the eyes of any resident in Millsap, not because of his race, culture, or creed, but because of his shoulder-length red hair. Additionally, Johnny wore a single, pirate-style earring dangling from one of his ears. He wore slacks and dress shoes along with a clean, stylish, dress shirt, the epitome of life in the big city. He showed no intention of changing the lifestyle and presentation he projected to the other students or the entire community.

Johnny's credentials preceded his entry into Millsap High School. Therefore, the coach was eager to invite the star player to join forces with his struggling group of cowboys who had been unable to win more than a few games in their position as a 1A high school. However, once the new player entered the coach's office he found himself facing a formidable foe. The head coach of the Millsap football team immediately told the boy who had brought fame and recognition to his 5A team in Houston, that he could only play football if he cut off his long hair and tossed the earring into the trash as well as learn to blend in with the country way of life all other citizens of Millsap enjoyed. To add insult to injury, the coach recruited the other players to torment Johnny through bullying tactics, which included simple assault of pulling the boy's hair to group attacks against the boy. Even the coach joined in on the physical and mental attacks.

To encourage further peer pressure bullying against Johnny, the coach passed word throughout the school encouraging the student body and other teachers to join in on the pressure to convert the new student to a good, old, country boy. Soon Johnny could not even step on the school property without encountering bullying tactics from the entire school, save one boy who chose to defend him. The bullying also followed him to his home.

The boy turned to his parents with a plea to return to Houston, but to no avail. His father's promotion from his employer forced the move to the branch in Millsap. Johnny's parents assured him that the bullying would cease once he proved that he was indeed an excellent student and a star athlete. The relentless tormenting from the citizens of Millsap drove him to a reclusive state as he vainly sought for an end to the mental and physical torture he was forced to endure, even by his parents.

Months after his first day in class, Johnny resorted to a dangerous decision by turning to the only solution he felt would genuinely relieve his pain: his father's .45 caliber, semi-automatic pistol. Both parents worked, which made it easy to access the weapon before his parents came home that evening. He placed the .45, along with four, loaded, spare magazines and a box of ammo on the top of his school books in his backpack. He set the backpack next to his bedroom door as he had always done, hoping his parents would not feel a need to secure the weapon before they went to bed that evening.

He lay in his bed, sleepless the entire night as his young mind reviewed various scenarios that would unfold the next day. Johnny promised himself that if one person chose to bully him, he would make sure they did not live to torture another soul. He knew what he was about to do was morally and ethically wrong because the act was entirely against his nature. Johnny always perceived himself as a kind person taught from birth to be kind to others. However, his tortured soul assured him that he could not withstand the torment a moment longer. Death was the only answer since no one, not even his parents, would stand against those who oppressed him.

The next morning, Johnny was ready for school early. He dropped the backpack into his car, driving to the school with only one thought on his mind, to gain retribution against his oppressors, which included everyone in the high school save one, the one boy who understood his plight and shared his concerns about the bullying, a friend who could offer no help without incurring the same abuse.

Johnny arrived early to ensure he entered the school before most of the other students and parked on the street to avoid confrontation with any bullies in the parking lot. Deep within, he was hoping beyond hope that the torture would not raise its ugly head that day, that life would finally return to normal as his parents had suggested.

His friend met him as he approached the school and Johnny opened the backpack and showed the boy the weapon within easy reach, along with the extra magazines and ammo. He assured his friend that he would no longer tolerate any form of oppression from student or teacher. His friend tried to convince him to return home, but Johnny knew that was not the answer. Johnny closed the backpack and continued into the school.

The motivated friend, engulfed by fear, chose not to lose a good friend, classmates, teachers, and others that day as he discreetly waited for the principal's arrival to share his concerns about Johnny and the threats he was prepared to fulfill that day. Fortunately, he did manage to share his fear with the principal before the classes began. Johnny was already in his first-period class where he sat silently, waiting for his first oppressor to make that fatal mistake. Luckily, no football players were in his class.

As the principal completed her story, I was already on my way, running full code so that I could make it to the school before Johnny made his fatal decision. I had advised the principal to extend first period based on extenuating circumstances and to pass a note to all teachers to not dismiss or allow any students to leave their classroom until further notice and to lock their classroom doors as well. I felt, with any luck, no one would confront the boy during class and that my arrival would prevent Johnny from resorting to deadly action. I arrived at the school about twenty minutes later and made my way, immediately, to the school office.

I met briefly with the principal, who assured me that all was quiet. I asked her to empty the office of all other staff, and then to send a note to Johnny's teacher asking him to come to the office and to bring all his books and personal belongings, hoping Johnny fostered no real desire to shoot anyone. I told her to ask Johnny to wait for her in her office, while I remained out of view in another office.

A few minutes passed as I waited in the assistant principal's office and the principal entered assuring me that Johnny and his backpack were seated in her office. I told her to wait outside and to ensure she was not in plain view and turned toward the closed office door of the principal's office, pondering what would be the best strategy. Being a combat veteran, I had faced many an enemy, up close and personal, with a loaded weapon. However, the idea of walking into a room where a mentally wounded boy sat with a loaded pistol created a multitude of scenarios that I did not care to face. The idea of shooting a child simply remained a challenge I refused to accept. I turned the door handle and stepped into the room with Johnny.

He looked up as the door swung open. However, he sat in a chair off to the right side of the room, which left him little chance to see the Colt .45 and badge on my left side. Being left-handed throws off many offenders as they search an officer's right side for the weapon they hope to take away during a violent altercation. We were required to wear our badge near our pistol instead of on our chest because the weapon is typically the first thing a person concentrates on when confronted by an officer. Therefore, Johnny could not readily see that I was an officer until I turned toward him.

I immediately observed that the backpack sitting on the floor to the right of Johnny, but the top remained closed. I stopped and smiled as I extended my hand to offer a handshake. Johnny stood up and grabbed my right hand to return the handshake. As he did so, he noticed my weapon and badge. Ignoring the obvious fear in his eyes I asked him if I could sit down so we could talk. He waved a hand toward the principal's desk and said, "Sure, officer. What's up?" Instead of following his lead to the principal's chair behind the desk, I sat in the chair beside him so that I could resort to less than lethal force to keep him from reaching into the backpack. I began to share the story I recalled from the principal. As my words echoed in the small office, Johnny's head dropped into his hands as he succumbed to the mental anguish engulfing him for so many months. I put my hand on his shoulder and waited for him to release the pain.

Moments later, he lifted his head, tears rolling from his eyes, and just looked at me. "What happens now?" he asked. I looked at him for a moment and then told him that I would like to hear his side of the story before I decided to take any action. He immediately unleashed the pain tormenting his very soul. Several minutes slid into history as Johnny related the endless days of harassment and bullying he endured along with the fact that he had gained no help when he took the problem to his teachers, the principal, or his parents. He said that he felt that he had nowhere to turn.

As Johnny finished his story, I put my right hand on his shoulder once again, offering my apology for the absence of any form of help from the adults who were responsible for his safety and sanctity. I assured him, that had I known the situation existed, his months of torture would have never occurred and the bullies, all of them, would have suffered consequences based on the laws of the land. I explained the application of the law to every offense against him and encouraged him to always rely on law enforcement if any such violence prevailed against him or his family in the future. He assured me that he would but reminded me that he had no idea that he could take the problem to any law enforcement entity. Millsap was too small to incorporate its own law enforcement agency and was entirely dependent on the Parker County Sheriff's Office.

We sat in silence for a moment and then I said, "Johnny. Where is the weapon?" His eyes shot to the backpack, and then he turned toward me. "In my backpack," he offered. I asked him if I could search his backpack and he readily agreed, offering to open it for me. I assured him that all I needed was his permission. He reached down and picked up the backpack by the straps and carefully handed it over to me as he said, "Please feel free to open it. The pistol is in there along with four magazines and extra ammo." I accepted the bag, stood up, and placed it on the principal's desk. I briefly opened the top glancing inside to ensure the weapon was on safe. It was. I closed the backpack, keeping it in my possession.

Johnny looked up at me and asked again, "What happens now?" I sat back down in the chair beside him, placing the backpack on the floor beside me as I began explaining the laws he had violated, which included bringing a loaded weapon onto school property and issuing a terroristic threat to his classmate and friend, who would be a witness against him as well as for him. I assured him that the crimes he had committed were felonies in the State of Texas. However, in the same breath, I assured Johnny that his impeccable record before arriving in Millsap would be in his favor when he stood before the judge. Additionally, I assured Johnny that my report would include his written statement along with witness statements from his friend and his parents, which would substantiate the charges against those who oppressed him during the past few months.

Johnny's eyes locked on mine and he asked, "Charges against them?" I allowed a brief chuckle at his response and said, "Sure, Johnny. We do not allow such criminal actions in this county. These people all know they committed crimes against you and will need to stand before a judge to answer for their crimes, just as you will in your effort toward retaliation."

He was astounded that his oppressors would face criminal charges and was equally bewildered when I assured him that my report would share statements that would not justify his actions, but at least make the judge and juvenile probation aware of the relentless torture that compelled him to commit the crimes he chose to undertake. I assured him once again that he could have avoided the entire situation had he or his parents contacted law enforcement in the first place. He assured me that he would indeed rely on law enforcement help in the future.

I asked Johnny to stand up and empty his pockets on top of the principal's desk. He tossed a handful of currency onto the top of the desk. I asked him to lean against the desk while I completed a pat down for my safety and his. Once again, he complied. I returned his money to him, picked up the backpack, and asked him to follow me out to my car. He looked at me for a moment and asked, "No handcuffs?" I looked at him for a moment, laughed, and said, "Johnny, you are no threat to me or anyone else. I have no reason to place you in handcuffs and embarrass you before your peers."

With that, I turned and walked out of the principal's office with Johnny following along behind. I grabbed the door leaving the school offices and asked him to walk beside me as we made our way out of the school. The halls were still empty. As we exited the building, I noticed the principal still sitting in her car. I motioned for her to remain where she was as I ushered Johnny to the rear seat of my car, securing the backpack in the trunk of the vehicle.

I turned back to the principal and waved for her to join us. She joined me as I stood beside the open driver's door of my vehicle. I wanted Johnny to hear what I was about to say. I assured her that all was well and that Johnny and I had shared many thoughts and concerns. I told her that I was taking Johnny into custody for felony possession of a firearm on school property with the intent to harm others. Her eyes darted to Johnny. I waited for her to return her focus toward me. I told her that additionally, I would be filing charges against every individual involved in the bullying tactics against Johnny, including teachers and other staff members.

With that statement, the principal's eyes dropped to the ground. I had no doubt she was hoping to be rid of Johnny, and the entire incident would merely fade into the past. She was equally unprepared for my next statement. I told her that I wanted her to call for a general assembly of not only her entire staff and students but for all parents as well. I based the request on my decision to provide a presentation that next morning that would make everyone in Millsap aware of the fact that bullying was a crime that would result in criminal charges against all offenders. We set the presentation for 9:00 am the next day. She agreed to take the proposal before the school board immediately. I advised dispatch that I had the offender in custody and asked them to notify juvenile probation that I would like to talk with them before they took any action against the offender. The probation officer was waiting in my office when I arrived.

I fulfilled my promise to Johnny with a written report expressing my opinion concerning the events leading up to Johnny's decision to turn to violence. I never saw Johnny again, but do not doubt that he still carries the mental wounds he suffered from those few months in the Millsap High School. I did follow up with his Juvenile Probation Officer who assured me the judge accepted no charges against Johnny and that he successfully transferred to the Weatherford High School, which was a strong 5A high school, with a coach that was more than eager to see such talent land in his lap.

The Millsap principal did comply with my request for the opportunity to share my thoughts with the residents of Millsap, which I have no doubt, mostly remained ignored. Regardless, I assured all the students, staff, and parents, that the actions they had taken were criminal by nature and by definition of the law, and that charges were filed against known perpetrators. I delivered handouts portraying scenes from the Columbine massacre in Colorado and told them how close they came to a similar massacre in their own backyard. I left the high school without receiving a thank you for the presentation or for saving the lives of their children and staff, which assured me that all they wanted was to put the entire event in the past.

A brief review of the Internet today reveals the fact that bullying remains a significant issue not only in the United States but also around the world. It is a crime that haunts homes in the form of domestic violence in every community across America. Throughout the past decade, bullying has expanded through online chat rooms and video services. Valorizing bullies for being so brave as to torture a hapless soul, a person who either chooses not to fight back or lacks the skills to do so, is a crime.

As mentioned earlier, most states have passed laws making bullying a criminal offense today even though statutes already did exist to empower law enforcement to deal with bullying. However, until school administrators, law enforcement personnel, and the courts in the land stand firm against bullying, the laws remain powerless against this crime. Every bully's victim or parent of a victim should commit to extensive research to ensure that he or she is fully aware of the local, state, and federal laws that empower legal actions against their oppressor and should be encouraged to pursue the maximum penalty.

In contrast to serving as Crimes against Children Investigator, my service as a Juvenile Investigator remains one of the more important highlights of my law enforcement career. Too many families foster hidden crimes that perpetuate juvenile crimes and encourage violence against others. Until America comes to grip with domestic violence, all related offenses such as bullying will haunt America's schools and communities with relative impunity. I worked too many cases involving abuse where the victim evolved into becoming the very type of person they hated, repeating the cycle of violence.

Even as I complete this writing, another school shooting has claimed more lives. The media and liberal radicals immediately purport the cause to be the presence of guns in our society, which is nothing more than a knee-jerk, politically motivated reaction to support the never-ending push to abolish the 2nd Amendment. Allowing such destruction of our inalienable rights would indeed allow the final victory for those who long to see our country fall, which can only happen through the total abolition of our Bill of Rights.

The solution to school shootings rests not with removing firearms from the equation. World history boasts heinous crimes where offenders use numerous other weapons against innocent victims, one such being weapons of mass destruction. Therefore, forcing the removal of the 2nd Amendment brings no resolution to the problem, which is the unbridled violence within our homes, our communities, and our schools. Parents are forced to overburden themselves with work to merely provide for the needs of their family. Unfortunately, those parents are neglecting the very ones they care about the most. This neglect exists not by choice but is forced by the new design of the family unit to fit the needs required to maintain proper support of the family in contrast to social demands today.

Only through proper safety measures will schools return to the safe learning centers we need. The future of our children, grandchildren, and America depends highly on the appropriate response to these and other threats against the safety and sanctity of Americans.

Chapter Ten

Burglary Investigations

The Criminal Investigations Division (CID) is an umbrella title given to the group of officers who are transferred from patrol to process the cases filed by those on patrol, which makes it a natural transition for officer promotion. Some agencies, however, rotate patrol officers in and out of CID as a training opportunity until they develop sufficient expertise to remain permanently assigned to CID.

Each agency or sheriff's office establishes investigative organizations that best facilitate the investigation of each crime, dictated by caseload as well. Lesser offenses typically dominate most crimes in any community. Many of these crimes offer little or no hope of being resolved merely because of the lack of evidence, with the exception of the crime of graffiti, which provides the investigator with a photo library of all previous graffiti crimes. The photographs allow one to associate an offender with prior offenses based on a comparison of the present crime with the photos of past, unsolved crimes. Of course, this applies to the method of operation employed by offenders as well, such as tools used by a burglar to force entry to a home or the items stolen once inside the home or business.

In our department, crimes were assigned based on common clusters such as criminal mischief and arson, which were typically juvenile offenders committing crimes of value less than $500. Of course, an occasional arson crime included a body, which elevated the offense to the homicide division. All deaths in our county were treated as murders until cleared by the investigator or the medical examiner's ruling of natural causes. Although criminal mischief is typically a property crime, we restricted property crime investigations to include burglary of a habitation, burglary of a business, burglary of a vehicle or vending machine, and theft. Many of these crimes involved juvenile offenders as well, which encouraged cooperative efforts between property and juvenile investigations.

The next division dealt with crimes of assault, which subdivided equally into misdemeanor and felony assaults. Homicide, of course, stood on its own and involved any form of attack against another human causing the death of that person, which ranged from involuntary manslaughter and natural causes to capital murder.

The final separation of investigations rested with crimes against children and the elderly, which I deemed as some of the more heinous crimes. The sheriff recognized my motivation to combat these crimes during my years on patrol, which eventually led to my final promotion to second in command of the Criminal Investigations Division and lead investigator of Crimes against Children, which included management of the law enforcement function of the Crimes against Children Task Force.

In our department, the natural transition from patrol to criminal investigations stemmed from each officer's focus toward a specific type of crime or criminal offender, which the sheriff or chief deputy could easily glean from the case reports filed daily, at the end of each shift. For example, one officer, Tim Olgesby, started as a dispatcher with the county and from the moment he signed on, he noticeably held a strong desire to rid the county of drugs. Quite often one's motivation to move toward a career in law enforcement spawns from a close encounter with a specific type of crime. I always wondered if Tim lost a loved one to drugs, which indeed would tend to provide such motivation.

Regardless, Tim completed his academy training and was soon promoted to patrol, where he immediately began drug interdiction efforts that were heralded by each sheriff, present, and future. Therefore, Tim's natural transition was to move into advanced stages of drug investigation as well as become the sheriff's representative to work with the Federal Drug Enforcement Agency (DEA). Tim indeed was one of the better officers to serve with the Parker County Sheriff's Office. As mentioned in Chapter Five, Tim retired from the Parker County Sheriff's Office as a primary member of the Weatherford/Parker County Special Crimes Unit.

Officers Brett Lane and Dwight "DD" Stevens served as burglary and felony property crime investigators. DD and Brett were veteran officers when I joined the sheriff's office and had long since served their time on patrol. Both men were the epitome of the wild west portrayal of the deputy sheriff, by appearance and demeanor. Both were highly professional officers. I rarely worked burglaries or thefts with the exception of during service as a patrol officer or as a juvenile investigator.

Burglary is difficult to investigate because offenders range from young children to the elderly, each harboring personal reasons for committing the crimes. Young children and juvenile offenders typically pursue the crime solely for the thrill of the moment and the knowledge that they can enter someone's home or business without that person's knowledge or consent. However, investigators easily separate child and juvenile offenses from felony adult offenders based on the type of property taken as well as the damage left behind.

Most child and juvenile offenders usually focus on liquor cabinets and the refrigerator in search of food or drink forbidden to them by the law or in their own home. Children, regardless of age, also search for tobacco products, game players, DVDs, and video games. Adult offenders fall into two categories: quite often they are drug addicts searching for an immediate source of income, but others are professional burglars and cat burglars who know precisely what items they want. The professional burglar identifies a prime target and precisely plans the commission of the crime.

The drug-addict or opportunistic burglar, on the other hand, typically searches for immediate opportunities with little concern about the threat of discovery. They choose their prey based on ease of entry and the probability of finding property that they may rapidly trade for drugs. Drug dealers take advantage of the addict by providing him or her with a shopping list of items that are easy to fence. Such offenders are very careless and often caught by the home or business owner, which may lead to a violent altercation resulting in additional charges of aggravated assault or murder against that offender.

The primary fencing operation for drug addicts remains the local pawn shops. The pawn shop owner/clerk pays the offender a fee that is far less than the value of the item because they know the offender will not argue since the stolen item leads to their next high. Such offenses lead to the rise of pawn shops, even in some of the better communities. Fortunately, Texas passed laws requiring pawn shops to register items they accept from individuals by make, model, and serial number as well as verify the item against a list of stolen items maintained by the State. Additionally, Texas law requires pawn shops to identify each customer by a Texas ID or other legal source of identification. However, many offenders carry fake IDs. Therefore, the state requirements only help identify the stolen property, with the offenders rarely being caught. Regardless, law enforcement may seize such property based on matching serial numbers provided by the victim.

Law enforcement agencies and state governments have created programs to ensure the public remains aware of the dangers of burglaries and thefts and the typical methods employed by such offenders. This information encourages homeowners to not only create a list of every item of value in the home but also to include the model and serial number and any distinguishing marks that would help prove that item belonged to the homeowner. Additionally, burglary and theft pamphlets suggest that property owners photograph or record by video every valuable object in their home ensuring the images include identifying marks and numbers. This method provides proper identification if investigators locate the property.

Officers Brett Lane and DD Stevens ensured that the community received important information so that homes and businesses provided fewer opportunities for future invasions.

To enhance this level of service, Sheriff Whiteman assigned me to specialized training so that I could offer a public service inspection to any business or homeowner concerning methods to defeat the average burglar. The service was an essential strategy since most homes in the county are isolated rural residences on private acreage affording burglars relative impunity to discovery, even if the house includes a monitored alarm system. The professional burglar knew, based on media reports, that the average response time of law enforcement to the crime scene was ten to fifteen minutes, providing plenty of time to force entry into a home or business, seize the exact items he or she wanted, and flee the scene, leaving virtually no clues except the form of entry and escape. Professional burglars rarely leave fingerprints at the crime scene but may indeed provide trace evidence from the tool used to force entry or tracks from tire and shoe prints on the property or roadside.

Through specialized training, business and homeowners learn the best practices in the use of technology to improve business and home security. They learn that, especially in a rural setting, the home offers three significant areas of protection against crime. The first regards the land surrounding the residence, which, in the country, typically includes a front gate. Numerous studies reveal that the average burglar will avoid a home if the owner will shut and lock the front entrance to the property. However, this level of protection decreases exponentially with the distance from a main road or highway as well as the distance from the nearest law enforcement office. Professional burglars conduct their research by observing how many patrol officers leave the station on each shift. Before committing the crime, professional burglars notoriously call in false alarms to any given address to assess the average length of law enforcement response to their chosen target. Regardless, the more technology one can employ in the gate construction as well as the monitoring of the gate opening will further enhance the ability to secure one's property.

The next level of defense rests with the exterior of the home, which relates directly to the structural design of the home. Burglars will access a house by the most accessible and timely means. However, professional burglars possess a working knowledge of alarm systems. Additionally, business and homeowners innocently broadcast the security company providing their alarm service, which empowers the enemy to research every product and type of installation employed by that specific security firm.

As a burglary prevention advisor, I performed home and business inspections, even for those already benefiting from an alarm system, to help identify weaknesses. Burglars are acutely aware that some security companies ignore skylights and attic entries when establishing a detected entrance into the home. Instead, they focus on the typical entry methods employed by the average burglar, which is to kick in or pry open the front, back, or side door. The second, most common entry method is through windows.

To prepare for the crime, a burglar will often seek temporary employment with a security service to gain firsthand knowledge of security designs and the eccentricities of each type of technology the system employs. Therefore, when that burglar enters a victim's property, he or she already knows the weaknesses that will facilitate an undetected entry, one of which is easy: to defeat the power supply to the alarm system. However, most security firms have learned to prevent this with the inclusion of a battery backup system that remains integral to the unit.

Professional burglars know that the average skylight is fastened to the roof framework with a handful of screws, making it easily removable with a cordless screw gun. With the screws removed, the seal, if any, on the skylight is easily defeated allowing clearing of the entire opening, providing a gaping, undetected hole into the home. The burglar either defeats or avoids interior motion detectors and secures the focus of his or her search within minutes, typically leaving the house by the front door, which does indeed activate the alarm but at that point the burglar has sufficient time to flee from the scene before law enforcement arrives.

Attic entrances to homes are usually inside the garage, but many builders prefer hallway entrances to offer more security. Most modern residences provide a pull-down, descending stairway making the house interior even more accessible for the burglar. One may ask how this opening is available to the burglar since both are inside the home. Unfortunately, many people leave their garage doors open or unlocked, which is an invitation to theft and provides the burglar with ready access to the interior of the home through the attic.

Of course, the burglar may kick or pry open the door to the home from the garage, but the professional knows that will set off the alarm. Therefore, the professional burglar will rely on access that defeats alarm surveillance. Even if there is no attic access from the garage, the ceilings of most garages are easily penetrated by a burglar with a ladder, thereby defeating the alarm at that point of entry unless the attic contains a motion sensor, which is rare.

Most residents assume their homes are relatively secure. Indeed, they are if the burglar is an opportunist, seeking quick access to gain the game player, TV, or another item they know one can quickly trade for drugs. However, the professional burglar studies the design structure of the homes in the area either by reviewing the designs and materials used by a given contractor or by observing the house construction. If the roof decking is nothing more than particle board, which is the typical choice of builders opting to cut construction costs, then the professional burglar knows access is easy by knocking a hole in the roof with a hammer. Regardless, even if the builder relies on quality grade plywood for roof decking, the professional burglar may employ a cordless circular saw to cut a hole through the shingles and plywood simultaneously, creating a considerable gap between rafters within minutes. Neighbors rarely pay attention to a person with power tools and may not even witness the burglar sawing a hole in the roof. As in the previous examples, the burglar has only to drop through the sheetrock ceiling to access the interior of the home. Therefore, a responsible homeowner who is serious about defeating home invasions should include motion sensors or surveillance cameras inside the attic as well as sensors on all attic entrances.

One professional burglary that I investigated while on patrol was of a residence that was completely emptied out by burglars employing an eighteen-wheel moving van. The home is located in a very affluent neighborhood of $500,000 to million-dollar homes. This house included a beautiful wrought-iron electronic security gate that should have barred entry of the offenders. However, during the investigation, the victim said that he and his wife grew weary of waiting for the gate to open, choosing to chance leaving the gate open since they were in plain view of their neighbors as well as the middle school, which was not a quarter of a mile west of their home.

Ironically, a neighbor across the road sat on his front porch watching the crime unfold and assured the victim that it took the men at least four hours to remove all the belongings from the house. They even removed the built-in ovens and cooktops as well as the refrigerator and freezer. The neighbor thought that the victim and his family were moving and never considered calling 911. Ironically, the members of this community never recognized the need for a community policing program because burglaries and other crimes were rare, and each house included a sophisticated alarm system.

To add insult to injury, the offenders stole the security equipment as well, which the victim had decided to disable as a waste of time because of the numerous false alarms he and his family endured. The home was on a major thoroughfare, which, as mentioned, was within plain view of the local middle school as well as in plain view of the passing school buses. The victims reported the crime after returning home from work that evening, having to rely on their cell phones to report the offense. The value of the crime totaled well over $1,000,000. This crime reveals the classic strategy of the professional burglar, which citizens could easily prevent if they recognized the need to organize a community policing effort.

Primarily, one of the best tools employed by an investigator to solve a burglary and one relied upon religiously by DD Stevens and Brett Lane is maintaining a database of every offender as well as the items taken by that offender. Although most burglars are familiar with various forms of entry, the tools of entry as well as the shoes they wear and the items they choose to steal quite often remain unique to each offender. Therefore, when an investigator reviews property missing from the crime scene, a comparison with previous burglaries may reveal a probable suspect. The offender's unique style will be readily recognizable, leading the investigator to the criminal's front door.

Burglaries of businesses present other unique challenges, which relate directly to the value of the product within the store as well as the proximity of the store to responding law enforcement agencies. Over the years, burglars have relied on an inexpensive car that runs well enough to get them to the targeted store. The burglar drives the clunker through the glass storefront, committing what is known as a smash and grab burglary. The large poles one sees in front of store entrances today defeat this crime. The junk car is the primary evidence left at the scene. The entire offense typically requires less than a few minutes with little concern that responding police will prevent their escape. Spray paint eliminates video surveillance to some degree as does a mask-covered face on the recording. While one crew commits the burglary, an escape vehicle waits adjacent to the targeted store to facilitate a rapid getaway.

Years ago, offenders from Tarrant County discovered that Weatherford, Texas, even though only a few miles from downtown Ft. Worth, offered a casual, virtually unprotected environment that encouraged burglary and theft. Many retail stores in the past never considered alarm systems because burglaries rarely occurred. However, as the smash and grab scenarios continued to rise across our nation, such stores found themselves easy prey.

Gang members from the adjoining Dallas and Tarrant Counties, mostly in their late teens and early twenties, chose one retail clothing store on the Courthouse Square in Weatherford as their target. The first burglaries occurred around 11:00 p.m., which corresponded to the shift change for city and county officers. The criminals forced entry into the store, which had no alarm, and stole clothing from all the racks near the entrance to the store. We advised the owners to commit to an alarm system as well as turn some of the hangers in opposing directions to defeat the immediate removal of the garments. They chose to invest in a low-end, monitored alarm system.

One night, just as I was entering Weatherford from the north, dispatch issued a 911 call to all available officers, alerting responding officers that the alarm company reported someone was burglarizing the clothing store a third time and the offenders were still on the scene. As I entered the Courthouse Square, I saw a four-door vehicle speeding away from the store with a Weatherford Police unit in full pursuit. I fell in behind the Weatherford officer as he rounded the courthouse, observing the offender turn right onto Santa Fe Street, which led directly to highway I-20 about five miles south. As we turned onto Santa Fe, we increased our speed to close the gap with the fleeing suspects. I remained silent other than advising dispatch that I was involved in the pursuit as an assisting unit. Suddenly, the driver of the suspect vehicle turned off his lights. We could only follow their direction as the driver hit the brakes to negotiate a curve or avoid collision with another late-night car.

At the junction of I-20 and Santa Fe is a large truck stop known as Petros. An eighteen-wheel driver pulled his rig out from the truck stop, unaware of the approaching high speed, no-lights vehicle. The truck driver never saw the fleeing car traveling toward him at over 100 mph. The offender veered his vehicle to the right to miss the massive truck now blocking the entire roadway. He continued along the gravel shoulder, missing the bridge crossing I-20 and forcing him on to the embankment leading up to the bridge and into the air.

Unfortunately, the offender's car twisted in the air as it crossed the embankment, falling in a spinning motion to the highway about fifty feet below. Landing upside down, the car hit nose-first, sliding across both lanes, coming to a stop against the highway divider. Fortunately, no other traffic was present, and the vehicle did not erupt into flames. The driver and the front passenger were thrown through the windshield with the initial impact, killing them instantly. The right, rear passenger was thrown through the windshield and fortunately landed on top of the front passenger, cushioning his fall and saving his life. However, he still suffered severe back and neck injuries. He was the only survivor.

The fourth offender never made it out of the vehicle. The impact crushed his body between the roof of the car and the interior with his body creating an X-shape against the roof line. We relied on hydraulic jaws to remove his body after the wrecker service flipped the demolished car over. Care Flight helo-lifted the solitary survivor to a Fort Worth hospital. Sadly, the oldest of the four offenders was only seventeen years old. All four were known offenders in Ft. Worth with extensive burglary, theft, and violent criminal records.

Remote businesses and churches were primary victims of nighttime burglaries with residential burglaries typically occurring during the day shift. Many churches were left unlocked to encourage members to enter the sanctuary for a moment of prayer regardless of the time. Church burglaries were extremely invasive to the congregation and church leadership and one that bewildered those of us in law enforcement. Of course, a burglary is equally invasive to a resident, if not more.

Ironically, most actual calls for patrol investigation of burglary, as well as calls for burglar alarm investigations, stemmed from residents returning home from a long day at work only to discover their home emptied or ransacked. However, a high percentage of the burglar alarm calls I received throughout my tenure in law enforcement were accidental activation of the alarm by a child returning home from school, a parent returning home from work, or occasionally, a large pet tripping the motion detection devices in the alarm system. Each false alarm burglary call is burdensome for law enforcement officers who are concentrating on preventing actual crimes, which is why many major law enforcement agencies presently issue fines against businesses or homeowners after a certain number of false alarms. Allan Lengel and Clarence Williams of the *Washington Post* reported that the city of Washington, D.C., "has about 4,600 burglaries a year, officials said. D.C. police get about 60,000 false alarms a year— more than half of them from businesses."[1] The city government is considering stiffer fines for business and homeowners because of the apparent waste of government resources and endangerment of those who were indeed in need for help during each officer's investigation of the false alarm.[2] Cities across the country are dealing with the same issue as media sources, through advertising and news releases, instill fear in America's public based on statistics developed from alarm calls.

Only once did we work a burglary in progress, which consisted of one man forcing entry into a business in the western part of Parker County, right off westbound I-20. DPS Trooper Reggie Barnett was the first to make the scene, discovering the offender coming out of the building. The man immediately fled in a green pickup with a white camper shell on the bed of the truck. Reggie initiated a pursuit as the driver crossed a nearby bridge and headed eastbound on I-20. I joined the pursuit right behind Reggie. We were about ten miles west of Weatherford.

The fleeing felon left I-20 at the Ranger Highway exit leading us on a chase that would take us to downtown Weatherford. Reggie quickly forced the offender to pull over. I arrived seconds later to witness Trooper Barnett forcing the offender from the car at gunpoint, which is a wise move for an officer completing a felony stop alone. Reggie ordered the man to lie on the ground as I approached. I asked Reggie if the man was the only offender in the vehicle and he assured me that he was unaware of another and urged me to handcuff the driver immediately. I cuffed the man, completed a pat down to ensure he possessed no weapons or other contraband, and placed him in the back of Reggie's patrol vehicle.

We then proceeded to advance on the pickup to ensure no other offenders were hiding inside. None existed, nor did the truck include any stolen items to our knowledge. Regardless, I completed an inventory incident to arrest while Trooper Barnett transported the offender to the county jail. We never received a notice of the trial of the offender, whom the courts released on bond. The offender assured us that he and a partner were feuding over the contents of the building and he was only securing what rightfully belonged to him before the partner sold the building. I assumed his story might have been true. Regardless, his method of recovery remained felonious.

Burglaries remain one of the plagues of any county or city and require a tremendous amount of time from either one officer or an entire crime scene unit to accurately identify, photograph, and gather all the evidence, including latent fingerprints. Burglaries and thefts are frustrating for business and homeowners because the crimes rarely afford the opportunity to catch the offender in the act. All the officers can do is ensure proper evidence is recovered to ensure the offender enjoys his or her moment before a judge and jury.

Fraud is another cause for burglary as is the case of arson in many instances. I worked a case where the only offense committed was to empty a large drinking water container the victim used to store his excess coins, which he assured me must have contained more than $1000 of coins. I dusted the container for prints although I questioned the truth of the fact that the container was full of coins. The neck of the container would have restricted rapid removal of the coins, which would have encouraged the offender to roll the large container out the front door to load it into his or her vehicle. The dusting effort did nothing but spread black dust onto the victim's white carpet. I asked the victim to check all other areas of the house and garage to ensure no other items were missing.

I received a phone call from an insurance investigator a few days later asking for a copy of the report. By law, we were required to release the front page of the report, which did not identify the name of the victim or the items stolen. I asked him why he was interested in the case. His response confirmed my suspicion that the victim of the burglary was committing fraud. The investigator told me that in addition to the empty water container allegedly full of coins, the victim reported a missing firearm (pistol), numerous high-valued jewelry items, and a riding lawn mower from the garage, none of which were previously reported.

I encouraged the investigator to file a fraud case with our agency, but he never called us back. Quite often, insurance companies and retail stores refrain from filing charges against shoplifters and fraudulent customers since it is much simpler to increase the client's insurance costs on the next year's policy. Additionally, many retail store owners or managers assured me that filing a burglary or theft was bad publicity for a store. The more positive reaction by the store owner was to file a criminal trespassing warning against the offender, which required the presence of law enforcement to remove that offender from the premises in the future.

In one particular case, with a major retailer, I uncovered a bicycle theft ring that stole bicycles from the store. One offender was a store employee whose responsibility was to assemble the bicycles for display in the athletic department. Once the young man completed the assembly, he would leave a chosen bike on the receiving dock where a second offender would pick up the bicycle and place it in his van. The bikes were sold through Craigslist and at First Monday sales held in the county or an adjacent county. I approached the store manager and we confirmed the criminal action through the security videos. The manager's reaction was that he would fire the employee. Even though the video revealed the license plate of the van, the manager refused to proceed with charges, being only interested in firing the employee. I encountered the same challenge with pastors and other church leaders. They preferred to simply move forward with strategies to prevent future invasive criminal efforts. Sadly, these victims fail to recognize the fact that refusing to file charges against an offender encourages that offender to continue his or her devotion to the crime because of the absence of consequences.

Chapter Eleven

Death Investigations

Death investigations cover a broad spectrum of causes with natural causes being the only ones that might fall outside the category of crimes. However, unless a physician provides a death certificate verifying the cause of death to be natural causes, investigators must proceed under the assumption of foul play. I investigated numerous deaths requiring confirmation of natural causes. However, I only understood the true importance of the declaration when dispatch sent me to an address in Aledo. The victim was a man to whom I owed my life. His actions during one battle in the Viet Nam War saved not only my life but the lives of all but one Marine when the enemy surrounded our position on the night of TET 1969. Colonel Larry Beale retired to Aledo from the U.S. Army as an honored officer in multiple wars. His wife passed a few years before him. He once told me he felt lucky to have survived to live into his sixties because he lost his father to heart failure, a family curse, when his father was only in his thirties. Larry's heart failed as well, at the age of sixty-two.

I stepped from my vehicle, observing the beloved flag of our country flying proudly in front of Larry's home. Guilt tore at me for not checking on him after he returned from his latest adventure out of the country, still serving his country by sharing his knowledge and experience with organizations supporting our troops in Afghanistan. I suppose his love for our country led me to join the cause as well when I chose to serve in the ANCOP program in Afghanistan in 2006.

A fellow investigator and good friend, Al Jones drove up just as I reached for the door handle. EMT personnel were already inside. Al knew Larry was a close friend and offered to take over the investigation, understanding the emotional toll awaiting me. I thanked him for his consideration but assured him that it was an honor, regardless, to investigate the death of one of Parker County's heroes. Al agreed and assisted with the investigation. Unfortunately, we lost Al as well just a few years later, another good man and Parker County hero. In the past, although I sympathized with the loved ones left behind, delivering a death notice was a part of the job. This notice haunted me for years, however.

Homicide investigations relate to any death created by unnatural causes ranging from unintentional death to premeditated murder. Patrol officers quite often serve as the first responders to accidental death investigations. Some prove to be accidents, while others include bizarre incidents such as one death in Millsap where a man attempted to prune a massive pecan tree with a chainsaw atop a tall wooden ladder. The rickety ladder buckled as the man tried to reach a limb far above his head. The chainsaw fell free, but the fall of twenty feet took his life.

Arson remains an enticement for many juveniles, especially in rural areas where wide open territories offer opportunities and the materials to create quite a blaze. However, occasionally, arson becomes a felony offense with the perpetrator being a home or business owner seeking insurance money to settle unwelcome debts. Some involve the more sinister crime of murder.

One such arson case was worked by Investigator Bobby Youngblood and other Parker County Officers during my rookie years as a deputy sheriff. Bobby informed me of the details of the case, but my direct involvement came only during the preliminary hearings and final trials of each offender. One suspect escaped after assaulting one of our corrections officers during a routine visit to the local hospital. Skylar, the offender, faked a minor injury. Overpowering the officer as they walked from the vehicle toward the hospital entrance, Skylar fled in the officer's car. This offender, a lot like Ted Bundy, possessed a disarming personality that readily encouraged the unwary officer to forget the fact that Skylar was a murderer.

The offender ditched the transport car in another county and stole clothing from a small retail store to complete his disguise. Through hitchhiking, Skylar fled toward Houston where he flagged down a motorist who kept a shotgun in a gun rack behind the seat. During a break at a truck stop, Skylar grabbed the weapon and killed the driver. Using the dead man's pickup, he continued to Houston where he committed numerous other crimes before being caught by Houston police. Houston PD returned him to Parker County where Sheriff Whiteman placed him in my charge throughout the trials, with orders to use deadly force if Skylar tried to escape again.

The crime for which Skylar had been arrested initially involved a senior man, George, living in a single-wide trailer on the far west side of Parker County. George decided it was time to rid himself of the nagging old woman who had been his wife for so many years. Instead of divorcing her, he chose to make money from her departure by purchasing a one-million-dollar life insurance policy. George hired a hitman from California to murder his wife, Mary. He set up the crime with the help of a neighbor, Sammy, who was on parole for aggravated assault. Sammy bragged to George about crimes that he had committed that law enforcement never discovered. Sammy, an older man as well, was no longer capable of harming anyone. He remained confined to a wheelchair most of the time, only able to walk short distances with the aid of a wooden cane.

Sammy helped George connect with Skylar, who was a seasoned assassin and offered to complete the job for $10,000 and would accept payment once George collected the insurance. Liking the idea, George partnered with the two men to ensure his nagging wife would disappear.

The men met in Skylar's motel room in Mineral Wells, the nearest town to George's house.

The three men decided it would be best to make it appear that Mary died from a drug overdose since neighbors and law enforcement already considered her an addict and fully expected to discover she succumbed to drugs. To the three men, it was a perfect crime. George contacted Mary's supplier and purchased a couple of syringes of crack cocaine. Although injecting crack cocaine is a rare method, Mary preferred it because she detested smoking dope, finding it more comfortable and quicker to realize the effects of the drug intravenously. The men were sure they had a fool-proof plan as they discussed personal plans for the insurance money. Unknown to the three men, however, the drug dealer had diluted the drug to increase his profit.

Sammy and George developed an alibi with plans for a fishing trip to nearby Lake Mineral Wells. They shared trip plans with neighbors, informing them they would return two days later. Before George and Sammy left for their alleged fishing trip, George drank a few shots of tequila with his lovely wife to ensure that she was in no shape to battle Skylar. The two men left as Skylar moved in for the kill through Mary's unlocked back door. Unaware of the stalking offender, she lay in the bed watching her favorite show on television.

Skylar overpowered Mary with little or no resistance. After injecting both needles into her arm, he sat on the bed beside her, watching TV as he waited for her body to succumb to the overdose. The diluted drug foiled the plan. Enraged, Skylar's racing mind conjured another method to ensure it would appear as an accidental death. He grabbed a pillow and attempted to suffocate Mary, but she fought back. Logic then assured him that suffocation left evidence of homicide and he tossed the pillow aside. Mary drifted into a deep sleep under the influence of the drug and alcohol. Skylar searched for a solution. A pack of cigarettes lying on a nightstand beside the bed provided the answer.

Leaving Mary alone in her drunken, drug-induced state, Skylar searched a storage shed for anything he could use as an accelerant. Minutes later, he returned to the bedroom with a five-gallon can of gasoline, which he poured on Mary's body, the bed, the surrounding walls, and the carpeted floor. He knew that the old trailer with its particle board construction would instantly turn into a flaming inferno.

Wisely, he let the fumes die down to a safe level, lit a cigarette, and tossed it on the bed beside Mary. The flames engulfed Mary's body as the fuel ignited, following the vapor trail to the floor and walls. Within seconds, the entire room became engulfed in flames. Realizing his success, Skylar fled from the home, hoping the discovery of her body with the remains of the cigarette lying beside her would encourage the medical examiner to rule the death accidental. Mary's friends knew she notoriously smoked in bed.

The flames and intense heat all but consumed Mary's body, and the heat intensity forced Mary's rib cage to burst open. As the arson investigator and the medical examiner sifted through the remains, they found a cigarette butt lying next to the body. Only the remains of the filter were left. The investigator collected the cigarette filter as evidence of Mary's deadly decision to smoke in bed, and the medical examiner ruled Mary's death as accidental. The three men had succeeded in their murderous insurance scam. They sat on Sammy's front porch sharing a beer and a toast to their victory and enjoying the view of the burnt ruins of the trailer next door. Even the local papers substantiated the medical examiner's ruling, encouraging the men to make plans for their future wealth.

A week later, the Parker County Sheriff's Office received a call from the Tarrant County Coroner's Office. Bobby Youngblood took the call. Moments later, Bobby was driving back to what he now felt must be a crime scene. The coroner had told Bobby that he found a bullet in the chest cavity of Mary's body, lodged in the unburnt portion of her back.

Rain and wind had spread remaining trace evidence among the ashes. Regardless, Bobby and the arson investigator began a systematic study of the debris. The arson investigator found an unburnt piece of carpet, photographed it in place, held the piece of carpet to his nose and then shared it with Bobby. The odor of gasoline filled his nostrils. At that point, Bobby knew someone had murdered Mary. His eyes fell on a partially covered object that appeared to be metallic. Brushing the debris aside, he discovered a rifle shell casing lying on the floor. After photographing the shell in place, he picked up the cartridge using the point of his pen, and placed it in an evidence bag. The piece of carpet was placed in a separate paper bag to prevent further contamination. Before they left the scene, Bobby checked the nearby storage shed where he found a near-empty five-gallon can of gasoline. He stepped back to ensure a photograph confirmed the origin of the gas can and then correctly secured the can as evidence as he carried it to his car. He drove to the coroner's office where he could immediately access their lab services as well as share concerns with the coroner.

The coroner presented Bobby with a surprise as soon as he walked into the office as he dropped the bullet he had found lodged in Mary's back into Bobby's open hand. Bobby looked at the round for a moment. It appeared to be the same diameter as the shell casing he discovered. However, the bullet showed no markings from the rifling as evidence of the weapon firing the bullet.[1] He was bewildered. The coroner offered an explanation, which he felt he could confirm upon examination of the shell casing. He assumed someone had left the complete round (shell casing and bullet) on the nightstand beside the bed, pointing upward in perfect alignment with Mary's body. Cooking off from the heat of the fire, the round bounced off the ceiling and lodged in Mary's back shortly after her rib cage broke open. The nightstand provided a solid base that kept the shell casing from falling over during the fire. Had it not been for the bullet, the case would have remained unsolved and the men would have received their pay off from the insurance company.

However, Bobby was not encouraged because, if the coroner's theory was correct, that meant that the round did not kill Mary, which left them with the original ruling of accidental death. Bobby produced the two remaining pieces of evidence: the burnt carpet and the gasoline can. The coroner turned them over to the lab for analysis. The lab confirmed that gasoline was the accelerant used to set the fire and the professional hitman had forgotten to wear gloves when handling the gas can. The latent prints led to a match with Skylar's fingerprints that were on file in the FBI database. All three men were tried and convicted of First-Degree Murder.

Murder in all forms haunted law enforcement jurisdictions throughout the United States and remained more than a challenge to Parker County patrol and investigation divisions. One of the more heinous crimes I worked as a patrol sergeant stemmed from another offense involving a man wanting to be free of his wife, who chose murder instead of divorce. Alfonzo was an illegal alien, who worked on one of the ranches in the southern part of Parker County. He and his wife lived in a small home about two miles south of I-20, with his employer's ranch being about five miles further south, just off Old Dennis Rd.

I received a call from dispatch around 5:00 pm on a cool spring evening. Dispatch advised that a woman called alleging that she had discovered her sister lying in the front seat of a car in front of her sister's residence. The complainant, a young Hispanic woman, was leaning against the hood of her own car, which she had parked on the shoulder of Dennis Road, near the driveway entrance to her sister's home. She was nervously fidgeting with a cigarette, which she tossed to the ground as I rolled to a stop. As I stepped out of the patrol car, the woman immediately burst into tears. Speaking broken English she managed to tell me that someone had brutally murdered her sister, pointing toward the small, country home nestled in a spread of cedar trees at the end of the road. I asked her to remain where she was and advised dispatch that I was continuing to the scene and would be out of the car on a signal 51 (investigation).

I stopped my vehicle about fifty yards shy of the house and waited a moment to observe the surroundings for movements warning me that an offender may still be at the scene. Nothing moved with the exception of the cedars swaying in the gentle spring breeze. I remained a bit wary as I stepped from the vehicle and made my approach to the scene. In a similar situation in Bexar County, a deputy sheriff had answered a domestic violence call deep in the rural section of the county. The offender murdered the officer before he could even step from the car. The deputy made the fatal mistake of driving right up to the residence without considering the potential dangers that often accompany any domestic violence situation, especially one in a remote area with only one responding officer. The 1,000 square miles encompassing Parker County spread deputies across the county with little hope of immediate backup, with exception to a DPS trooper or constable who may be in the area.

In the Bexar County case, the offender had already murdered his family and remained committed to taking out anyone approaching his home, his last hope of refuge. He easily took out the deputy with one round from his high-powered rifle with the aid of the scope that enabled an easy kill of less than 100 yards. Dispatch checked on the deputy a few moments later, and after receiving no reply, she closed the channel to emergency traffic only and asked for a nearby unit to respond. A DPS officer a few miles away volunteered to assist and as he arrived at the scene, he observed the deputy still sitting in his car and assured dispatch that all was well as he parked his car beside the deputy's vehicle. As he stepped from the car, the offender took him out as well. The scenario repeated itself as the dispatcher searched in vain for a reply from either officer. A SWAT team was finally activated to bring resolution to the situation.

Keeping this recent event in mind, I cautiously approached the scene, turning my radio down to a barely audible level. As I approached the home, I observed a forest green, four-door Chevy Impala sitting adjacent to the front of the home. The passenger door was wide open. I could see no one on the inside of the vehicle and then turned my attention to the house. The front door was closed with no indication there was anyone inside the home, which offered no reassurance, however. An open pasture stretched westward away from the front of the house, with no trees or undergrowth available to offer any cover for an offender lying in wait.

Slowly, I checked the trunk to make sure that it was locked to ensure the offender was not lying in wait there, then moved to the driver's side of the car, relatively comfortable with the fact that I left my back exposed to a sudden assault. I could see the body of a woman lying on the front bench seat with what appeared to be something wrapped around her throat. Ensuring no one was in the back seat, I opened the driver's door. The scene before me was horrific.

I initially thought the offender had choked the woman to death with the towel that remained twisted around her neck. However, lying on the passenger-side floorboard was a short piece of 2x4 wood about two feet in length with numerous, long bloody nails sticking out. I was horrified as I envisioned the offender wrapping the towel around the victim's throat, holding her head in place as he used the nail-studded 2x4 to turn her head to a bloody pulp. Her head and body were covered in blood, leaving her face a mangled, distorted mass of crushed bone and flesh. Her body was lying with her legs and feet positioned as if she had been attempting to drive away before the assailant opened the passenger door and grabbed her with the towel. The nails in the board assured me that the murder was a cold, calculated, premeditated assault.

I stepped away from the scene with my eyes still locked on the mangled corpse as I keyed up the mike on my handheld radio. I advised dispatch that the victim was deceased and asked her to notify the on-call investigator as well as the county coroner to meet me at the scene. Additionally, I asked her to close the channel as I conducted a search of the home and all out-buildings to ensure the offender was not still at the scene.

Searching a crime scene to secure a deadly offender remains one of the more challenging duties of a solitary officer. However, awaiting assistance can be equally daunting based on the probability that the offender may be maneuvering for a position of opportunity to subdue the officer.

Therefore, an effort must be exerted to secure the crime scene so that dispatch could notify approaching officers if I discovered the offender.

The front door of the home was unlocked. Standing to one side, I gently turned the handle until the latch was completely free. I pushed the door aside, stepping inside the home and quickly moving to a position against the living room wall to ensure I did not allow the offender much time to sight in on my body, briefly silhouetted against the evening sky, which is commonly referred to in law enforcement as the tunnel of death.

I searched the immediate interior as I dropped to a crouching position to minimize myself as a target. Momentarily, I remained motionless, my ears and eyes searching for warnings of any movement inside the home. The silence was my friend. Glancing outside, I ensured no one was approaching from the front yard, then moved forward to the next room, relying on the same technique to enter each room. A few minutes later, I walked outside, leaving an empty house and attic behind. My eyes focused on a small storage shed in the backyard. No other buildings or vehicles were on the property. I approached the shed and observed a padlock in place and barring entry. I walked around the building to ensure no one was hiding behind the structure. With the area secure, I turned up the radio, advising dispatch the area was clear. She assured me that the coroner and the on-call investigator were en route.

Returning to the front of the home, I removed crime scene tape from my trunk and began stretching the tape across the driveway entrance to the residence. Since there was no threat of anyone coming from any location on the rest of the property, I decided not to waste tape creating a complete perimeter. I began a visual search for clues in and around the victim's car.

I remembered the victim's sister who remained at the driveway entrance to the property. I contacted dispatch and asked her to send the sister to the scene. Moments later, the sister arrived with another woman, who identified herself as a neighbor and volunteered to serve as an interpreter. I was grateful for her presence. The victim's sister asked to be allowed to see her sister once again. I assured her I was sorry, but I could not allow her to re-enter the crime scene. I encouraged the neighbor to tell the woman that her sister was indeed deceased and there was nothing she or I could do to help her at this point and that we needed to keep people away until the investigator and coroner processed the scene.

My interest in bringing the sister forward rested with the need for clues as to where the offender might be. Through the interpreter, the sister told me that the victim's husband was a very jealous man and that he had called earlier looking for his wife, but she had told him she was unaware of her sister's whereabouts. Her husband told her to let his wife know that he was waiting for her at home. She dropped her gaze to the ground, then looking up at me with tears rolling down her cheeks her eyes focused on the car where she knew her sister lay. She began sobbing uncontrollably with the neighbor making every effort to console her.

Waiting patiently until she regained control, I asked her if she had any idea where the husband may have fled. She thought for a moment. Suddenly, her eyes brightened as she voiced a memory of a bunkhouse that served as temporary quarters for workers living on the rancher's property. She volunteered to lead the way to the ranch and point out the bunkhouse location, which, fortunately, remained hidden from view of the rancher's home. We waited for the on-call investigator and the coroner to arrive.

The investigator, a retired Fort Worth PD officer, was about ten years my senior, a knowledgeable officer, whom I held in the highest regard. He was new to the department, and I only knew him by the name of Dennis. I assisted him with processing the crime scene.

During the process, I asked the sister and the neighbor to stand by as I shared my concerns with the investigator. Knowing the offender was an illegal alien assured me of the probability that he was attempting to return to Mexico as soon as possible, leaving a narrow window of opportunity to locate and bring him in for questioning. Dennis agreed. Upon completing the processing of the scene and securing all evidence in his trunk, Dennis requested a wrecker to seize and deliver the vehicle to the sheriff's office sally port, where it could remain locked and protected for further forensic investigation. We left the car in the care, custody, and control of another patrol officer and followed the victim's sister to the ranch. Making sure I had all her and the neighbor's identification information, I told the sister that I only wanted her to reveal the location of the bunkhouse and nothing more.

We arrived at the ranch after darkness covered our approach. The complainant stepped out of the car long enough to point to a small structure about one hundred yards on the other side of the barbed-wire fence. Nothing but open pasture stood between us and the bunkhouse. We excused the sister and her friend, who were indeed anxious to leave, with good reason. The victim's sister was a witness to the threat of violence from the victim's husband.

Dennis and I checked out with dispatch but did not ask her to close the channel because the distance from the fence line to bunkhouse required too much time to cross to justify negating normal radio traffic. Climbing over the fence, we approached the bunkhouse in silence. Being a seasoned officer, I had no concern about Dennis giving our approach away. As a former combat special ops Marine, approaching an enemy position with stealth under cover of darkness was an easy task.

As we narrowed the gap, we stopped momentarily to study the structure, which had only one door, on the north side of the house. Our approach from the south and the moonless night helped lower the threat of detection. As we stopped beside the front door, we could hear a television along with laughter and conversations, assuring us that numerous people were inside the home. We decided that the best approach was to conduct a knock and talk strategy with one of us watching the sides of the house to ensure the offender did not flee out a window. I was not too concerned, because our approach offered nothing to alarm the offender or his friends to this point.

Dennis knocked on the front door and stepped to one side revealing his experience in dangerous entries. I watched the outside walls to see if any sudden light revealed the raising of a window. I checked my shotgun to assure myself, once again, that it was armed and ready.

The door opened, and I immediately began walking toward the front door as Dennis stood in the doorway chatting with the man answering the door. I walked up wielding the shotgun, and the man automatically pointed to the back of the house. None of the men spoke English, but they apparently knew why we were there. The bunkhouse contained only a living room, a bathroom, and a small bedroom off to the south side. Ignoring the bathroom, I followed the pointing fingers to the back bedroom. I moved forward with Dennis standing guard with his back to the edge of the bedroom doorway as he watched the four other men in the living room.

The bedroom was barely large enough to enter with most of the room filled with bunkbeds along each wall. The only window was on the west side of the bedroom, and it was covered and locked. I yelled out for the man to come out from hiding. A scuffing noise sounded from under the bunk against the back wall. I yelled out to warn him to show his hands or risk death from the shotgun. A head peered out from under the bunk. I pointed my shotgun at his head and commanded, "Salir ahora" (Come out now).

He immediately crawled out from under the bed and remained face down on the floor. I handed my shotgun to Dennis. He remained alert as I dropped one knee on top of the alleged offender's back and completed a speed-cuff technique to ensure immediate, secure custody. Following handcuffing the suspect, I searched him to secure any form of identification, weapons, or contraband. His pockets were empty. We managed to communicate the identification of the suspect as the husband of the victim and left the other men to return to their TV and their *cerveza*. They offered no threat as we departed.

We found a gated opening in the fence and led the man to the patrol vehicle. I placed him in the back seat of the car and advised dispatch that we were returning to the station with one suspect in custody. I dropped Dennis off at the original crime scene to enable him to return to his vehicle and then met him back at the sheriff's office where we ushered the man inside for immediate interrogation. Dennis contacted a Weatherford (WPD) Hispanic officer for assistance with the interrogation and the Miranda Warning.

I returned to patrol and received a call from Dennis about six hours later advising that the man finally confessed to the murder of his wife and that he would be booking him into the Parker County Jail with a request for no bond based on the man being a flight risk. Since the interrogation time fell within the time allowed to retain custody of a suspect of a crime and we had proceeded with all laws governing evidence collection and processing, we were confident the DA would accept the man's written confession, which was confirmed by the WPD Hispanic officer.

Not every death case filed with the Parker County Sheriff's Office provided a ready solution. One of the more troubling was that of suicide or alleged suicide. During my tenure with the homicide division as well as on patrol, I shared my concerns about the numerous suicide calls in Parker County with an emergency room nurse at the hospital in Azle. She assured me that the ones I witnessed paled in comparison to the number of cases she treated almost daily, cases never reported to the Parker County Sheriff's Office or any other law enforcement agency in the area for one reason or another. I worked two troubling suicide cases as a junior investigator.

The first case involved a gay triangle. The gay couple, George and Joe, lived in a single-wide trailer in a slumlord district on the eastern border of Parker County, not five miles north of I-20. The community offered the typical slumlord scenario with broken-down vehicles littering the street, many used for spare parts for another broken-down car. Kids as young as eight were smoking cigarettes as we drove down the road; most appeared homeless or at least severe cases of being latchkey children.

George and Joe lived at the end of a horseshoe drive with another trashed-out single-wide next to theirs and a double-wide trailer that was much cleaner and well-maintained, on the other side of their dilapidated home. An elderly gentleman walked out on the porch as Slim and I stepped from our vehicles. A stench of burning rubber reminded me of the days on patrol spent hunting down the source of that odor, based on the probability that the stench was an attempt to cover up the chemical odors emitting from a local drug lab. I felt that was true in this case and made a note to notify the Narcotics Task Force.

Slim and I walked up the remains of a wooden deck that threatened to collapse as we approached the front door of the home where the offense occurred, more evidence that the home was in pressing need of maintenance. However, since George and Joe only rented the trailer, they were far from interested in repairing the property, and apparently so was the slumlord. A rustling inside caught our attention. A few minutes later, the door swung open to reveal a man about thirty-five to forty years-old, dressed in sweats, a T-shirt, and bathroom slippers. He waved us inside where his partner, identified as Joe, was lying on a couch.

A .410, break-action shotgun lay across the crook of Joe's right arm, which dangled off the side of the couch along with his right leg. Joe's face revealed a dark hole where his right eye used to be with gunpowder burns radiating out from the hole and covering his entire face as well as his upper chest. Additionally, even though the exit wound was rather large, about three inches wide, the only blood and brain splatter was on the pillow underneath Joe's head. His left arm lay by his side with the left leg lying against the back of the couch. It appeared to me that Joe had been asleep when shot, which served to arouse my suspicions immediately.

We photographed the body from numerous positions, bagged the hands to ensure the medical examiner could collect trace evidence, if any existed, and then secured the weapon and other evidence.

Using a rag, I picked up the weapon, noticing oil covered the gun's exterior. As we entered the living room, I had observed a shotgun cleaning kit sitting, open, with the contents spread out on the table. George assured me that Joe had cleaned the weapon the evening before, while they were watching shows on a new TV that had been a gift from Joe's new friend. We identified the new friend as Larry with an address out of the west side of Tarrant County. According to George, Larry dropped by about 10:00 pm the night before and surprised them with the wonderful gift, which was a 40-inch big screen design and still sat in the new location. George was watching it when we arrived. George told us that Larry hung around until shortly after midnight and then left and that he went to bed shortly afterward, leaving Joe still cleaning his shotgun and watching TV.

I excused myself and left Slim to continue questioning the surviving friend. The house next door on the south side of the victim's residence appeared abandoned, but I noticed an elderly man sitting on the front porch of the home on the opposite side. He waved me over. I introduced myself and shared the reason for our presence at the gay residence. The old man looked at me for a minute then told his story about being awakened in the dead of night by loud screaming from the gay couple's house.

He said that he looked out his bedroom window to see three men, including George and Joe, arguing and shoving each other on the front porch. I asked him who was pushing whom and he told me that at first, the fight was between George and Joe, but then George started shoving the new guy around and almost shoved him off the porch. He told me that the new guy stumbled down the steps and ran to his car, a white, two-door sedan. He said the make or model was not visible, but it looked foreign. He said that the new guy sped off and never returned to his knowledge. He thought about calling 911, but so many people get in fights in their little community that he just passed it off as another domestic violence. He said the other two men argued a bit more, then entered their home, closing the door behind them.

He told me that he decided to stay up and watch the late-night news because it was almost 2:00 in the morning. He looked concerned for a moment as his eyes studied the distance. I asked him what was troubling him. He looked up and said, "Well officer, I'm just not sure what I heard, but while I was watching the news, I heard a loud bang that sounded like a gunshot, but it was over as quick as I heard it." I asked the man if he would be willing to provide a witness statement and he assured me he would. I thanked him for his time and returned to Slim and the single survivor.

I asked George what time he went to bed, and he said that it was shortly after midnight. However, according to the neighbor, George was involved in an altercation with the other two men on the front porch of the home between 1:00 and 2:00 am. I asked George if he was jealous of the fact that a new friend showed up with such a fantastic gift. George's eyes shot to the ceiling as he searched for his answer, followed by an adamant "No." He claimed he was delighted to have such a beautiful TV and that he and the newcomer became instant friends. He thought for a moment and then told me that Joe and Larry had gotten into an argument, which caused Larry to become so upset that he stormed out of the house and left. He claimed the argument ensued over whether Larry should have bought such an expensive gift for someone he barely knew. However, it was obvious that no one made any effort to reject the gift.

Slim was satisfied with George's story and determined that the cause of death was a single shot from the shotgun to the victim's right eye. The Parker County Medical Examiner arrived and took over the care, custody, and control of the body while Slim and I headed back to the sheriff's office. During the twenty-minute ride, I shared my suspicion that George had killed Joe in a jealous rage based on the information I received from the neighbor. Slim assured me he would file the case as a suicide, but would hold onto my notes until he received the report from the medical examiner.

Once we arrived back at the station, I immediately put my thoughts down on paper in the form of a supplemental report that would accompany Slim's report. In addition to George lying about being involved in the altercation on the front porch, my concerns were numerous. First, the position of the victim compared with the dimensions of the shotgun remained very questionable. The .410 shotgun had a 28-inch barrel, measured from the breach of the weapon. This suggested that the victim had to have a reach of at least that length to reach the trigger to fire the weapon. Additionally, the discharge end of the barrel must have been embedded into the victim's eye socket even to hope to match that reach.

However, evidence left by the shotgun blast ruled out that possibility. The gunpowder burns on the victim's entire facial area, his neck, and chest as well as the pillow behind his head informed me that the discharge end of the barrel was approximately twelve inches away from the victim's eye socket. As a man of 6'-3", my reach from my shoulder to the area that would still allow activating the trigger on a long-weapon is only twenty-three inches. I would have been challenged to place that barrel in my eye socket and still be able to reach the trigger. The victim was only 5'-9".

Another area of concern was the position of the body. Every long-weapon suicide I worked during my career involved the decision of the victim to place the weapon on the floor while he sat on a couch, chair, or another item of convenience. It was apparent the victims did not want to attempt to hold the weapon over their head while they lay down on the floor or couch. Even a teenage suicide victim in southern Parker County made the same choice.

The evidence, in this case, dictated that the victim was lying down when the shotgun blast occurred, based on the full containment of blood and brain matter within the pillow underneath his head. His body was stretched out entirely on the couch with his left arm by his side and the left leg lying on the couch. The right leg was bent slightly at the knee with the foot flat on the floor. The right arm lay outstretched, hanging off the side of the couch with the weapon lying in the crook of the right arm.

From my line of reasoning, the man had to hold the weapon with his left hand holding the barrel, while he hoisted the gun over his head to a position twelve inches away from his face and still manage to hit the trigger. According to Garavaglia and Talkington of *The American Journal of Forensic Medicine and Pathology*, "For individuals using long guns, the firearm was in the hand of the decedent in 19.5% of cases."[2] These facts lend some support to the theory Slim expressed concerning the fact that we found the weapon lying in the crook of the victim's right arm. However, the drop of the shotgun should have caused bruising or cuts to the victim's face, arms, or hands.

I never saw the final report as newer cases pushed resolved cases into the past. However, Slim told me that the coroner's final report confirmed that the weapon had fired only one shot and the death was ruled a suicide. We moved forward to the next crime.

The next case Slim and I worked together stemmed from another suicide relating to ongoing domestic violence between a husband and a wife who attended his church. I arrived at the crime scene several minutes before Slim and decided to go ahead and meet with the surviving wife. Other than the wife, the house was empty, but dispatch informed me there were three children in the family. Mom told me that the children were staying with her parents at the moment. When she answered the door, I observed that she was neatly dressed, but her dress shoes revealed blood splatter, which told me that she was in proximity to the victim when the offense occurred. I asked her to lead me to her husband's body, which was on the patio in the backyard. The victim was still in the patio chair with his body slumped backward. Both arms lay across each armrest on the chair with the palms facing up. He had a small entrance wound on the right side of his head, with the exit wound breaking through the skull about ½-inch above his left ear. A semi-automatic, .45 caliber pistol lay on the deck below his right hand. Evidence of the exit wound was on all the windows and the deck area from the left side to about 180 degrees from the exit wound. I quizzed the woman about her appearance, and she told me that she could not stand the blood and brain matter on her person, so she removed the clothing and placed the bloody clothing in the washing machine. She then took a shower. She assured me that she then put on fresh clothing and had time to replace her make up before calling 911. She was not sure why she chose not to change the shoes as well.

Slim made the scene and offered his sympathies to the surviving spouse. They chatted for a moment and then Slim photographed the scene and we secured all the evidence. The coroner's report ruled the death a suicide even though the lab found no prints on the weapon. The victim wore no gloves when he committed suicide. However, the report failed to address gunpowder evidence on the hands of the victim. I shared my concerns about the wife cleaning up before calling 911 and expressed the specific concern that she tossed the clothing into the washing machine instead of holding the clothes as evidence of the suicide. Regardless, the coroner ruled the death a suicide.

Every death investigation offers an emotional challenge to the investigator and medical examiner. The homicide or death by natural causes of children remain the most vivid memories. One case I worked involved a solitary death of a teenage boy who was hit by a train while sitting on a railroad track. The boy's body offered no signs of being bound or gagged and the body was in a position against the inside of the railroad track when discovered by the patrol deputy.

I met with the Santa Fe Railroad Investigators to gain their knowledge and expertise in the investigation based on my concern that the boy may have been coerced or distracted from recognizing the approaching train. The path of the train revealed at least one-half-mile of track before the train hit the boy. One would assume the boy, even though he was under the influence of marijuana at the time, would have heard the approaching train and moved away from the tracks before the train arrived. The railroad representative told me, though, that approaching trains rarely make enough noise to warn even a fully alert person even when the train has a clear approach to the victim. He mentioned that a train was scheduled to approach within a few minutes and suggested that I wait and listen. I agreed, even though I felt confident that my training and experience would indeed provide sufficient warning. We stood facing away from the direction from which the train would approach. Suddenly, I heard a noise behind me and turned expecting to see the train coming around the bend about a half-mile away. As the investigator predicted, the train was upon us before I heard any sound at all. I turned just in time to see the train conductor wave as the massive engine roared past us at seventy to eighty miles per hour. The medical examiner ruled the death as accidental. I could not argue.

Throughout my career murders ranged from the body of a baby boy being discovered in a shallow grave in a pasture to gang-type slayings involving bodies found wrapped in a carpet and dumped along the roadside or off a bridge. Many dropped to the cold files with the victim only known as Jane or John Doe. It remains a challenge to every investigator to ensure that he or she conducts a proper search of the crime scene following all rules of evidence. We all sympathized with the surviving loved ones and took a personal interest in bringing each case to resolution. To send a case to cold files meant that one more unsolved crime would haunt those investigators forever.

Chapter Twelve

Public Relations

A Part of Crime Prevention

Every officer, regardless of his or her position as a law enforcement officer and irrespective of the agency holding that officer's certification, must consider that everything he or she says or does, on or off-duty, projects an image of his or her agency. In other words, every officer is a public relations officer, 24/7, even when he or she is alone with the family or friends. Additionally, all law enforcement officers are required, by written policy, to stand against crime regardless of his or her location at the time, even outside jurisdictional boundaries, with the exception of crossing state or national borders. Even then, that officer is duty-bound to protect the oppressed within the limits of the laws of that land. To say this responsibility is overwhelming at times, would be an understatement.

Inherent dangers arise with this responsibility as well. Some officers prefer not to remain armed and ready to defend against deadly assault when they are off-duty. Unfortunately, violence never takes a holiday. One of the best examples I recall from my training as a rookie is a video provided by a store owner revealing a scene recorded by video-surveillance during regular store hours. Because of an increase in theft from his store, he installed hidden surveillance monitoring every cash register.

The video shows a line of customers waiting patiently for their turn. Suddenly, the next person in line, a male about twenty-five years old, pulled out a pistol and demanded that the cashier empty the cash register. An off-duty law enforcement officer stood right beside the offender. The cashier laughed and said, "Seriously, you can't rob me. That man behind you is a cop!" The officer behind the robber was ill-prepared, since he did not carry his weapon off-duty. The robber turned the gun on the officer, firing multiple shots at close range. The officer died at the scene.

The cashier should have relied on more forethought before making her bold statement. Usually, a law enforcement officer would have already committed to decisive action when the offender produced the weapon. Unfortunately, since he did not carry his firearm, the situation forced him to rely on his training concerning disarming a suspect with only personal weapons (hands, feet, and body). This decision would have required action within a millisecond. His choice to not always carry his duty weapon remains questionable, but his failure to appropriately react to the presence of the gun cost him his life and could have enabled the offender to kill all those present as well.

Officer safety remains paramount in all situations. If an officer jeopardizes his or her own life recklessly, the ability to ensure the safety and security of the people he or she swore to protect becomes endangered as well.

There is no doubt that the cashier's level of expectation was that she felt the officer would be her instant hero and instantly remove the threat leveled against her. Instead, she watched him fall to the floor, leaving her and the store customers in dire danger from the assailant. Fortunately, in this case, the offender fled without further action. However, based on the brazen attitude of offenders today, one would expect that offender to turn the situation into a mass murder before fleeing the scene. Therefore, the importance of officer training and safety remains paramount, maybe even more so today.

Some may ask how does this relate to public relations? Citizens of a community rightfully expect that an officer of the law will stand ready to protect them at any time against any threat. When an officer is ill-prepared and becomes a victim as well, citizens experience an increased level of fear. Lack of decisive action rapidly equates to public relations issues as fear spreads throughout the community.

In Temple, Texas, in the 1990s, George Jo Hennard drove his vehicle through a large, plate-glass window of a restaurant. He then stepped out with a semi-automatic pistol and began systematically shooting patrons inside. Officers attending a convention in Temple responded to the shooting and entered the restaurant to deal with the offender, who suffered multiple gunshot wounds from officer firearms, but turned his weapon on himself leaving in his wake twenty-two people killed and several others wounded.[1]

During the subsequent investigation, news surfaced alleging that Mr. Hennard wrote a threatening letter that was forwarded to the Temple Police Department long before the shooting, but the Chief of Police needed probable cause to act against the suspect. According to Chief Francis L. Giacomozzi, the letter contained no actual threat against a specific person. Therefore, the absence of probable cause negated an arrest warrant. The release of this news hampered public relations between law enforcement and the citizens of Temple, Texas.

A psychological review commitment of Mr. Hennard to ensure he benefited from a twenty-four-hour psychiatric evaluation may have helped community leaders deal with his emotional trauma before the incident. However, hindsight is 20/20. Law enforcement officers and leadership regularly receive threatening letters and occasional threatening phone calls, most of which are harmless.[2]

For example, dispatch once informed me that she had just received a pay phone call from an unidentified male parolee who planned to ambush officers in retaliation for sending him to prison. He boldly revealed that he lived on Quail Run Road in the northeastern sector of the county. I asked dispatch to check the records for known offenders with an address on Quail Run. Moments later she advised that numerous parolees and ex-cons lived on or right off Quail Run. During the transmission, a DPS Officer recalled that he knew of one felon residing in that area who, during his trial, had threatened to kill the officer when released on parole. We checked out the residence, but the house was empty. Without probable cause, no action could be taken against the unidentified suspect. All we could do was keep a watchful eye as we drove through that area.

One may assume that patrol officers are the only officers serving as the voice of public relations within a community. However, many law enforcement agencies create an entire public relations department explicitly designed to build, maintain, and repair public relations. They provide guest speakers and other public services on behalf of that law enforcement entity every day as well as during critical incidents. When one considers the elected position of the county sheriff, public relations remains paramount.

In 1997, Sheriff Ben Whiteman approached me with the idea of serving as the public relations officer on his behalf. I assured him that as a Viet Nam combat veteran, I would probably not be the most desirable choice because of open resentment and distrust some community members fostered against Viet Nam veterans. He assured me that the good citizens in Parker County held all veterans in the highest regard as he urged me to accept his offer. I could not envision myself attending all the social events in Parker County and never considered myself as a public speaker. Regardless, I accepted the challenge. Soon, Sheriff Whiteman forwarded a list of all public relations events I was required to attend, especially those asking for a guest speaker from the Parker County Sheriff's Office. Before each meeting, Sheriff Whiteman reminded me of the importance of creating a positive image of the work we were doing for the county as well as being responsive to every question with a positive response. Every sheriff understands public image directly affects the longevity of his or her service as the sheriff.

Serving as a guest speaker with the local schools, all the major business and other community organizations, the school superintendent's monthly meetings, and being the voice for the sheriff's office during the monthly Parker County Monthly Crime Report on the local radio station remain the highlights of my memories as the Public Relations Officer. Sheriff Whiteman once commented that he needed to assume responsibility for a few speaking engagements because my name showed up in the local newspaper and on the radio more often than his. I assured him that I was far from being a politician and harbored no desire to run for sheriff.

One of the more memorable meetings was with a local mental health facility providing care, custody, and control for MHMR patients who could function, to some degree, in public. They asked for guest speakers to join them in a luncheon, especially law enforcement officers. I was pleasantly surprised to discover the residents in that meeting to be highly responsive and overwhelmingly respectful throughout the speech, which centered around the services we provide to the MHMR community. They were proud to know that we worked diligently to ensure the safety and security of all citizens in the county, regardless of their needs. A few of them qualified for release to their family as functional members of society who could take on menial labor positions such as cleaning tables or even assembly-line work. I left the meeting with each patient and employee begging me to return for a visit someday. I added that request to my list to ensure I remembered to drop by regularly.

Women's and youth organizations asking for a guest speaker to discuss the legality of self-defense were more challenging. Of course, their prevailing question always returned to the use of a firearm.

One self-defense meeting required meeting in their clubhouse in Mineral Wells. I advised the Palo Pinto County Sheriff's Office and Mineral

Wells Police Department that I would be poaching in their territory and invited them to send an officer to join the meeting if they chose to. They declined the offer and expressed their appreciation of my efforts to meet with citizens regardless of their residence. During the meeting, we discussed the various forms of assault while relating each level of force with the use-of-force continuum. The State of Texas provides the Use of Force Continuum that guides the level of force a person may legally employ against another in self-defense. The law allows individuals to use only the amount of force justified to stop the assault. The National Institute of Justice describes the use-of-force continuum standards in the specific, following order:

1. Officer Presence
2. Verbal Commands
3. Personal weapons — Empty-hand techniques
4. Less-than-lethal force
5. Lethal force[3]

The increase in attacks on and murders of law enforcement in our country suggests that the first level of force seems to have not only lost its impact on those citizens who find themselves on the opposite side of the law but also empowered offenders to justify illegal actions against law enforcement officers. Lack of presidential support in the past, as well as the continued media hype encouraging citizens to revolt against our law enforcement community, effectively diminishes the first level in the use-of-force continuum. It is no longer safe to assume that an officer's presence is going to resolve any given situation. The absence of public support and the lack of court support of officers in their daily interactions with the public have all but rendered our law enforcement community defenseless. One must question the applicability of the first level of force.

However, during the meeting in Mineral Wells in the 1990s, the presence of an officer still commanded respect. Explaining the definition of "presence," I helped the ladies understand the level of influence they brought to the equation as well. These words surprised many of the women and left me wondering if some of them lived in an abusive relationship. Additionally, I assured them that their knowledge, as it applies to self-defense, provided the tools they needed to stand against any oppressor legally. I encouraged them always to call 911 as soon as practical.

The power generated by a 911 call today, even if the victim never utters a word but merely places the phone in his or her pocket, is more significant than many realize. The 911 dispatcher can quite often hear the offender's threats or even the sound of the assault. If the perpetrator is not capable of retrieving the phone and destroying it or turning the phone off, the dispatcher and the recording of the call provide a level of presence to the situation. Additionally, the GPS function in the phone can direct officers to the immediate location.

Cell phones made their debut during the mid to late 1990s, initially only as bulky bag phones that could not be carried by a patrol officer. But even with a cordless phone, the victim could call 911 and then shove the phone into a hidden area that would still enable the recording and dispatcher's overhearing of the assault.

Many people do not realize the level of presence they bring to any given scenario. For example, the presence of a wife returning home to discover her husband physically or sexually abusing their children should strike fear in the mind of the offending husband. Of course, the level of threat against the offender's security rests with the probability that he abuses his wife as well, which may also alter the influence of presence in the situation.

I worked numerous domestic violence and child aggravated sexual assault cases where mom provided no defense of her children because of the emotional and physical control over her enjoyed by the offender. However, once counselors empower mom with the knowledge that law enforcement can help her, and her children escape the clutches of the offender, she indeed can become a force that weakens the level of control the offender has over that family.

The ladies in the meeting received the information well, asking a few questions concerning the law but remaining eager to discuss the level of force they could use against a rapist, robber, or anyone bent on causing harm to them or a member in his or her family. These questions prompted us to move from verbal commands to personal weapons, which describes any part of one's physical anatomy that one may reasonably employ against another in self-defense. However, before we moved forward in the discussion, I impressed upon the women the importance of the first level in the use-of-force continuum, assuring them that if they said, "Leave me alone," and the offender complied, then they were not empowered to resort to any level of force past that point. I reminded them that they were only allowed to use the level of force necessary to stop an assault against them or another.

As we proceeded, the discussion concerning the use of personal weapons led, as it always does, to the apparent fact that most men possess strength far superior to women. This fact often leads women to the next level of defense, which is the use of non-lethal weapons. Tasers did not exist in those days. However, women and other victims could rely on two options in the use of non-lethal force. The first was the use of Pepper Spray or the lesser form known as Mace, which is profoundly limited because of multiple factors. First, if the attack is outside, prevailing winds may blow the spray back onto the victim. Secondly, the proximity of the offender to the victim creates a similar concern since the spray may deflect from the offender onto the victim. The one with the stronger resistance to the chemical will retain the upper hand.

When my wife (Cindy) and I first started dating, she voiced her concern for her safety since she lived in an apartment complex. She pulled a large can of pepper spray out of her purse to show me she was ready to take on anyone with harmful intent. She thought I would support the use of the chemical. However, if the offender is a veteran, he or she probably knows how to react to the debilitating effects of the gas. I guaranteed her that I was a prime example.

During Marine Corps combat infantry training we were forced to remain seated inside a tear-gas chamber without any protection against the gas for at least five minutes. If a Marine tried to flee, the Drill Instructors, who wore gas masks, followed the Marine outside and forced him to return to the chamber. Sadly, squad leaders had to remain in the gas chamber until their entire squad completed the exercise, which meant that I stayed in place for about fifteen to twenty minutes.

After sharing this information with Cindy, I realized that I had destroyed her feeling of security to some degree. However, she reassured me that the pepper spray she purchased guaranteed no one could stand against it.

One evening upon returning from another date, Cindy opened her purse, searching in the dark for her door key. She commented about something falling off and then pulled the Pepper Spray canister out of her purse, minus the top cover, which is the firing mechanism for the spray. When she attempted to force the top cover back in place, she activated the spray in full force against my face. The Pepper Spray engulfed her as well. She dropped to the pavement, rubbing her eyes and yelling in pain. I grabbed her purse, located the house key, scooped her into my arms, opened the front door, and helped her wash the chemicals from her eyes and exposed skin.

My own eyes were watering profusely so that my vision was all but blurry as well. However, I knew how to react to the spray, which is to do nothing. Do not touch any part of your body and especially your eyes, ears, and nose. Any exposed skin, especially freshly shaved skin, will create an almost unbearable burning sensation. To say my face and eyes were on fire cannot begin to explain the pain introduced by the full effect of the spray.

The next day, I met her at her apartment and began teaching her self-defense, continuing the practice throughout the following months to provide her with some level of confidence that she could survive an attack long enough to call 911 as well as contact me. However, I promised her that the more important part of self-defense was to teach her mind to become more cognizant of her immediate environment and to recognize her *red flags*.

During the meeting in Mineral Wells, I started the discussion of the God-given ability to recognize *red flags*. None of the women recalled the term. Therefore, I spent considerable time explaining the internal signals our mind presents to us to warn us of impending doom. During the session, I asked everyone to share an example of when she felt something was just not right and how listening to the feeling saved her life or at least prevented injury. Even though their minds had indeed warned them in the past, the idea that they could cultivate and train their mind to a higher level of awareness left them in awe. I felt confident that these women would move forward with that mental exercise to contribute to their safety.

As the discussion began to wrap up and we had covered the use of deadly force as well as the variety of weapons, including personal weapons, one woman, who had remained quiet throughout the meeting, very meekly raised her hand. I invited her to share her thoughts, and her words did not surprise me. Her question always remained on the heart and mind of at least one person in the crowd. "Officer," she said, "Should I purchase a firearm?" I repeated her question aloud, and then provided the following response. "That is an excellent question, ma'am," I told her. "The question you must ask yourself and provide an honest answer to is, can you see yourself killing someone?" I aimed the question at every member of the group. No one immediately raised her hand. I continued to tell them that unless they could answer with a confident yes, then they should refrain from purchasing a firearm. Their hesitation during the moment they needed the weapon to save a life may allow the offender to take the gun away and kill the entire family with that weapon. I warned them that when an offender was threatening their life that the moment to act required action within a millisecond.

One older lady sitting in the back row offered another challenging statement. She stood up, looked around at her friends and said, "I know I could not kill anyone and feel that my best approach would be to simply allow them to beat me up and take my money or to offer no resistance if that person chose to rape me." The group fell silent as each member considered her words. This response was typical as well since most people, especially women, cannot fathom the idea of taking another person's life. I decided, for the benefit of the other women present who may be entertaining the same question, to pose another challenge to the woman claiming she would allow herself to be raped or assaulted.

"Ma'am." I paused to make sure everyone was listening. "What if the offender was raping your granddaughter?" The instant fury in the woman's eyes revealed her answer before she uttered a word. The very picture of her dearest granddaughter being raped and killed by a heinous offender was more than her mind could bear. She returned to her feet, looked around the room, sweeping her hands and arms to include every woman in the room. She looked at me with tears in her eyes and said in a very stern voice, with no hesitation, "I would kill them."

I apologized for painting such a vivid picture concerning harm to her granddaughter but assured her and her friends that it is easy to accept injury against ourselves, but not against those we hold dear, especially those who are entirely defenseless. I continued by sharing the fact that all my life, I had endured personal attacks regardless of whether I could win a fight or not, and never felt true hatred against the offender, with the exception of the Viet Nam War. I stopped for a moment, moving my gaze from one woman to the next and then continued. "However, once my children were born, who are presently under ten years old, my thoughts concerning protecting them offer no resistance against killing to ensure their safety." The women rose to their feet clapping their hands, many with tears in their eyes.

I held up my hand to encourage them to return to their seats. I told them that as we brought the meeting to a close, we needed to revisit the primary rule governing the use of force, which commands us to use whatever level of power we must employ to stop the assault and no more. I reminded them that the use of deadly force remains the more challenging because one cannot retract such force once delivered. If one threatens another with a deadly weapon and an assailant possessing an equally lethal weapon suddenly drops that weapon and retreats, then one can only use that threat of deadly force to secure the offender's gun and keep the offender in retreat. I reminded each woman that we were compelled to call 911 as soon as practical, if we had not already done so to advise law enforcement of the situation and that we had the suspect in custody at gunpoint.

The next question, which I anticipated as well, related to the offender's willingness to remain in custody. What if he or she decided to flee the scene? Could we or should we use deadly force to stop that person from escaping? I reminded them that we could only use the level of force we felt justified to use against a person who was assaulting us. If that threat against us no longer existed, we could not resort to deadly force to stop a fleeing felon. I stated, "However, if you sincerely feel that the offender is fleeing to gain access to your grandchildren or children with the intent to kill them or cause severe injury, then the use of deadly force may be justified, but we must be prepared to stand before a judge and jury and offer evidence that probable cause existed."

Too many variables enter into each scenario we conjure up, and such scenes rarely equal the actual threat when that situation does arise. Therefore, providing advice to the average citizen is risky at best. Regardless, the actual importance of such meetings with members of the community is to provide them with facts of law that will govern their actions as well as impress them with the knowledge that everyone responds in the way they practice. Most untrained people will respond with the fight or flight response, but military personnel or law enforcement officers are trained to overcome the fight or flight and respond more effectively. Therefore, if we fail to prepare ourselves mentally and physically for the worst-case scenario, we will probably fail to escape the assailant or to provide protection for our loved ones.

Another question law enforcement officers often hear regards the type of weapon one should choose for personal protection. Women are a bit easier to coach than men because many men prefer a gun that offers the most lethal force, which means a magnum pistol. However, when it comes to self-defense, one must realize that most of your battles with that weapon are going to be three feet or less away, which means that a magnum is overkill. Additionally, some firearms have double-action capability, especially revolvers—and a double-action pistol requires more strength to force the hammer to cock and release to fire the weapon. Therefore, if the person does not practice regularly, his or her ability to shoot the gun with any accuracy is minimal.

The next thing one must consider in weapon choice is the killing power of the round leaving the barrel. Most pistol and rifle rounds will easily penetrate a double sheetrock wall with enough velocity to kill or injure the person in the next room. Therefore, if you keep a .44 or .357 magnum by your bed and an offender enters your home and you begin firing that weapon at the assailant, you must remain aware of the bullets missing your intended target as those rounds penetrate the walls into the next room. The projectile can hit your children or other loved ones in the adjoining room.

Therefore, when choosing a weapon for protection in the home one should select a cartridge that offers the least probability of passing through a wall. It may be wise to carry a rat shot round in the chamber in contrast to the typical bullet. Rat shot is nothing more than tiny steel or lead pellets that will probably not penetrate a wall, but is highly effective against rats, mice, and felons. The probability that it will kill an offender is slim, but the rat shot will carry enough force to discourage the offender less than three feet away. Additionally, he or she has no idea if the next round is deadly.

My personal choice of a weapon inside the home is a legal length, short-barrel, pump shotgun, loaded with game loads for quail or dove. The beauty of this defense is that the game load should fall short of penetrating the wall but will severely injure any offender. Additionally, if the weapon expends all its ammo, it can still be used as a deadly defense if the owner trains in the use of the shotgun for thrust and parry strategies. A pistol serves little purpose for assault unless the assailant is already on top of you. Therefore, my recommendation to any citizen is to purchase a pump shotgun and rely on the game load to take out the offender as well as self-defense tactics using the empty weapon.

Other public relations meetings might be with businesses and community crime watch groups to share practical ways to protect one's home or business. Of course, the first line of defense while someone is away on a business trip or vacation is to request extra patrol. Additionally, the owner should provide dispatch with photos or at least license plate numbers and physical descriptions of all vehicles that may be present during their absence. This information helps any deputy driving by to determine if the car parked at that location is or is not a suspect vehicle. Additionally, the owner should stop all mail and other deliveries to the home or business. One telltale clue to burglars is the pile of newspapers at the entrance gate or front door of the property.

Most conversation revolves around the security of the business or home, which is a tough call in a rural setting. Even if a home or business includes the latest in technology for the security alarm systems and video surveillance, one must face the reality of the distance a law enforcement officer must travel to respond to an alarm call. The fastest response time for a Parker County Deputy responding to an alarm call was at least fifteen minutes, with the exception of already being in the immediate area when the request was received. The probability of that happening is slim to none, since the county is large and law enforcement is understaffed and must focus on high-crime areas.

One must develop other levels of security that will discourage a burglar or thief and encourage him or her to move down the road to an easier target. Law enforcement and military forces refer to this as hardening the target. One's focus is on making it more difficult to access the home, business, or outbuildings, which serves as a useful tool to discourage any prospective burglar. Although one may assume a burglar alarm system is one of the best tools to rely on, the actual effort starts with the entry to the property.

In a rural setting, the front gate to the property is the primary blockade against illegal entry and most country homes include some form of front gate, which may be nothing more than a single pipe locked to a vertical pole on the opposite side, which only blocks a vehicle. However, the more effective gates are those discouraging climbing as well as forced entry, on foot or from a vehicle. If the offender has reason to believe that the home or business will provide sufficient returns from the effort, he or she may push through the gate or pull it open with a rope or chain.

The gate, as your first line of defense, can also have two types of alarms as well as send a notice to the alarm company. The first type of warning is the notice of arrival of someone outside your gate. Many systems enable the owner to talk with that person from any location in the world if sufficient Internet service is available. The second alarm is a notification that someone has passed through the gate. The beauty of having both alarm functions rests with narrowing the response time because the offender still must drive to and find access to the interior of the home or business.

Lighting for the gate offers another critical facet of personal security. Gate lighting should be placed above, shining down onto the gate, exposing anyone hiding in the bushes or behind a gate post. Lighting must never shine in the eyes of the driver because that would temporarily blind them. Of course, most gated entrances include an electric motor to open the gate as well as mailboxes that are easily accessed by the driver as he or she drives up to the gate. One must keep in mind, however, that electrical service to the gate may be easily defeated by an offender who lies in wait for a victim.

The second line of defense for a home or business depends on the exterior of the building. All lighting should be focused down or up against the side of the building to reveal anyone hiding next to the exterior walls. Floodlights and spotlights aimed at a person approaching prevent that person from seeing anyone who may be lurking. Therefore, positioning and choice of lighting remain paramount to security.

Exterior doors should include a deadbolt with a full one-inch penetration into the door jamb. Additionally, the door jamb should be constructed of steel or a steel plate and can be attached to the back side of the door frame to provide added strength to the deadbolt closure. Some people turn to a double-key deadbolt, and many insurance companies require such when a window or door glass is three feet or less from the deadbolt. However, this requirement conflicts with fire code in many cities because of the inherent danger of a lost key preventing opening that door from the inside or outside. Many alarm companies address this challenge with the inclusion of an intrusion alarm reacting to breaking glass in or near the doorway.

Garages and garage doors offer easy entry if the burglar carries numerous garage door openers with various codes for each opener. With luck, the garage door code will match, and the door will move out of the way. The public relations officer's duty is to share this knowledge with every home and business within that officer's jurisdiction. With such information in hand, homeowners and businesses can move forward with efforts that will indeed reduce the impact of burglars within the community.

Quite often, the public relations officer is the official voice that provides public service information relating to progress in a significant crime or information relating to traffic issues arising from a major accident or construction. Additionally, the public relations officer may deliver weekly crime reports describing the most wanted offenders who may be hiding somewhere in the county. More importantly, this officer is the first line of communication of community needs, opinions, concerns, fears, and distrust back to the sheriff or other law enforcement leaders of the county, city, or state.

Another equally important facet of public relations includes media relations or meeting with anyone requiring information concerning a specific case. This is especially true with high-profile cases. One such case involved a local businessman who was charged with DWI Manslaughter. The man allegedly drove a vehicle while intoxicated on a major thoroughfare, where he failed to avoid oncoming traffic. The result was the death of four teenage girls who were killed in the head-on collision. The media was reporting every bit of information they received, regardless of the facts, which presented the offender as a wanton murderer. Although he admittedly made a mistake, the media led the call for the death penalty in the case.

This was a difficult case to handle as the public relations officer because unless one stays focused on the facts as well as the rights of all citizens during a trial, especially those of the offender and the victim, the case may be falsely influenced by public pressure causing a wrong person to be freed or a person with no true ill intent against the victims to be persecuted for his or her participation in the crime. In this instance, the District Attorney filed for a change of venue, which allowed the case to be transferred to another jurisdiction where attorneys could expect to receive more impartial jurors and judges.

Another aspect of public relations rests with dealing with crowds. Crowds can become hostile and offer extreme challenges to a law enforcement officer who must protect citizens while ensuring the rights of all people. Such incidents can turn deadly.

Dispatch sent me to investigate a loud music call in the northeastern sector of our county, a well-known high-crime area. I received the call about 10:15 on a Sunday evening. The county did not have an established noise ordinance, which forced an officer to search for other reasons to bring peace to the neighborhood during such altercations. Parties in the county ranged from typical teenage loud music issues to major, adult gatherings involving bands of a different genre. This event was a gathering of approximately 300 Hispanic people celebrating the Cinco de Mayo. As I approached the private property from about a half-a-mile away, I could hear the music filtering through the cool night air. The music offered the typical, festive mood one grows to expect from such celebrations. However, each party always seems to provide the chosen few who opt to enhance their pleasure by becoming thoroughly intoxicated or consumed by drugs to the degree that their behavior becomes offensive to everyone, even those who attend the party merely to enjoy the hospitality of their hosts.

As I pulled into the long driveway entrance to the residence, I could see a home on a hill about 100 yards further down the road. The terrain on either side of my car was open prairie of coastal Bermuda, which told me that the owner was deeply involved in livestock or at least a provider of hay to the livestock profession. The music increased in volume as I drove further down the dirt road. I could now see a bonfire radiating flames high into the evening air. Fear of spreading flames was not a consideration because the spring rains had resulted in strong growth of crops and coastal Bermuda pastures. Additionally, it was a peaceful spring night with nothing but stars and only a gentle breeze. The guests virtually surrounded the home enjoying the frivolity of the evening; some were even inside the barn participating in a dance that had moved away from the crowd to its liking.

I stepped from the vehicle, one man alone, walking into a large group of people who could easily ignore the presence of the officer walking among them. As I advanced toward the house, I greeted each small group with, "Buenas tardes. Espero que estés disfrutando la fiesta," hoping no one perceived my presence as threatening.

Initially, I wondered if my choice of words was correct. My mastery of Spanish offered knowledge of salutations, and just enough of the language to sort out words relating to weapons one may employ against me, but otherwise, I knew very little of the language. However, all the people replied with kind words in turn, and some even insisted on answering in English, which served to return the respect I attempted to show to them.

As I neared the house, an elderly gentleman stepped forward, extending his hand. I shook his hand with a firm grip as he asked if he could help me in any way. I told him that I had been dispatched to investigate a loud music call but had no idea that he offered such a large party gathering. He smiled and said, "Yes, I have a host of friends," as he waved both arms in opposite directions. He then looked concerned and asked if my presence meant the party was over.

I reassured him that I had no intention of ruining his festivities, but that ordinances against disorderly conduct required that I ensure that the noise level was lowered to a more acceptable level. Being Sunday evening, the law was more applicable because most people were trying to get a good night's rest before returning to the grind in the workplace tomorrow. He agreed that the music was loud and shared his concern that the party had outgrown his original intention to have a few friends over for the evening.

Assuming this was my opportunity, I asked him if he would mind moving the party indoors by either moving the band inside the barn and closing the doors or merely moving the live music inside his home. The elderly gentleman liked the barn party idea and welcomed my presence as the opportunity to ask those who were burdensome to leave.

He interrupted the music as he made his way to one of the microphones where he issued an edict dismissing the people from the party. He told his close friends that he would be moving the party to the barn. He used my presence as the catalyst to downsize the party. I could tell, from some of the looks I received, that a few of the men and women did not appreciate my intrusion. However, they heeded the elderly landowner's request as the entire party of 300 men and women disbanded, with some returning to their cars and leaving while a small group helped the band gather their instruments and equipment to facilitate the move to the barn.

Soon the party returned to full swing, but behind closed doors. Some of the people invited me to dance as I tapped a foot to the tune. I politely refused by holding up my radio to help them understand I was on call. Only the muffled sound of the band radiated from the interior of the barn. Even the night sounds of a typical spring night returned to their rightful place. The old man approached me with an extended hand once again and thanked me for my help. We enjoyed mutual respect and that was all that mattered; we both knew and appreciated that. It is doubtful that today, one officer could walk into a similar situation and enjoy the same level of respect from the participants.

On another day, during the day shift, dispatch contacted me, advising that Sheriff Whiteman wanted me to meet him in his office. Sadly, one typically searches his or her memory of recent interactions with the public to wonder why the sheriff would want him or her to report to his office.

The sheriff is the top law enforcement officer of the entire county, basically meaning he is the law of the land. Therefore, the position alone commanded a healthy measure of respect. In the case of Sheriff Ben Whiteman, that respect included personal awe and admiration. Sheriff Whiteman was not only the elected sheriff of the county, which meant he carried the honor of the average citizen in the county, but additionally, Sheriff Whiteman offered a mile marker, an achieved goal in life that I longed to attain: a Master of Science Degree in Criminal Justice. I entered law enforcement with a Bachelor's Degree in business administration and little to no knowledge of the law short of what I gathered during my training with the academy. To achieve the level of professionalism I hoped to attain, I knew I must at least master a level of education equivalent to that reached by Sheriff Ben Whiteman. He was my motivator.

I entered his office with my hat in my hand, searching his eyes for clues telling me what wrong I committed. He stood leaning against his desk when I entered the room. We completed a cursory handshake, and then he dropped my hand as he walked across the room, obviously studying something on his mind. My thoughts could trace no grievous errors in my interaction with the public, and I knew my written reports were immaculate. He stopped pacing and looked at me momentarily, and then he shared his concerns.

He had just received a notice from the County Commissioners informing him that a Ku Klux Klan rally had been approved to take place at 10:00 am that morning on the County Courthouse Square. Legally, the KKK leadership had met all the qualifications to hold a rally as would any other citizen. Sheriff Whiteman knew he had to provide security for the Klan during the ceremony, which we both knew was nothing more than a membership drive. However, we both also realized the propensity for such a gathering to erupt in violence, bringing harm to all those in and around the ceremony.

Sheriff Whiteman told me that he called me in because he felt I had the calm demeanor as well as the commanding presence to ensure safety and security throughout the event. I felt humbled by his vote of confidence. He told me that no other officer had the experience I had under the pressure of extreme violence, because of my experience as a special ops combat veteran. I assured him that I fostered the same contempt for the KKK as did just about every other citizen in our county and asked him if I could call in my patrol officers to assist with security measures. Sheriff Whiteman looked at me for a moment and then told me to do what I felt I had to do without bringing too much focus on the KKK rally. I reassured him that I would employ every ounce of my training and experience to ensure the rally proceeded without incident.

I asked dispatch to recall all dayshift officers to the station. Fortunately, the shift had just begun operations and all the officers were still nearby. Following the briefing, the officers headed to the County Courthouse Square to set up on each corner of the square. I only had four men and myself to deal with whatever challenges arose during the rally. I would soon find that we faced a formidable foe... hatred. I ordered the men to refrain from any physical encounters and only to ensure that those stopping to listen to the crowd chose not to incite a riot. I placed myself in front of the podium, which I felt would probably be a strategic location for any violence against the speaker.

The leader of the Ku Klux Klan gathering thanked me for my presence and told me that they were merely there to recruit members and share their concerns. I convinced him that my presence was to ensure the safety and security of the members of our community and to make sure that he and his Klan members enjoyed their right to free speech as guaranteed by the Bill of Rights, and nothing more. He readily perceived that he did not have a friend in the ranks of local law enforcement. He proceeded to complete the establishment of the perimeter with numerous KKK banners proclaiming various controversial subjects.

I checked with my officers by handheld to ensure that all was secure. A small crowd was already gathering across the street from the Courthouse Square. The man, dressed in his Klan attire, stepped up to the microphone and began a speech that related to the racial bigotry that we have all grown to detest. My skin crawled with the knowledge that I had to stand there and force others to leave this man and his followers alone to ensure the protection of their inalienable rights.

All Americans are guaranteed the right to speak their piece as long as it does not incite harm against others. This man's speech was borderline, in my opinion. I focused my attention on the crowd, which had already increased to about fifty people, all of which seemed to express displeasure toward the presence of the Klan in their community. They did not perceive it as such, but I was on their side. Soon, men and women were hurling obscenities, not only at the speaker but towards the presence of sheriff deputies for protecting for such atrocious people.

I noticed one man moving from one small group to the next, obviously with the intent to create problems for the unwanted visitors. I decided it was time to gain control instead of waiting for violence to erupt. I watched as the man made his way to a large group where they momentarily engaged in a heated conversation with some pointing fingers toward the podium and my protective perimeter. I left my position, advising my personnel that I was going to mingle with the crowd for a moment. They each acknowledged and remained steadfast. A couple of them were talking with some of the bystanders.

I made my way to the group and approached the man I had observed talking with every group. He yelled out, “Look, it’s one of the traitors!” I walked straight toward him, grabbed him by the elbow and ushered him to the side, but still within hearing range of everyone in the large group. The man looked at me and voiced his concern that the sheriff would allow such people even to cross the county line.

I asked him if he had ever heard of the 1st Amendment. He assured me that he had but stated that in his opinion people like the KKK should not have that right. I told him that, fortunately, or unfortunately, that right exists for all Americans, and we have no power to stop them, either verbally or physically, from accessing that right. He looked at me for a moment and asked, “Well Deputy, what would you suggest we do?” His words were loud enough to fall on the ears of all those in the large group.

The crowd grew silent as they each awaited my reply. I looked at the crowd’s presumed leader, then back toward the Parker County citizens who were gaining momentum and anger every second. I offered a solution, “What if the crowd simply was not here? What if we all just ignored these jerks and left? Are we not empowering and encouraging their speech with our mere presence? Does not our presence condone the existence of the KKK?” The man looked at me in disbelief, and then my words filtered past the hatred in his mind as he realized the truth behind them.

What would the Klan leader do if no people were present to listen to his racial, anti-government slurs? He turned to the crowd and yelled out, “This is ridiculous. Let’s all go home or at least leave the square. Let them preach to themselves.” Within moments, the rally was over. Word to disband passed throughout the crowd that had swollen around the entire perimeter of the Square. The group rapidly disbursed, and traffic and business resumed as if the KKK presence was nothing more than a mere nuisance that would soon disappear, which it did.

The KKK leader was livid, demanding to know why I ordered the people to leave. He promised he was filing a complaint that I had compromised his right to free speech. I reassured him that I did nothing to usurp his command of the audience gathered around the Square and encouraged him to continue speaking to his heart's desire. He waved to the empty square and said, "Speak? Speak to what? They are all gone." I told him that I only suggested that they may have something better to do than stand around listening to some racist bigot share his warped sense of being. Once again, he promised to file a report with the sheriff and the town mayor for intervening in his 1st Amendment rights. Once again, I promised him that the people left based on their own volition, with no coercion or orders from me. He scowled at me as he and his fellow Klansmen packed their belongings, returned to their cars, and headed east, leaving Parker County behind. The rally had lasted no more than twenty minutes from the moment of inception.

I advised dispatch that the party was over, and all participants had cleared the scene. I further informed her that all business and traffic had returned to normal. I released my men to return to duty and returned to the sheriff's office to assure Sheriff Whiteman, personally, that all was well. He was standing at his office door chatting with Chief Deputy Shumaker when I returned to the office.

He waved me forward and asked what I had done to end the rally so soon. I assured him that I did not issue any orders. I merely adopted the age-old strategy of picking out the ringleader in the crowd, the one who was focusing on inciting the crowd to violence, and suggested an alternative solution to him. I told Sheriff Whiteman and Chief Shumaker that I, fortunately, encountered a man who listened to reason and one not blinded by hatred and fear. I shared my solution with the sheriff and the chief, and they both laughed at the simplicity of the plan. Sheriff

Whiteman slapped me on the back and told me to return to patrol and do something constructive for once. I left them in the hall musing over things and headed north, in search of criminals.

Both these incidents relate to the absence of respect perpetuated by negative press from media sources across our land today. The KKK rally on the Courthouse Square in Parker County that morning could have turned into a bloody riot. The acts could have spilled onto the streets or even against the businesses, creating more damage and panic. Every law enforcement officer within radio distance would have been called to the scene, leaving the criminal element free to commit their chosen crimes against the communities vacated by those officers. An all-points bulletin issued as a cry for help assures offenders listening to scanners that they have a window of opportunity to commit their crimes without deterrence.

One should note that the local news was the only one to file a report concerning the presence of the KKK in Parker County that day. The story nestled quietly on the inside pages, saying nothing about the rally other than its brevity. However, if the leader of the citizenry had refused to be discouraged that day and succeeded in inciting the crowd to riot, then not only would the local press have reported the incident, but also helicopters from large news agencies in Ft. Worth and Dallas would have been covering the event from their airspace above until the ground crew could arrive to gain firsthand encounters from the rioters and their victims. Parker County would have made history as a source of riots involving the KKK.

My service as the Parker County Public Relations Officer revealed the importance of building relationships with home and business owners in the county. Communication barriers disappear as the level of trust takes a more positive turn. Therefore, one may easily understand why every law enforcement officer in the city, county, or state must realize the importance of building a positive relationship with everyone he or she encounters on patrol and yes, sometimes that includes an offender. How much would it mean to a male offender who is not a murderer or other heinous offender to hear words of encouragement from an officer assuring him that you would drop by and check on the family occasionally to ensure they were safe and secure while he was in jail. One may assume that an officer certainly has nothing to lose and the community may gain a person more willing to work toward moving away from a life of crime.

Chapter Thirteen

Investigating Crimes Against Children

Crimes against Children (CAC) remain among the more challenging and mentally exhausting crimes for any investigator and leave victims scarred for life. They can exacerbate PTSD issues an officer already endures from years investigating other heinous crimes as well. Because the victims are so young and innocent, the vivid memories that flood one's mind and nightmares of past cases trigger imposing, uncontrolled and unpredictable reactions stemming from law enforcement PTSD.

Quite often, this career path leads to issues in one's personal life as the investigator notices telltale signs of abuse in children belonging to friends, relatives, or neighbors. Merely observing actions of people in a mall or other public areas may trigger warnings of offenders or victims among them. Such knowledge and experience forces one to remain more aware, even intrusively aware, of his or her children as they interact with other children or an adult, alienating one from family and friends if the officer cannot resolve his or her suspicions.

However, this writing relates to the victim, not the investigator, and is intended to make the average citizen, law enforcement recruits, and criminal justice students aware of the horrors some children endure behind closed doors. The cycle of abuse, as well as the mental instabilities of some individuals, create motivation to prey upon the innocence of children with acts of crime that often drive their victims to suicide or murder.

I must admit that my introduction to Child Protective Services (CPS) as a patrol officer created a love/hate relationship until I genuinely began to focus on the importance of this agency along with the challenges each CPS investigator faces. Patrol officers may encounter situations where children face potential dangers but discover that CPS refuses to allow an emergency extraction of those children because of written policy or state or federal laws. However, law enforcement officers must not believe the false perception of this agency promulgated by the media. The perception that CPS won't assist with endangered children rapidly disappears once an officer accepts the CAC Investigation position.

In the mid-1990s, dispatch sent me to a domestic violence call at a single-wide trailer in northern Parker County, just north of Springtown. As I made my way through the foot-high Johnson grass and other weeds to the front porch, I observed countless beer cans scattered on the porch and throughout the visible areas of the yard. I did not doubt that mowing the yard would produce evidence of even more. I could hear screaming inside the home, which provoked a loud knock and announcement from me as I strained to decipher the conversation behind the closed door. "Sheriff's Office!" I commanded.

The yelling ceased immediately. Footsteps rumbled from inside as someone ran toward the door, which rapidly swung open. A young woman about twenty years old stood in the doorway with tears running down her cheeks. She had a toddler settled on her hip. She pointed across the living room to the kitchen area to a man standing with a beer clutched in one hand and a cigarette in the other. She proclaimed that she wanted him out of her home.

As I stepped into the home, I noticed fleas and ticks already seeking fresh prey. The floor was alive with thousands of insects. A bundle of joy on the carpeted interior caught my eye. The baby, barely three or four months old, was lying, unclothed, on the bug-infested floor. I reached down and swooped the baby into my arms, brushing all unattached insects from her body in an attempt to free her from the biting ticks and fleas.

I ordered both parents to stop their verbal assault and to sit down while I contacted CPS. I asked dispatch to have a CPS investigator call me on their landline immediately. Moments later the phone rang, and I hastened to pick up the receiver before either parent could move. I told the CPS investigator what I had found and asked for permission to conduct an emergency extraction based on the nude baby and the insect invasion against her weak, infested body.

The kitchen and living room offered similar décor, including leftover food overgrown with mold sitting on top of the TV, end tables, and floor. Incensed at the lack of parenting and caring for their young, I wanted CPS to intervene immediately. However, the CPS investigator explained how such conditions did not, on their own, justify an emergency extraction, but assured me she would investigate the home the next day. I hung up the phone, frustrated with the entire situation but understood written departmental policies.

I assured the parents it was their lucky day. Further investigation revealed that neither parent had harmed or threatened the other and that the call originated from a concerned neighbor. Consequently, the situation required no further action. By a written policy we were to ensure no one was in immediate danger and, if not, to clear the scene and make an incident report. A few years later, the Texas laws changed, encouraging officers to either force one person to leave the residence for the night or to complete an arrest to ensure no further violence ensued in the home. Regardless of the officer's decision, the new law required the officer to file an incident report to secure a permanent record of violence in that residence.

Before leaving, I told both parents that they needed to treat the home for infestation immediately. The wife started crying, alleging that fumigating the house was too costly and an unaffordable luxury. I encouraged her and her husband to stop drinking and smoking and use that money to rid their home of pests. Promising both parents a return visit the next day to ensure they immaculately cleaned the house and yard, I cleared the scene.

I kept my promise, heading straight for their home at the beginning of the evening shift the next day. As I neared the house, I could see that the situation remained unchanged. I pulled into the driveway, stepping out without even checking with dispatch. I was infuriated at the arrogance of the parents to ignore my warning. The door immediately swung open with my knock. I prepared for a confrontation with the worthless parents, but the home was empty, no furniture, nothing but the insect infestation. The couple had fled the county or to another part of the county where they could hide until the scenario repeated itself. I feared Lyme Disease might claim the baby but remained powerless to intervene. As I chatted with CPS to cancel their visit, the receptionist informed me that they were used to people on the run.

Over the years, I became close friends with the Parker County CPS officers and recognized the challenges and dangers they each encountered with every entry into homes that I entered armed for instant defense. CPS investigators lack any weapons and face irate parents. The officers' only option is to flee the residence. It takes a lot of courage and love for children to inspire a person to walk into a home, unarmed, with no expectation of safety during an altercation.[1] CPS officers earned my utmost respect and those in Parker County learned they could count on me to accompany them to ensure their safety with just a phone call.

There exist two levels of sexual offenders in crimes against children. One, of course, is the classic pedophile who intentionally preys upon our children. True pedophilia is a mental condition that may be caused by a psychological imbalance due to genetic characteristics or other form of mental health issues. [2]

States create penal code laws based on varying levels of victim age, which increase or decrease the severity of the offense and the sanctions imposed upon the offenders, and in turn determine how to file a case. In many states the law considers anyone under the age of seventeen to be below the age of consent. Therefore, a child cannot legally comply with the actions or requests of an offender. This lack of legal consent relates to the next type of offender, the man or woman who is enticed to commit offenses against a child who commits acts to attract that adult. Most of these cases involve post-puberty children who are discovering their sexuality, based on media presentations, encouragement by peers, or through an inherent interest in their ability to attract the opposite sex. Regardless, such action does not excuse the offender's invasive response. However, the child's activities do lower the offender's culpable mental state. This adult may be in a frustrating relationship with the child's natural parent making him or her more vulnerable to the enticements offered by the teenager. He or she may resist initially, lowering defenses with the teenager's increasing, explorative nature. Poor decisions lead to a dangerous combination encouraging the child to develop unnatural attractions.

In one such case, the written confession from a fourteen-year-old-girl alleged that she posed nude in plain view of her stepfather, to intentionally entice him to return her advances. She varied locations to the surprise of the offender, serving to increase the enticement leading to the offense. Additionally, the girl chose to share a blanket with her stepfather while watching TV in the living room, allowing her to offer physical enticements as well.

The girl's mom discovered her husband, a thirty-five-year-old male with no criminal record, molesting her daughter one afternoon. Mom confirmed her daughter's promiscuity in her statement agreeing that she caught her daughter standing in front of a window with the curtains drawn open numerous times while the stepfather was mowing the yard or playing outside with her younger siblings. Mom informed me that each event involved some level of parental counseling that excluded her husband and without professional counseling for her daughter. Additionally, mom admitted she lost physical attraction for her husband for various reasons, and this led to his sexual frustration. The offender admitted that he was frustrated with the relationship with his wife but agreed that nothing could justify his actions.

The teenage daughter was aware of the tension between her parents, which encouraged her to tease her stepfather. Each refusal of her advances fueled an increase in the levels of enticement of her stepfather. The overall circumstances fortified terrible decisions to lower his boundaries, opening the door for a physical, sexual encounter with the child. Mom, although compelled by jealous rage more than an outcry against the sexual assault of her child, contacted the Parker County Sheriff's Office to file the complaint.

During the interrogation, the stepfather's guilt remained obvious based on his non-verbal clues alone. Remorse engulfed him, reducing him to a sobbing mass for several minutes. Upon regaining composure, he provided a written confession, throwing himself on the mercy of the court. I filed the case based on the Texas Penal Code listing of the sexual assault of a child defining a child being less than seventeen years old but older than thirteen.[3] If the stepdaughter had been less than fourteen, the case would have been filed as Aggravated Sexual Assault of a Child, which carries a much higher penalty. The judge, jury, and the District Attorney felt empathy for but did not condone the offender's actions. He received a ten-year probated sentence requiring substantive counseling.

Millsap High School demanded my attention once again. This next case was more sinister than the one with the teenager taking a gun to school. This crime stemmed from a male student's father who enticed prepubescent and teenage girls to not only pose nude for photographs and videos but also to engage in forms of perverted sex with each other.

The boy's father recorded the videos and still shots on DVDs, which his son sold to other students during class sessions at the high school.

Fortunately, none of the boys engaged in any reported sexual activity with the girls. However, the investigation revealed the names and locations of each female student, which empowered me to approach the parents for full identification to file the appropriate charges against the offenders (father and son). An interview with the victims led to the recovery of evidence and statements confirming the actions of the father and the son. I filed Sale, Distribution, or Display of Harmful Material to a Minor, a Class A Misdemeanor in the State of Texas, against the teenage son. I charged the father with Sexual Performance by a Child, which is a Second-Degree Felony.[4]

The teenage boy was found guilty of the offense of distribution of pornography and served a probated six-month sentence under the care, custody, and control of Parker County Juvenile Probation. The father, not so fortunate, threw himself on the mercy of the court and received a ten-year probated sentence with severe penalties and fines as well as stringent counseling requirements and registration as a sex offender. His saving grace stemmed from the fact that none of the girls offered evidence that he ever touched them.

In a remote area of Parker County, near the Veal Station Cemetery, another case was reported by the local school district. This case, forwarded by the Springtown Middle School counselor, offered insight into a unique, inbred culture. Child Protective Services became involved immediately and withdrew two prepubescent girls from the home to facilitate an offsite interview of the alleged victims. The discussions led to the discovery that the father decided it was his duty to train his two girls in various acts of sex to ensure they would become good wives to future husbands. He adamantly denied that he was a sex offender and continually asserted that he was merely doing his duty as a father. The courts disagreed and gave him a chance to think about his perversion with a forty-year sentence.

The leading businesses in Parker County contributed funding to create the Parker County CAC Task Force, the first of its kind in Parker County. The sheriff at that time, Jay Brown, asked me to accept the leadership of the sheriff's office participation in the Task Force. I readily agreed and welcomed the opportunity to work closely with other professionals, who included the DA, counselors, private attorneys, psychiatrists, doctors, nurses, and others.

The business consortium provided funding to purchase a Victorian-style home on the southwest side of Weatherford, Texas. CAC divided the house into three major sections. The first section, the foyer, catered to the public, serving as the reception area for parents/guardians and victims. On rare occasions, CPS employed a strategy to encourage the perpetrator to come in with the family, without providing any notice that he or she was considered a suspect.

The lobby included a play area for the children to help engage them so that they wouldn't worry about why they were in a strange place. Typically, CPS never told child victims they were going to talk to anyone about the suspected offenses. This strategy ensured that the children did not become defensive and fearful that their parent, guardian, or another relative would get in trouble. CPS extended every effort to make the reception area a non-threatening environment. Even sex offense and child abuse pamphlets were kept hidden inside the receptionist's desk. Each receptionist was a CPS officer as well, which ensured that if the perpetrator uttered a confession or committed any offense in plain view, he or she faced additional charges. The immediate probable cause enabled a warrant, quite often before the suspect attempted to leave.

The second area consisted of two separate rooms complete with soft, comfortable couches and chairs as well as more toys and books than most children ever see. The oak plank floors of the building encouraged the inclusion of area rugs offering further comfort for the child victims. CPS did not allow parents, guardians, or relatives into the room with the children. The entire purpose created an ambiance of comfort that encouraged children to relax. CPS always stimulated each child to choose one toy to take home before he or she left, further enhancing that child's positive reaction to the encounter.

Additionally, the interview room included a hidden nanny cam providing a clear, uninterrupted view of the entire room. A phone on an end table next to the chair provided communication between the CPS investigator and the CAC investigator. The nanny cam supplied real-time videos, complete with audio, to the law enforcement officer sitting at a desk located in a rear entrance room. The room allowed law enforcement officers to come and go from the building without being seen by the children or suspects. Each officer (city, county, or state) parked in the parking lot in the rear of the building with shrubbery blocking any view of the presence of the officers or their vehicles as they entered or left the small room housing the video monitor as well as a second phone, which provided instant communication with the CPS.

Investigators observed the interview via video and heard everything the children and CPS investigator said as well as any action they took while being interviewed. The officer could call the other phone, which the CPS investigator would answer as a call from a friend or relative, excusing herself for a moment and allowing the kids to return to playing. The officer shared observations or questions he or she felt may encourage the children to talk about the experiences they suffered at the hands of the perpetrator. The CPS investigator relied on anatomically correct dolls, which enabled children to point to the body part with which they were forced to interact.

Fortunately, each child victim typically changes his or her entire countenance when asked if anyone ever harmed or inappropriately touched them or if the child shared information concerning any sexual contact with an offender. Once CPS completes the interview, he or she provides a video and transcript of the interview to the law enforcement officer, along with a copy of the CPS report. With that information, the law enforcement officer pursues a case and a probable cause warrant against the suspect.

If the suspect was present during the interview, he or she was always allowed to leave without knowledge of the allegations provided by the victim. However, the probable cause warrant issued by the magistrate shortly after law enforcement submitted the probable cause affidavit empowered the arrest. Quite often, the offender discovered a patrol vehicle waiting for him when he and the family returned home. Patrol officers typically secured the capture by asking the offender to step outside. Additionally, unless the offender resisted arrest, the officer would usually complete a frisk out of plain view from the windows of the home and seat the offender in the back seat of the car without being handcuffed in plain sight of his or her children. Patrol booked the offender into jail where the CAC Investigator followed up with the interrogation, confronting him or her with the evidence provided by CPS.

I assumed responsibility for CAC investigations upon appointment from Sheriff Brown, following the transfer of the other investigator to another position within CID. He expressed a desire to move out of the CAC section for health purposes and assured me that I was entering an investigative position that challenges one's soul. The assignment had left him emotionally drained because of witnessing so many heinous crimes against children.

After my first year in service as the CAC investigator, the District Attorney (DA) called me into her office one day without giving a reason. I feared that the DA would challenge the accuracy of my case filings, which was her duty when preparing a case for trial. However, as I entered her office, she stepped from behind her desk, offering a friendly smile, and congratulated me for filing more successful cases in one year than the accumulated case filings of abused children in the history of the county. I shook her hand and walked away with her high praise ringing in my ears. "Think of all of the children you have set free from oppression and harm," she said as I turned to leave. As we reviewed prior cases, the vigorous action we both expended helped me understand the importance of our duties to protect our children.

All the cases I worked up to that point had fallen into place without much effort. The perpetrators typically cooperated without the need for lengthy interrogations or other strategies to wear down their natural defenses. However, confronting a pedophile who openly and deliberately preys upon children will challenge any investigator with the strong desire to ensure all regulations and rules of evidence are correctly addressed to avoid giving the defense attorney an opportunity to call for a mistrial. A child's life remains endangered if the investigator or patrol officer disrupts any portion of the investigative process.

One of the pedophile cases I worked with the CAC Task Force focused on a repeat offender who was highly knowledgeable and skilled in the methods he employed to entice children. He convinced parents that he cared only to provide his community with child care services that engaged the latest technology, books, and learning-aids, allowing their children, his prey, to become more advanced than other children who did not have the opportunities he could offer.

Three computer systems in his alleged school were located in separate rooms, enabling him to work independently with children, away from prying eyes. The computer systems employed large monitors to ensure the children were easily enticed by the screensavers, which showed other children enjoying time with the computers and playing with other children. The pedophile made sure nothing showing through the screen saver process revealed his true intentions. Additionally, only he could access the hidden software that connected the children to gradual enticements grooming them in preparation for sexual adventures.

The systems being in three different rooms allowed him to separate the children, lowering their resistance, without the temptation to share thoughts or concerns with other children. Additionally, he groomed the children through various means of manipulation to ensure that all actions within the alleged school for toddlers would remain their little secret, undetected and never shared with outsiders.

The offender placed bookshelves on each side of the computers to serve as an enticement for the children as well. Each shelf layout offered eye-level temptations with the upper shelves providing known and approved children's books that he knew the parents would welcome. Of course, those books were at adult eye-level while the illicit enticements remained below in plain view for the children to access and view.

The lower levels were filled with typical approved child education-oriented books as well. However, every other text contained cartoon-style child pornography designed to make the contents more interesting. As he groomed each child, he slowly advanced the process until the children showed interest in exploring each other. He relied on hidden video equipment to record the child-on-child actions, turning the recorder off when he became involved. To ensure complete privacy, he kept the front door of the alleged school locked, which the parents perceived to be on behalf of child safety. As a final part of the grooming, he threatened the children that he would release the videos to their parents as well as to their friends if they ever told anyone about the secret education methods he employed.

Fortuitously, one little girl had been thoroughly warned by her parents to remain alert concerning such encounters, which included warnings concerning grooming, placement of child pornography at her eye-level, and other strategies typically employed by sex offenders. She resisted the enticements and reported her fear to her parents, begging them not to force her to return to the school. They tried to investigate on their own, but found the doors locked. Unknown to the parents, the pedophile kept hidden cameras providing a 360-degree view of the exterior of the school and an alert system that would make him aware of anyone approaching the school.

Fortunately, the parents took their child and their suspicions to CPS, where the CPS investigators interviewed the child under the watchful eye of law enforcement. With the completion of the interview, we had sufficient evidence to pursue a warrant not only for the pedophile, but also to search his alleged school and seize all computers and all peripheral equipment. Based on the child's information, we located all the child pornography as well as every form of enticement the offender created, some of which we found in the attic of his alleged school as well as in his home. The man stood trial for multiple counts of Child Enticement and Aggravated Sexual Assault of a Child with every child he ever touched or enticed in the past. The jury found him guilty on all counts, and he received a forty-year sentence with no opportunity for parole.

One final case before I chose to retire from law enforcement was even more heinous. Unknown to the outside world, a family had moved into a slumlord trailer park on the far northwest side of Parker County. What makes this situation more heinous than the others is the fact that the offenders were the children's parents, both in their early thirties. They conveniently produced numerous offspring with the intention to use and abuse each child from a six-month-old baby to a nine-year-old girl, with a total of seven children victimized daily. The parents employed foreign objects as their tools of abuse to sexually assault each child and forced the children to abuse each other as well. The parents never allowed the children outside the home, keeping them locked in rooms until the parents were ready to subject the children to more deviant filming.

Luckily, one child escaped one day, fleeing to a neighbor's trailer. However, the offenders kept the children so heavily sedated that the child was unable to vocalize the horrors hidden behind closed doors. The parents located the boy and settled the neighbor's concerns, a mother of two small children as well, by assuring her that the boy suffered from mental issues and was kept anesthetized to ensure he was not a danger to himself or others. However, the woman remained suspicious and reported her concerns to CPS. CPS responded by sending a Child Protective Services investigator to the home to complete a knock-and-talk to ensure the safety of the children.

As the CPS investigator stood patiently waiting for someone to open the door, a man suddenly stepped through the open door, pointing a shotgun at her and ordering her to leave, telling her she was trespassing. She assured the man that she was there on official business as a CPS investigator, but the man would not back down. He increased his threat by pointing the shotgun at the CPS investigator's head. The man's wife stepped onto the porch to support her husband's ominous warning. The CPS investigator wisely backed away, slowly, to ensure the man did not fire his weapon as she considered her next move.

As the Head of the Parker County CAC investigations and a close friend with all the CPS investigator, I had stood ready to accompany any CPS worker to protect them during hazardous contact with potential offenders. Dispatch contacted me immediately as soon as the call came in from CPS. The CPS representative, Wendy, and I talked on the phone briefly as she described the encounter. I asked her if she had left the scene, and she assured me she had, but that she was waiting at the junction of Highway 199 and the adjacent road leading to the trailer park. She expressed grave concern for the safety of the children within the home. I asked her to remain in her vehicle and wait for my arrival but to phone me if the people tried to flee. I provided the magistrate in our office, Honorable Judge Melvin Simons, with my handwritten probable cause affidavit and explained the need for haste. After reading the supporting documentation, he signed the document without hesitation, encouraging me to bring the scoundrels to justice.

With the warrant approved, I drove immediately to Springtown, hoping the offenders would make the mistake of meeting me at the door with their shotgun. I suppose that was the Marine side of me, but I was incensed with the idea that they would threaten anyone, much less a CPS investigator who was merely fulfilling her duties of protecting our little ones.

I made the drive in good time. Wendy was waiting for me at the junction of Hwy. 199. I pulled over briefly to ensure she did not choose to follow me back to the scene. I wanted her to remain in a secure safety zone until I cleared the path for her to take possession of the children. I assured her that dispatch would contact her very shortly.

Driving to the home, I stopped my vehicle about 100 yards from the property to ensure my arrival remained undetected. I checked out with dispatch, advising her that I was investigating a hostile situation involving a firearm and that I would be available on my handheld radio. Fortunately, the western part of Parker County offered strong signals back to the station, raising no communication concerns. Additionally, dispatch made all the units in my vicinity aware of the situation, but did not ask for a backup officer, nor did she close the channel to emergency traffic only, upon my request. I did not want numerous patrol cars showing up at the scene, which would alert the offenders and possibly create a standoff situation with the children caught in the middle of gunfire. Since I was not in uniform, I felt the best approach was to approach on foot. Of course, my ten-gallon hat and the .45 on my hip, accompanied by the gold star sheriff's badge, somewhat hindered my stealthy approach. Regardless, it was still a better chance than inviting the entire army.

My eyes searched the perimeter of the property as I negotiated my path to the front door of the single-wide mobile home. I was in luck. Based on the aluminum foil covering all their windows, I assumed the residents were drug addicts as well. The foil hampered their view of my approach, but also my view of the home's interior. I walked as quietly as possible, making sure of every step to minimize external noises, something I picked up during the Viet Nam War. I walked up the rickety wooden steps, keeping my feet against the far edge of each level to reduce the chance of noise from a creaking step. Moments later, I stood beside the front door of the suspect's home.

This mobile home offered the same unique challenge mentioned earlier in this book. The front and back doors opened to the outside; meaning that the door had to swing open outward, leaving anyone inside the opportunity to seize a weapon or create some other defensive measure before the officer could enter. The doorway in a conventional home offered the standard door swinging to the inside, which readily facilitated immediate entrance with a swift kick from the officer.

Additionally, the single-wide and double-wide trailers were simply constructed with little or no concern given to multiple studs on either side of the doorway to enhance the strength of the opening. Therefore, to force entry, one had to pry the door open with a crowbar or other tool to break the door handle off, which rarely facilitated a useful entry. I merely turned sideways alongside the door, instead of standing directly in front of the door. However, this protective stance still provided little protection against a hail of lead flying from the barrel of a shotgun.

I knocked on the door as I cast a quick glance at each corner of the trailer as well as toward the windows. There was only silence from inside the home. I knocked again. The door suddenly pushed open as a man stepped onto the porch. I was prepared for his exit and moved a couple of steps further to the side to keep distance between us. He was unarmed as far as I could tell; no shotgun after all. Luckily, his wife followed him. I asked them to go ahead and step onto the lawn so that we could talk for a moment. They complied without question, keeping quiet.

I watched them walking down the steps and witnessed no sign of resistance or any telltale evidence of a weapon on either one. I shut the front door to ensure my back was covered to some degree and followed them down the steps. The man turned toward me as I negotiated the last porch step. "What do you need, officer?" His eyes glanced at the badge on my side and then fixed, momentarily, on the weapon on my side as well. I redirected his attention away from my pistol. I did not doubt that he and his wife were planning to jump me. I smiled and told them that they were both under arrest. They acted surprised.

"Arrest? For what?!" the wife bellowed out. The man turned to her and told her that it was probably because of that bitch CPS worker. I assured them they guessed right. I confirmed that in addition to charges of interfering with the duties of a public official, I was charging them with Aggravated Assault with a deadly weapon with the intent to kill the CPS investigator.[5]

They tried to deny anything as I encouraged both to bend over and put their hands on the side of the porch and spread their feet apart as wide as possible. The woman protested that she had children inside as I handcuffed her husband and forced him to sit on the ground. I pushed her back against the porch and grabbed both hands as I completed a speed-cuffing technique. I helped her join her husband as I told them about forgetting to warn them about the other charges. I smiled and said, "How about Aggravated Sexual Assault of a Child as well as numerous other charges creating and selling child pornography." Silence welcomed my words.

Forgetting to inform them of the other charges was far from the truth. I wanted to see the look on their faces when they realized they were about to face a judge and jury to explain the heinous crimes they committed. I read the Miranda Warning to each suspect separately and provided each with a Miranda Warning card as well to ensure they understood the charges they faced. I grabbed my handheld, keyed up the mike, and advised dispatch that both suspects were in custody and asked that she send the CPS investigator to my location, assuring her the scene was secure. I had not entered the home at this point. Therefore, I was unsure if the scene was genuinely protected. However, I doubted that anyone but the children were in the home and felt we would probably find them locked away in each room or held captive by some other heinous method.

I completed a search of each suspect, once again to ensure they were not hiding any handcuff keys, weapons, or contraband on their person. I ushered both suspects to my vehicle and secured them in the rear seat. The grid and the locked doors in the rear passenger area assured me that they would not be able to escape as I searched the house for the children as well as any other adults who might be a threat to CPS. I drove my vehicle to the driveway of their home and left the suspects locked in the rear of the car, with their hands secured behind them.

Moments later, Wendy arrived. She stepped from her car, momentarily glaring at the two suspects and stopping long enough to soak in her moment of victory against the man and woman who had threatened her life. She then turned to me and we entered the home, encountering a memory that would last a lifetime. The scene reminded me of the house mentioned earlier in this chapter, which was consumed in trash and insects, but this one was far worse. The living room was alive with roaches, fleas, and ticks making the carpet appear to be alive as the insects attempted to either flee or attack us as we entered the home. Beer and whiskey bottles were scattered across the floor as well as every flat surface in the house. Leftover food lay on the countertops and floors, long ago consumed by the mold growing around the remains of what was once a tasty morsel. The scene seemed to repeat itself with every major crime we encountered.

The stench within permeated your very soul, defying definition or classification. Every room in the home presented similar scenarios with the addition of a baby lying naked on a bedroom floor, and numerous small children cowering against a corner in each room in anticipation of the torture they knew awaited them at the hands of dad and mom. Most of the doors required a swift kick to defeat the lock barring entry. Some of the children were locked in closets, while others were chained to a piece of furniture. The CPS investigator and I took photos of the children in their horrible condition.

Only one room in the home was in pristine condition. It was a back room that had been added onto the single-wide trailer and served as the room where the children were forced to perform before the camera, delivering the offensive material direct to some viewers while being recorded on DVDs.

I photographed each room but left the evidence untouched. I wanted the Crime Scene Specialists to correctly process the entire scene to ensure every piece of evidence was adequately located, photographed, and secured per all evidentiary rules and regulations. I wanted to make sure that the evidence deprived the defense attorney of any opportunity to have this case dismissed.

I advised dispatch that I had one male and one female suspect in custody and was returning to the station, providing her with my starting mileage, following Sheriff Brown's written policy, when transporting females or children. I had dispatch send an EMT unit to the scene to assist CPS with the care, custody, and control over all the heavily sedated children.

About halfway back to the Parker County Sheriff's Office, my thoughts were interrupted by laughter erupting from the female suspect. She said, "I'll tell you something, officer. You can put us in jail, but we will bond out and start making new babies to take the place of the ones you have taken away, and after the courts release us, we are going to start our business all over again."

I smiled and said nothing. I had provided the Miranda Warning to both suspects earlier. Her words sealed her fate with the judge and jury as I made a mental note to include her res gestae statement in my report.[6] I did not respond, allowing her to continue to offer further words of incrimination. Her husband remained silent.

This case went before the 43rd District Court of Parker County in early 2000 with a predictable ending. Usually, the District Attorney allows an offender to take the opportunity to plea bargain. However, the crime scene evidence, as well as the statements from all the children, coupled with my report providing the mother's final words during transport back to the jail, assured the District Attorney that she had a solid case.

The jury found both suspects guilty on all counts, and the judge delivered forty-year sentences for each offense, stacked on each other, with no hope of parole. The woman's threat echoed into history as the reality hit home. She would never enjoy the embrace of any male for the rest of her life, which would indeed be spent behind bars.

The children moved forward with their lives with counseling and foster care provided by the county. However, I found in my career that foster care homes were not necessarily a safe-haven—I filed charges on two foster care homes for endangering the children in their care through providing alcohol and illicit drugs to the children.[7]

Chapter Fourteen

Epilogue

Service as a deputy sheriff has evolved since my retirement in 2004. Technology enjoys a more prominent place in the daily affairs of the average deputy and other officers even though some may perceive those technologies as being more of a nuisance than a contribution. Technology certainly has contributed significantly to the advancement of the criminal justice system globally. However, it has also empowered a rise in criminal enterprises. The Internet alone has given birth to the Darknet where criminals enjoy relative freedom from detection and impunity to prosecution for years as they expand sinister crimes such as drug and human trafficking as well as terrorism.

With the average patrol officer, such contributions from technology include the use of less-than-lethal-weapons. During my tenure, Tasers, water cannons, and other similar weapons remained in the future. We stood against any crimes with only a handful of tools. We either had to rely on our baton or the more advanced weapon known as the ASP, which was nothing more than a steel baton that expanded with proper forward thrusting. Our only other option before turning to deadly force rested with a can of Mace or what is known as Pepper Spray today.

These less-than-lethal-weapons served their purpose but offered counter-productive results as well. Either of these does indeed subdue most offenders. However, those offenders who are high on drugs or alcohol are less susceptible to the chemicals as are former military personnel who experienced such weaponry in training and combat. Additionally, a strong wind can turn the spray back on the officer as can a scuffle with the offender after he or she comes in contact with the spray.

Years ago, we had a felon escape from the Parker County Jail. Dispatch notified every available officer to help locate the offender who possessed a significant propensity toward violence. We cornered the escapee in a creek bed in the southern part of our county. One officer sprayed the man as he attempted to lunge toward him, covering him with pepper spray. The rest of us struggled to carry him out of the muddy waters onto dry land. During the process, some of the spray residues transferred from the offender onto my face and eyes. Fortunately, my combat training prevailed as I ignored the effects of the spray and managed to handcuff the felon and place him in the patrol vehicle for transport back to jail. Therefore, one cannot rely 100 percent on the effectiveness of sprays.

The ASP and baton can and will create a harmful impact on offenders if not used properly. Even when appropriately used such self-defense weapons may cause severe bodily injuries such as a broken bone or even death. The possibility also exists with the use of the Taser, which is a standard tool in law enforcement today. The Taser can create undue stress in individuals with pacemakers or other sensitivity to electric shock. Additionally, if the offender is standing in a precarious location such as on a balcony or along a roadside, the Taser may cause that individual to fall from the height or into oncoming traffic. Therefore, the use of less-than-lethal-weapons remains a challenge today.

Another issue involves training. During my tenure in law enforcement, I observed too many altercations where the officer relied on his or her dominant hand to use the ASP or baton against an offender. This mistake applies to the flashlight as well. We always respond in the manner that we train. I suppose that is something that fell back on my combat training and experience as well. I always remained acutely aware of the need to keep my weapon-hand free. I trained to fire with either hand but focused similar training with less-than-lethal weapons in my weaker hand.

Another addition to the arsenal of today's law enforcement officer is the use of the body-mounted or dash-mounted cameras, which have been adopted by most law enforcement agencies. These cameras provide the opportunity to review events during encounters with law enforcement by recording video and audio. Allegedly, these cameras were introduced to ensure proper reactions/actions from law enforcement officers based on the theory that officers become more aware of the need to assure superiors, taxpayers, and the courts that lawful use of force remained within legal parameters during all encounters with the public. Based on reports I have read, these devices are serving more as evidence in court for or against the officers' actions on the street as well as confirmation of the illegal actions of the offender(s). The true challenge with the use of body and dash cameras rests with the fact that only that which falls in plain view of the camera or within the audible range of the recording device may be viewed during the replay. Therefore, some judgment calls remain when analyzing each officer's use of force or offender's level of resistance or violence during an altercation.

I harbor the ultimate respect for all law enforcement today because of their tenacity and commitment to the cause during harsh media attacks as well as overwhelming distrust from the community. Violent encounters and death prevail against our officers today because of an extreme lack of respect from the public in some areas of our country. Our law enforcement leaders and the average patrol officer face formidable challenges and dangers that officers in the past rarely encountered. Violence on the street, within our homes, schools, and religious institutions appears to be out of control. Officers face such dangers daily and should be commended for their dedication to the public and devotion to duty.

As I look back on my career in law enforcement and review the numerous duties of a deputy sheriff, I am well satisfied with my decision to pursue that career path regardless of the low pay. Men and women throughout America remain drawn to that career, which confirms my commitment to the career path as well. Some people receive more motivation to pursue and remain in a career because of their commitment to serve and protect the public than any monetary offer could hope to stimulate. The job requires an energetic individual who is willing to leave his or her family to fend for themselves while he or she risks life and injury to serve and protect the rest of the community. Throughout my career, one Biblical quote held me steadfast in my duty as a deputy sheriff: "Greater love hath no man than this, that a man lay down his life for his friends." (Holy Bible King James Version 2018). This famous quote defines the emotional and physical commitment our law enforcement officers and military personnel foster in their service to our country. Fortunately, we never lost a law enforcement officer during my tenure as a deputy with the Parker County Sheriff's Office, with the exception of natural causes, but the risk remains. Other agencies throughout the United States did not fare so well with officers lost to violent encounters or as traffic fatalities.

The Director of the University of North Texas Press, Ron Chrisman, asked why I chose to never fire my weapon in the line of duty during my tenure in law enforcement even though I admittedly had taken the lives of others during my tour of duty as a CAP Marine during the Viet Nam War. My only answer is that although each level of duty was significantly different, I never felt compelled to resort to deadly force while with PCSO. I am proud of my decisions against the use of deadly force, but equally, understand the probability that I may have made the wrong choice. I suppose the burden of the decision falls back on the offender's choice to not force me to turn to deadly force. If the level of threat levied against me or others increased to that unknown level, I would probably not be able to stand before humankind today and attest to the fact that I never chose deadly force during my tenure in law enforcement. The deadly threat did indeed exist in a few encounters, and I did indeed draw my weapon with the intent to use deadly force if necessary. However, a more viable alternative always provided the opportunity to turn away from deadly force. Every officer must make his or her personal decision concerning the level of force to employ against an offender. Whether he or she survives the altercation depends on many variables as well as merely... the grace of God. The decisions we make in a millisecond, whether in combat or law enforcement, do indeed live with us or die with us.

My files contain a lifetime of records from the awards I received as the Officer or Sergeant of the Year on many occasions. One may say the same about the countless letters from citizens voicing their appreciation for the protection or action officers extended on their behalf. None of those records offers any dollar value. However, each one does provide justification and confirmation of my decisions as a law enforcement officer serving on behalf of the citizens of the State of Texas. Lives were changed, harm was averted, and the oppressed were set free. However, I served only as the catalyst to allow such freedom from oppression. The counselors, probation and parole officers, medical personnel, attorneys, and countless others are the ones who indeed led the victims and offenders I encountered to a more favorable lifestyle. The duties of a law enforcement officer force him or her to move from one call to the next, stepping in and out of the lives of victims and offenders daily, carrying away nothing but memories, some good, some bad.

Before my career with the Parker County Sheriff's Office faded into the past, I found myself recruited to move into the field of education to help a local school district create a Criminal Justice Program for their Career and Technology Department. I enjoyed that career path briefly, as I found myself teaching our youth rather than dealing only with offenders. Being able to help students understand how to depend upon the laws of the land to empower them against oppression remains the most significant influence that arose from the five years I spent as a high school teacher. Through their studies and teachings, students learned to use the laws to combat bullies or invoke changes in their school or communities through proper channels instead of open rebellion.

During my service as a criminal justice teacher, a friend recruited me to consider joining the cause of sharing my law enforcement experience as a mentor with DynCorp International during the war in Afghanistan. From 2006 to 2008, I served as a mentor and Central Region Commander of the ANCOP Program in that war-torn country. Initially, I served as a mentor in Kunduz, Afghanistan, which led me to travels throughout the northern provinces. After only a few months, Command transferred me to the capital city of Kabul where I completed my service as the Central Region Commander in charge of over 300 personnel, two local camps, and four forward operating bases, which included a remote base commanded by the Kiwis troops and officers from New Zealand. In addition to command, while relying on the CAP Marine concept and community policing ideas, I created an intel cooperative that led to the recovery of numerous explosives, firearms, and other weaponry as well as intel concerning Taliban concentrations throughout central Afghanistan.

While serving as the Central Region Commander, I decided to pursue higher education in the field of criminal justice, which led to my present career as a criminal justice, homeland security, and forensic psychology professor. Through my position as a professor, I can impart my knowledge, experience, and expertise to those who are rising in the ranks behind me. I am empowered to contribute to their lives, even to the degree of possibly saving their life or the life of others through my scenario-based training.

At the time of this writing, I am fading into the age of seventy-one, facing the probability that my life in this world will probably last only a decade or two at best because of the injuries I have endured from combat and law enforcement. However, I remain steadfast in my commitment to duty as a professor as well as a civilian in my efforts to maintain my presence in the fight against crime.

In 2013, I met with Greg Bristol, retired FBI Special Agent, Ben Greer, an active California Attorney activist against human trafficking, and retired NCIS Special Agent Joe Martinez. Together we shared our desire to remain in the battle against the world's most heinous crime, human trafficking. Together we created the Human Trafficking Investigations & Training Institute (HTITI), which provides awareness and investigative training to law enforcement, other government entities, global security forces, and essential NGOs throughout the United States, the Caribbean, and globally as we contribute to the battle against human trafficking.

In late 2019, I furthered my efforts as a civilian volunteering for the cause of counterterrorism by joining the Department of Homeland Security (DHS) Bomb Making Materials Awareness Program (BMAP). Through DHS training, I am empowered to meet with major retailers, manufacturers, and average citizens to teach them about the strategies and techniques terrorists employ to gain access to volatile household products that can be used to create homemade explosives (HME). These services are strictly on a voluntary basis on behalf of DHS and all Americans. Hopefully, my efforts will help prevent future attacks on American soil.

In conclusion, I remain committed as a full-time professor with the Columbia Southern University and the University of the Virgin Islands in my efforts to empower students with knowledge and experience that will help them as they continue their lives as members of our criminal justice systems around the world. To each, I pray they will never give up the good fight for our cause is just, despite those who stand against. We must prevail in our mission to protect the oppressed.

Endnotes

Notes to Chapter 1

1. Civil Process is the action required to serve court papers to the person or persons named in a civil lawsuit, also known as a tort. Most civil process is handled by sheriffs or constables, depending on agreements between those entities and the courts. Constables usually serve on those civil papers developed through the Precinct Courts within each county, which deal with minor misdemeanor or county ordinance violations carrying a penalty in fines. The courts also handle civil cases not exceeding $10,000. Sheriffs typically handle civil process for all divorces and civil cases exceeding $10,000.

2. Shift work refers to typical 8-hour shifts with three shifts within a 24-hour period. The Sheriff rotated shifts on a fixed schedule or any time he felt a change in officers on a given shift would improve overall performance. Therefore, becoming accustomed to a shift was a rarity in law enforcement.

3. (Findlaw.com, 2017). State homestead protection laws help prevent people from becoming homeless in the event of a foreclosure or change in economic circumstances. In Texas, every family and every single adult person is entitled to a homestead exempt from seizure passed on the claims of creditors, except for a pre-existing mortgage or lien against a given property. Texas homestead law protects qualifying real property from forced sale by general creditors, and courts have interpreted the laws broadly to help accomplish their goals.

4. (Texas.gov, 2019): "a prejudgment process which orders the seizure or attachment of property to be maintained in the custody of the U.S. Marshal, County Sheriff or other designated official, under court order and supervision, until the court determines otherwise."

5. (findlaw.com, 2017). Homestead property includes up to 200 acres, if rural, and the home resting on that acreage. However, the owner must file the property as a homestead before the delivery of the papers to the owner. Additionally, implements of a person's trade remain protected if that seizure will deter from the livelihood of that person. An individual may also keep one vehicle for every licensed driver within the home as well as a specific value of furniture and other valuables within the home.

6. (Texas.gov, 2019). Typically, seizure of a child or children from one parent or guardian and delivering that child or children to a court for proper release to the person or persons declared by the court to be in proper receipt of the child or children. The Writ of Attachment may also apply to any person who has refused to comply with a court subpoena.

7. (Texas.gov, 2019). The property is seized either by the assignment of the delivery of the court papers to the defendant, which requires their presence in court to show just-cause for another form of settlement in the case or immediate delivery of the property to the plaintiff by the courts. Repossession requests are usually served by Writs of Execution.

8. The most apparent issues rest with the seizure of a vehicle. The state law only mandates that the vehicle seizure includes all attachments that were with the vehicle when the person received possession from the original seller. Therefore, the person in possession of the vehicle has every right to expect retention of any additions he or she completed to improve the vehicle with exception to any permanent changes that could not be easily removed, restoring the vehicle to the original condition. For example, if the buyer had purchased new tires for the vehicle, those tires would have to remain with the vehicle because tires came with the vehicle. However, if removing the additions causes no harm to the vehicle's original condition, then the person must be allowed the opportunity to complete those changes before the deputy takes possession.

9. To facilitate the removal of such items without the approval and knowledge of the owner is an act of theft, with the degree of the offense based on the value of the item. The relative ease of stealing one's property

explains why illegal property seizures attract burglary and theft offenders as a perceived *legal* career.

10. The typical process for pursuing a Writ of Execution for a vehicle costs the original owner anywhere from $1500 to around $5000 depending on the court costs and attorney fees, which encourages unscrupulous dealers to pursue an alternative, illegal source of recovery. The dealer provides a repossession individual with a duplicate key to the vehicle or relies on a wrecker service to merely hook up the vehicle and haul it away, with no attention or concern for the personal items that may be inside or installed on the vehicle, which equates to theft of those items.

11. The decision was based on the fact that I did not see the offense occur and the fact that the wrecker driver's wife and two young children were with him. The property owner was not happy with releasing the alleged offender, but since the offense did not occur in my plain view, I could not lawfully complete the arrest.

12. An easement is typically a section of land between two properties that the county, city, or state retains for government purposes such as utility services or access. The owner still owns that property but cannot create any form of permanent construction in that easement without filing for and receiving a variance.

13. The Sheriff's Department is responsible for the legal seizure of any and all types of personal property and real estate to satisfy debts such as back taxes or other matters deemed such sales by a city, county, or state court.

14. (Texas.gov, 2019). The Texas Homestead Act allows a resident to file for a Homestead Exemption, which allows that owner to set aside the home with up to a given acreage, depending on that property being in the city limits or a part of a larger plot of land in the county. This property cannot be seized to satisfy debt, with the exception of back taxes.

15. (Texas.gov, 2019). The Writ of Attachment is primarily designed to empower the courts to order immediate seizure of a person or persons

to bring that person or persons immediately before the judge issuing the Writ.

16. (Mullen, 2017). Drug mule is the term given to persons involved in accepting possession of drugs from a dealer or manufacturer for the purpose of delivering those drugs to the end user.

17. (Mullen, 2017). Children less than seventeen years old and as young as four or five years old may be used to commit crimes that would result in jail or prison commitment for adult offenders. Children are easy to manipulate and offered a given level of anonymity to the dealer or manufacturer.

18. (Pedrelli, Nyer, Yeung, Zulauf, & Wilens, 2015). Mental Health Problems and Treatment Considerations: Self-Mutilations.

19. A cutter is a layman's term we used in law enforcement for those individuals who inflict serious wounds on themselves allegedly as punishment for some previous sin.

20. (Helen Okoye, 2018). *Nonsuicidal Self-Injury DSM-5: Conditions for Further Study*

21. (Paxton, 2019). Renters Rights, Austin, Texas: Texas Attorney General.

NOTES TO CHAPTER 2

1. (Achenbach, Wan, Berman, & Balingit, July 8, 2016, para. 2) Protests turning violent in an effort to defeat violence defies logic.

2. (Fema.gov, 2013) National Response Framework, 2nd edition discusses common communication traffic nationwide.

3. *Armor* 80 (January-February 1971):84). Website is: https://books.google.com/books?id=GmNRAQAAMAAJ&printsec=frontcover#v=onepage&q&f=false

4. (Tijicon.com, 2018) One of the manufacturers of sights for pistols, shotguns, and rifles that empower the shooter to ensure the glowing sight pattern targets the dark outline of the suspect, aiding in a probable hit with the first shot.

Notes to Chapter 3

1. (Autism Research Institute, 2018, para. 2) Social interaction traits that limit autism victims' ability to interact with others outside a controlled environment.

2. (Touch Point Solutions, 2017, para. 2) Sensitivity to lights, noises, touch, and changes in temperature, is enough to cause avoidance, anxiety, and extreme meltdowns. In treatment, occupational therapists (OTs) and physical therapists (PTs) typically try to provide sensory information to organize the central nervous system to produce a more organized response to sensory stimuli.

3. (Touch Point Solutions, 2017, para. 5) ...users report they experience less pain, are more calm, are able to sleep better, and have improved performance. TouchPoints™ can be used for a short duration to spot treat stress, or they may be left on for longer periods of time to prevent it as well as 15 minutes in the morning and night to help improve sleep. (para. 5)

4. (CDC, 2017) Each drug we consume includes probable side-effects. Side-effects are proven issues that must be revealed to the public.

5. (webmed.com (2017) Uncontrollable suicidal thoughts remain one of the side effects of this drug resulting from one's belief that he or she no longer needs the drug. The absence of the drug creates a tremendous attack of depression leaving some people suicidal.

6. This was a few years before the first cellphone, known as a bag phone, was invented and provided to the public. Therefore, the salesman's only option was to use a pay phone.

7. (James & Glaze, 2006, para. 2) BJS statistics relating to mentally ill inmates.

8. (Torrey, 2011) A review of federal mandates to cut funding to mental health services nationwide.

9. (Torrey, 2011, para. 23) A report showing specific impact and increase of mental health issues in prisons as such relate to mental healthcare services.

10. (FNU.edu, 2014, para,6). Florida National University offers a Forensic Psychology Degree to encourage the criminal justice system to accept responsibility for the fact that the system remains liable for ensuring the rights of suspects are not violated at any stage in the criminal justice process.

NOTES TO CHAPTER 4

1. (History.com Editors, 2019) Constable's dash cam provides evidence to his murder during a traffic stop.

2. (History.com Editors, 2019) Dash cam shows the constable being stabbed and shot.

3. (Cipolla, 2017) Felony offenders' intent on defeating law enforcement efforts will hide in the trunk of a vehicle and shoot through the trunk, blindly, or wait for a plain view of the officer.

4. (Cipolla, 2017) A Texas DPS Trooper survives an encounter with drug dealers on a highway in south Texas as the offenders attempt to surround and overpower him during a traffic stop.

5. (Cipolla, 2017) DPS Trooper survives highway encounter and kills one offender. The others were convicted of related crimes and were incarcerated.

6. (Johnson, 2017) The Tijicon sights were contested during the 1990s but are an accepted asset in law enforcement today. One primary concern

rests with the reflective light revealing the officer's location during a building search situation.

7. (Johnson, 2017, para. 11) The inventor of the sights counters the concern with proof that training eliminates this concern.

8. (Cipolla, 2017) The trooper's focus on the immediate threat saved his life. The other offenders had weapons, but had not attempted to draw those weapons at the moment.

9. A White Warrant is a warrant created by a parole officer who works from probable cause that the parolee has violated the parole requirements. The parole officer files a complaint with the district judge, who issues the White Warrant, which orders the offender to be brought before the judge for consideration of revoking the offender's parole.

10. (UNODC.org, 2019, para. 5) Many victims of human trafficking are used to ferry drugs across international borders. Popularly known as "drug mules," the victims are made to swallow balloons containing illicit drugs and are then transported across borders. Once they have reached their destination, these balloons are retrieved from the victim's body.

11. (PCSOSCU.net, 2014).

12. (Mitchell, July 28, 2017, para. 1) This article reveals the continued, seeming, unchecked demand and supply of drugs from within Parker County and other counties surrounding the Dallas-Ft. Worth area.

13. (Brown, 2019) A significant difference arises when working DWI versus DUI. A basic coordination test alludes to drug influence, but a blood test is typically required to determine the presence of an illicit drug. An intoxilyzer exam validates alcohol content in the human body. A drug addict arrest typically requires accompaniment of alleged drug possession or offender consent to a blood test.

14. (Justice.gov, n.d.) The Three Strikes and You Are Out law was passed during Bill Clinton's administration as an effort to enhance punishment

for repeat offenders, which has led to significant increase in the elderly population in America's prisons.

15. (WWLTV.com, 2017) on I-10 in Louisiana, stranded motorists were attacked by robbers, who shot one of the three motorists as the robbers had completed their offense and were returning to their own vehicle.

Notes to Chapter 5

1. (Durose, Harlow, Langan, Motivans, Rantala & Smith, 2005, p.1) The Department of Justice report deals with murders only. Indeed, children are rarely murdered by their parents, but crimes against children remain widespread throughout the U.S. and globally and range from parental child abuse to the more heinous crime of human trafficking.

2. (Truman & Morgan, 2014, para. 2) The Department of Justice statistics reveals the dominance of domestic violence in the United States today.

3. (American Progress, 2011) This reference notes the life choices show an increase in domestic violence among same sexes as well. Interestingly, female violence in same-sex relationships dominates that sector of relationships.

4. (National Domestic Violence Hotline, n.d.) Confirms statistics from American Progress.

5. (CDV.org, 2014, para. 3) Noteworthy statistics, especially considering the fact that children offer a high propensity toward becoming violent adults.

6. (Nikolow, 2015, para. 5)

7. (Michelle Leonhart, 2013) DEA Report 2013 reveals the predictive influence of PCP and other drugs with a propensity toward violence.

8. (Demetriou, 2009) Author lists facts concerning dangers to officers during the moments of physically arresting an individual, which includes unnoticed weapons or sudden actions to avoid arrest.

9. (Demetriou, 2009, para. 1) Further discussion by the author relating to officers killed or seriously injured during the arrest.

10. (Quora.com, n.d.). Hinged handcuffs prevented any twisting action and empowered speed-cuffing of both wrists when the situation presented itself.

11. Medivac (abbreviation for Medical Evacuation) is a military term relating to calling for a helicopter to remove a victim from the battle scene.

12. (Nickolow, 2015)

Notes to Chapter 6

1. (law.jrank.org, 2018). The women's liberation and civil rights movements, especially the riots arising during these times, led to more political and agency awareness of the gap between citizenry and law enforcement.

2. It appears public outcry demanded changes in law enforcement and public relationships with more focus on community involvement instead of aggressively preventing crime.

3. (Policeone.com, 2016) Hong Kong Police travel to Texas to understand and copy community policing concepts.

4. "CID"—Criminal Investigation Division—is the section of law enforcement operations that investigates all crimes reported to that agency.

Notes to Chapter 7

1. Kaiserwillys.com, 2018). The Willys Jeep was employed by American forces for officer and other forms of transportation during both world wars, the Korean War, and the Viet Nam War.

2. Dale Pilcher was a veteran officer with the Parker County Sheriff's Office and a U.S. Army Veteran. Dale was compelled toward investigating crimes that were common to Parker County and remained unsolved

either because of the lack of investigative resources or lack of interest from Parker County investigators. Juvenile runaways or missing children received little attention because of being perceived as nothing more than runaways. Little concern was given to those children falling prey to sexual predators, human trafficking operations, or others focused on child victims. Livestock mutilations were chalked up as a cost of doing business by ranchers and farmers.

3. (Richardson, Best, & Bromley, 2017) Based on original works published in 1991 by Taylor & Francis providing a description of the alleged legal practices of those following the Church of Satan.

4. (Vallee, 2016) Jacques Vallee participated in cattle mutilation investigations throughout the 1980s and 1990s with his research taking place all over the world.

5. (McCue, 2016). The Skinwalker Ranch in the Uinta Basic in northeastern Utah is reported as a UFO/Paranormal hotspot involving numerous cases of cattle mutilation. The author relates historical reports alleging UFO activity in the area of the mutilations.

6. (Sieczkowski, 2013) Cattle mutilations are reported across the United States as well as in other countries. Some people claim to have seen alien aircraft involved in the crimes.

7. (Rempel, Gerhard, 1989). This research alludes to political and major corporation involvement in criminal cult activities across the United States.

8. (Otten, 1986). Charlotte Otten completed this research through a Calvin College Faculty Research Grant in 1986. Her research reveals numerous werewolf sects or individuals living lives based on Lycanthropy.

9. (Dnash.com, 2014). Internet search reveals numerous sources for fangs, ranging from false caps attaching to the front teeth to actual caps covering the entire tooth.

10. (Overton, 2011). The case ended up with an arrest of a law enforcement officer and other prominent citizens; the final result of that specific case was unsupported by the State of Texas and passed off as a witch hunt.

11. (Carlton, 2018). Wilkes.com is a national community blog, which offers no credibility to this writing, but does provide some validation that such threats did exist during that decade.

12. (justia.com, 2019) Timothy Bridges, defendant in the case mentioned in this chapter, appealed the trial facts, but the findings of the lower court were affirmed.

13. (Minor, 2010) David Minor provides a review of the history of the settlement known as Veal Station, which gained its name from the businessman who founded the settlement.

14. (McClure & Byrd, 2017). McClure & Byrd provide a brief review of blood moon theories and explanations in relation to the writings of John Hagee in 2013 who relates blood moons to Biblical prophecies.

15. (Texas.gov, 2018) Desecration of a grave includes destruction of any objects such as tombstones or other grave markers as well as digging in the earth above the grave without a court order of exhumation.

16. (Snider, 2014). Provided a review of the history of the glowing tombstone along with facts revealing the tombstone theory to be false news.

17. (Dallasnews.com, 2017) The newspaper reveals a story relating to the notorious gang known as MS-13, which has gained prominence during the past two decades with a membership covering all the Americas.

Notes to Chapter 8

1. (Robinson, 2019) Fort Wolters was famous for being a training base for helicopter pilots and other military personnel during the Vietnam War and slowly ebbed into history with the end of that war.

2. (Jimenez, 2017) C4 Explosive is a chemical explosive manufactured strictly for military use in training and combat. C-4 will not explode without a primary detonator.

3. Mortar rounds, much like artillery rounds, are rendered volatile (armed and dangerous) by the action occurring after the round drops into the cylinder and launches into the air.

4. EOD Refers to Explosive Ordnance Disposal, the title given to military personnel responsible for handling such dangerous devices.

NOTES TO CHAPTER 9

1. (Bartollas & Schmalleger, 2016). Discusses juvenile status offenders and juvenile delinquents.

2. (Texas Penal Code, 2018) Texas Penal Code 28.03 applies to criminal mischief, which designates four levels of offense: Class C 0- <$100, Class B $100- <$750, Class A $750- < $2500, Felony >$2500. Additionally, if an offender or offenders commits multiple crimes during the same criminal effort, it is known as a criminal episode and the case can be filed as one case even if multiple victims exist. This can enhance the crime from a lesser misdemeanor or felony as the case may be.

3. (Bartollas & Schmalleger, 2016). Quite often, the juvenile is nothing more than a rebellious child who is driven by personal desires that remain contradictory to the established parental or guardian rules within his or her home.

4. (City of Weatherford, 2018) Weatherford city limits include numerous small lakes offering opportunities for family outings. The city patrolled the parks during regular business hours.

5. (Lozano & Foltz,1990)

6. (Texas Penal Code, 2018)

7. (Hong, Sung, Hyunkag, Allen-Meares, & Espelage, 2011)

8. (Hong, Sung, Hyunkag, Allen-Meares, & Espelage, 2011)

Notes to Chapter 10

1. (Lengel & Williams, 2004, para. 5) Washington D.C. provides an inaccurate correlation to a county with a population far less than most major cities. However, the problem of false alarms permeates every law enforcement agency.

2. Lengel & Williams, 2004)

Notes to Chapter 11

1. Rifling refers to the grooves cut in the inside of the barrel of most firearms, which force the bullet to spin as it leaves the barrel. The rifling marks on a bullet match a bullet to a specific weapon.

2. (Garavaglia & Talkington, 1999, p. 2) This report primarily referred to handguns, but did mention long weapons as well. Generally, a pistol is indeed still clutched in the hand of the suicide victim, which equates to the shotgun lying in the crook of the victim's right arm in this case.

Notes to Chapter 12

1. (Hayes, 1991) Disturbed individual warned that he would murder numerous people in the future, but the threat was passed off as a hoax.

2. (Hayes, 1991)

3. (NIJ.gov, 2009). The National Institute of Justice is a federal agency that serves as a primary source for specific laws, regulations, and case law relating to the use of force.

NOTES TO CHAPTER 13

1. CPS investigators are civilian employees in contrast to certified law enforcement who are trained and mandated to deal with any violent threat in their jurisdiction and armed to do so.

2. (Vandiver, 2017) The pedophilia and pedophilia organizations around the world focus lobbying efforts and work to entice children away from parents for the express purpose of sexual gratification from the offender. These offenders and offending organizations are represented worldwide.

3. (Texas Penal Code, 2018)

4. (Texas Penal Code, 2018) Sexual offenses can be as minor as offensive contact, which is a Class C offense to Aggravated Sexual Assault of a Child, which is a First-Degree Felony.

5. (Texas Penal Code, 2018) This code is based on placing a victim in imminent fear of deadly assault even though the offender did not fire the weapon.

6. Texas Code of Criminal Procedure Sec. 5. "Nothing in this article precludes the admission of a statement made by the accused in open court at his trial, before a grand jury, or at an examining trial in compliance with Articles 16.03 and 16.04 of this code, or of a statement that is the res gestae of the arrest or of the offense, or of a statement that does not stem from custodial interrogation, or of a voluntary statement, whether or not the result of custodial interrogation, that has a bearing upon the credibility of the accused as a witness, or of any other statement that may be admissible under law."

7. Most foster care homes in Parker County were indeed caring individuals who ensured the safety and welfare of the children in their care, custody, and control. Some individuals pursued the service only for illicit profit, however.

Bibliography

Achenbach, Joel, William Wan, Mark Berman, and Moriah Balingit. "Five Dallas Police Officers Were Killed by a Lone Attacker, Authorities Say." *Washington Post,* July 8, 2016.

Americanprogress.org. *Domestic Violence in the LGBT Communityand Jail Inmates, Department of Justice Special Report.* Washington, D.C.: American Progress, 2011.

Autism Research Institute. *Is It Autism*? San Diego, CA: Autism Research Institute, 2018.

Bartollas, Clemens, and Frank Schmalleger. *Juvenile Delinquency,* 2nd ed., Justice Series. New York: Pearson Books, 2016.

Brown, David. *DUI and DWI Overview: What It Means to be Charged with a DUI (Driving Under the Influence of Drugs or Alcohol) Or DWI (Driving While Intoxicated).* Berkeley, CA: Nolo.com, 2019.

Carlton, J. *Threats of Satanist Attacks against Children.* Wilkesboro, NC: Gowilkes.com., 2018.

CDC.gov. *ASD Treatment.* Washington, D.C.: Center for Disease Control and Prevention, 2017.

CDV.org. *Startling Domestic Violence Statistics for Children.* New York: Childhood Domestic Violence, 2014.

Cipolla, Matthew. "Scary Police Shootout in Refugio, Texas, 1991." Refugio, TX: YouTube.com, 2017.

City of Weatherford. *Cartwright Park.* Weatherford, Texas: Weatherford, 2018.

Demetriou, George. *Be Mindful of the Handcuff Rip Tactic by Violent Offenders.* New York: Police One, 2009.

Durose, Matthew R., Caroline Wolf Harlow, Patrick A. Langan , Mark Motivans, Ramona R. Rantala, and Erica L. Smith. *Family Violence*

Statistics Including Statistics on Strangers and Acquaintances. Washington, D.C.: Bureau of Justice Statistics, 2005.

Dnash. *Custom Fangs: Traditional Vampire and Werewolf Dental Caps.* Stratford, CT: Dnash.com, 2014.

FEMA.gov. *National Response Framework.* Washington, D.C.: Department of Homeland Security, 2013.

Fortwolters.com. *U.S. Army Primary Helicopter Center/School.* Mineral Wells, TX: Fortwolters.com, 2017.

Findlaw.com. *Texas Homestead Law Overview.* United States: Thompson Reuters, 2019.

FNU.edu. *The Role of Forensic Psychology in Criminal Justice.* Hialeah, FL: Florida National University, 2014.

Garavaglia, Jan, and Billy Talkington. "Weapon Location Following Suicidal Gunshot Wounds." *The American Journal of Forensic Medicines and Pathology* (Riverwoods, IL) 20, no. 1 (1999): 1-5.

Hayes, Thomas. "Gunman Kills 22 and Himself in Texas Cafeteria." *The New York Times,* Oct. 17, 1991.

History.com Staff. *Videotaped Murder Leads to Convictions in Texas.* New York: A&E Television Networks, LLC, 2019.

Hong, Jun Sung, Hyunkag Cho, Paula Allen-Meares, and Dorothy L. Espelage. *The Social Ecology of the Columbine High School Shootings, Children and Youth Services Review.* New York: Elsevier Publishing, 2011.

James, Doris, and Lauren Glaze. *Mental Health Problems of Prison.* Washington, D.C.: U.S. Department of Justice, 2006.

Jimenez, Carlos. *EOD Techs Train for Explosive Situations.* Marine Corps Air Station, Iwakuni, Japan: U.S. Marine Corps, 2017.

Johnson. *Testimonies: The Tijicon Sights Were Contested during the 1990s But Are an Accepted Asset in Law Enforcement Today.* Wixom, MI: Trijicon, 2017.

Justia.com. *Timothy Ray Bridges v. The State of Texas—Appeal from 29th District Court of Palo Pinto County.* Mountain View, CA: Justi.com, 2018.

Justice.gov. *1032 Sentencing Enhancement Three Strikes Law*, Washington, D.C.: U.S. Department of Justice, N.D.

Kaiserwillys.com. *About Willys MB: Military and Civilian Models— A Brief Overview.* Aiken, SC: Kaiser Willys Auto Supply, 2018.

Law.jrank.org. *Police: Community Policing Origins, Evolution of Community Policing.* Los Angeles: Law Library, 2018.

Lengel, Allan, and Clarence Williams. "Police Resources Diverted by False Burglary Alarms." *The Washington Post,* November 7, 2004.

Leonhart, Michele M. *National Drug Threat Assessment Summary.* Washington, D.C.: Drug Enforcement Agency, 2013.

McCue, Peter A. *Private Investigation Case Types /Sect Occult or Cult Investigations.* Unita Basic, UT: EBSCO Information Services, 2016.

McClure, Bruce, and Deborah Byrd. *What's a Blood Moon: Astronomy Essentials/ Human World.* https://earthsky.org/human-world/what-is-a-blood-moon-lunar-eclipses-2014-2015, 2019.

Leonhart, Michele M. *National Drug Threat Assessment Summary.* Washington, D.C.: Drug Enforcement Agency, 2013.

Lozano, Wendy, and Tanice Foltz. *Into the Darkness.* Philadelphia, PA: Kluwer Academic Publishers-Human Sciences Press, 1990.

Minor, David. "Veal's Station, TX." In *Handbook of Texas Online.* Texas State Historical Association, 2010.

Mitchell, Mitch. "Meth, Date-Rape Drug, $14,000 and Guns Seized in Parker County Bust." *Weatherford Star-Telegram*, July 28, 2017.

Mullen, Ronan. "Children Being Used as Drug Mules in Dundalk Crime Ring." *Dundalk Democrat,* Oct. 4, 2017.

National Domestic Violence Hotline. *Domestic Violence Against Men.* Austin, TX: National Domestic Violence Hotline, n.d.

National Institute of Justice. *The Use of Force Continuum.* Washington, D.C.: Office of Justice Programs, 2009.

Nickolow, Jeremy. *The Challenges of Domestic Violence Investigations, In Public Safety.* Port Orange, FL: American Military University, 2015.

Okoye, Helen. *Nonsuicidal Self-Injury DSM-5: Conditions for Further Study.* https://www.theravive.com/therapedia/nonsuicidal-self--injury-dsm--5. Detroit, MI: 2018.

Otten, Charlotte F. *A Lycanthropy Reader: Werewolves in Western Culture.* Syracuse, NY: Syracuse University Press, 1986.

Overton, Mac. "Kelly Wilson Case Remains Unsolved." *Gilmer Mirror,* January 7, 2012.

Paxton, Kenneth. *Renters Rights,* Austin, TX: Texas Attorney General, 2019.

PCSOSCU.net. *The Tri-County Drug Task Force Evolved into the Weatherford-Parker County Special Crimes Unit.* Weatherford, TX: Weatherford/Parker County Special Crimes Unit, 2014.

Pedrelli, P., M. Nyer, A. Yeung, C. Zulauf, and T. Wilens. *College Students: Mental Health Problems and Treatment Considerations: Self-Mutilations.* Bethesda MD: Acad Psychiatry, 2015.

Policeone.com. "Hong Kong Officers Look to Texas for Community Policing Models." *Austin American Stateman,* March 5, 2016.

Quora.com. *What Are the Various Ways That Police Officers Can Cuff Someone and When Is Each Method Used?* Mountain View, CA: Quora.com, n.d.

Rempel, Gerhard. *Hitler's Children: The Hitler Youth and the SS.* Chapel Hill: University of North Carolina Press, 1989.

Richardson, James, Joel Best, and David Bromley. *The Satanism Scare.* Piscataway, NJ: Transaction Publishers, 2017.

Robinson, Keith. *Fort Wolters Photo Gallery.* Mineral Wells, Texas: Keith Robinson, 2019.

Sieczkowski, Cavan. "Lyn Mitchell, Missouri Rancher, Suspects Aliens Mutilated Her Cows." *Huffington Post,* Aug. 1, 2013.

Snider, Tui. *Press Release: North Texas Ghost Hunter Debunks Springtown's Glowing Tombstone.* San Francisco, California: WordPress.com, 2014.

Texas.gov. *The Texas Homestead Act.* Austin: Texas State Government, 2019.

Texas.gov. *Texas Penal Code 42.08 Desecration of a Grave.* Austin: Texas Historical Commission, 2018.

Texas.gov. *Writs of Attachment.* Austin: Texas State Government, 2019.

Texas.gov. *Writs of Execution.* Austin: Texas State Government, 2019.

Texas.gov. *Writs of Sequestration.* Austin: Texas State Government, 2019.

Texas Code of Criminal Procedure. *Res Gestae, Article 38.22: Section 5.* State of Texas: State of Texas, 2017.

Texas Penal Code. *Criminal Mischief 28.03.* State of Texas: State of Texas, 2018.

Texas Penal Code. *Title 9. Offenses Against Public Order and Decency, Chapter 42. Disorderly Conduct and Related Offenses Sec. 42.02. Riot and Sec. 42.03. Obstructing Highway or Other Passageway.* State of Texas: State of Texas, 2018.

Texas Penal Code. *Title 5. Offenses Against the Person: Chapter 22. Assaultive Offenses; Sec. 22.011. Sexual Assault of A Child.* State of Texas: State of Texas, 2018.

Texas Penal Code. *22.01: Assault by Threat.* Austin: State of Texas, 2017.

"Texas Teen Slain as Sacrifice to 'The Beast' After She Insulted MS-13 Gang's Satanic Shrine." *Dallas Morning News/Houston Chronicle,* 2017.

Torrey, E. Fuller. *A Review of Federal Mandates to Cut Funding to Mental Health Services Nationwide.* Arlington, VA: Treatment Advocacy Center, 2011.

Thetouchpointsolution.com. *From Sensory Avoidant to Sensory Tolerant.* Westchase, FL: TouchPoint, 2017.

Thetouchpointsolution.com. *Touchpoint FAQS.* Westchase, FL: TouchPoint, 2017.

Trijicon.com. *Bright and Tough Night Sights.* Wixom, MI: Trijicon, 2018.

Truman, Jennifer L., and Rachel E. Morgan. *Nonfatal Domestic Violence, 2003–2012.* Washington, D.C.: Bureau of Justice Statistics, 2014.

UNODC.org. *Drug Mules Swallowed by the Illicit Drug Trade*, New York: United Nations Office on Drugs and Crime, 2019.

Vallee, Jacques. *Forbidden Science,* 5th ed., Documatica Research, LLC, Morrisville, NC: Lulu.com (Self-Publishing), 2016.

Vandiver, Donna. *Sex Crimes and Sex Offenders.* New York: Routledge, 2017.

Web.com. *Prozac: Pro and Con.* New York: WebMed, LLC, 2017.

WWLTV.com. "Stranded Driver Robbed and Shot After Car Breaks Down." New Orleans, LA: WWLTV, April 21, 2017.

Index